Technology, Activism, and
Social Justice in a Digital Age

Technology, Activism, and Social Justice in a Digital Age

EDITED BY JOHN G. McNUTT

OXFORD
UNIVERSITY PRESS

OXFORD
UNIVERSITY PRESS

Oxford University Press is a department of the University of Oxford. It furthers
the University's objective of excellence in research, scholarship, and education
by publishing worldwide. Oxford is a registered trade mark of Oxford University
Press in the UK and certain other countries.

Published in the United States of America by Oxford University Press
198 Madison Avenue, New York, NY 10016, United States of America.

© Oxford University Press 2018

Library of Congress Cataloging-in-Publication Data
Names: McNutt, John G., 1951– editor.
Title: Technology, activism, and social justice in a digital age /
edited by John G. McNutt.
Description: New York, NY : Oxford University Press, [2018] |
Includes bibliographical references and index.
Identifiers: LCCN 2018007253 (print) | LCCN 2018015326 (ebook) |
ISBN 9780190904005 (updf) | ISBN 9780190904012 (epub) |
ISBN 9780190903992 (pbk. : alk. paper)
Subjects: LCSH: Information technology—Political aspects. |
Political participation. | Social justice.
Classification: LCC HM851 (ebook) | LCC HM851 .T42995 2018 (print) |
DDC 303.48/33—dc23
LC record available at https://lccn.loc.gov/2018007253

9 8 7 6 5 4 3 2 1

Printed by Webcom, Inc., Canada

CONTENTS

Information and Communications Technology (ICT) has emerged as a major driver of change in the world today. The emergence of the information economy, globalization, the development of smart cities and a host of other artifacts of our modern age are dependent on technology and technology tools. There are very few areas of our lives that technology does not affect.

It is clear that technology can do wonderful things. It can help us to communicate, solve problems and resolve conflicts. Precision medicine promises to help us defeat an entire range of intractable illnesses. We can make education available to far more people through online learning and distance education. Technology can help us follow public issues and address our government in profound ways. It can also enrich our social lives by facilitating contacts and relationships.

There is another side to the coin. As I write this, the news media reports that a woman was killed by an autonomous vehicle that failed to stop for her and millions of American are wondering if their Facebook data was compromised. Cybercrime and cyberterrorism are constant threats. People from all over the world are wondering if Artificial intelligence will eliminate their livelihoods.

Technology can also help produce the change that we need to create a vibrant future. New technologies blend with traditional methods to make the hard work of creating social change more productive and successful. We face new threats that previous generations have not had to deal with. This does not mean that traditional pressures have gone away. Advocates and activists have their work cut out for them. Fortunately, they have help.

The book you are holding your hands, *Technology, Activism, and Social Justice in a Digital Age* introduces you to the cutting edge of technology and social change. You'll learn about social media, civic technology, leaderless organizations, open data, political technology, data science. In addition, you will learn about more traditional approaches to social change such as lobbying and organizing. The book also looks at the changing nature of social change organizations and the issues that they face. This is not a technology book per se. It won't show you how to set up a social media account or program a computer. It examines how to use various technology applications in a social change context. It helps readers to think about advocacy and social change today and how technology will make a difference.

This book brings together a rich variety of perspectives to the issue of technology and social change. The authors are academics, pracademics, and practitioners. They share a common devotion to a possible future that is just and fair and supports human potential as well as an understanding that this goal can be achieved. They come from social work, public administration, journalism, law, philanthropy, urban affairs, planning and education. The chapter authors represent new voices and experienced researchers and practitioners.

This book was a long time coming. It builds on over 30 years of research and a network of people who contributed to the development of new and exciting ideas. Many of the contributors have been involved in traditional practice. This is a conversation that the readers can be a part of that will change how they look at changing the world. Consider this book at a tool. It introduces many new ideas about technology and social change. Each chapter brings you something new and provocative but it's up to you to make it part of your work (present or future).

John G. McNutt
Newark, DE

ACKNOWLEDGMENTS

The editor would like to thank my colleagues and students (past and present) for their help in formulating my ideas and supporting my work. I also would like to thank my dear friend David Follmer, Principle of the Follmer Group for all of his help and support on this project. None of this would be possible without the incredible help of the Oxford University Press.

Michael Ahn, PhD, MPA, is an associate professor at the John W. McCormack Graduate School of Policy and Global Studies, University of Massachusetts Boston.

Justine Augeri, PhD, is an analyst at US Government Accountability Office and has taught at George Washington University, Trachtenberg School of Public Policy and Public Administration.

Janice Barlow, MPA, is the director of KIDS COUNT in Delaware at the University of Delaware.

Katherine M. Boland, EdD, MSW, is a research analyst at the University of Connecticut.

Lori A. Brainard, PhD, is an associate professor at George Washington University, Trachtenberg School of Public Policy and Public Administration.

David B. Carter, PhD, is a community activist, independent scholar and adjunct faculty member at the University of Delaware.

Nina David, PhD, is an urban planner and assistant professor in the School of Public Policy and Administration at the University of Delaware.

Lauri Goldkind, PhD, MSW, is an associate professor of Social Work at Fordham University.

Jonathan B. Justice, PhD, MPA, is a professor in the School of Public Policy and Administration at the University of Delaware.

Stephen Kleinschmit, PhD, is a clinical assistant professor of public administration, College of Urban Planning and Public Affairs, University of Illinois at Chicago.

Patricia Libby, MS, is principle at Pat Libby Consulting. She was founder and director of the Caster Center at the University of San Diego. Her long career in nonprofit practice and policy included eight years as president/CEO of the Massachusetts Association of Community Development Corporations.

John G. McNutt, PhD, MSW, is professor in the School of Public Policy and Administration at the University of Delaware.

James Melitski, PhD, is a professor of public administration at Marist College.

Lauren Miltenberger, PhD, MPA, is an assistant professor of public administration and nonprofit coordinator at Villanova University.

Suzanne Marmo Roman, PhD, MSW, is an assistant professor at Sacred Heart University.

John C. Ronquillo, PhD, MPA, is an assistant professor of nonprofit and public management at the University of Colorado Denver School of Public Affairs.

Kryss Shane, MSW, is an independent practitioner.

Shariq Siddiqui, JD, PhD, is the executive director of Association for Research on Nonprofit Organizations and Voluntary Action (ARNOVA) and visiting director and assistant professor at the Muslim Philanthropy Initiative, Lilly Family School of Philanthropy at Indiana University.

Robert Warren, PhD, was professor emeritus at the University of Delaware. He passed away in 2016.

Yingying Zeng, PhD, is an independent scholar in Charleston, South Carolina. Prior to coming to the United States, she was a reporter in China.

Karen Zgoda, MSW, is a PhD student of public policy at the University of Massachusetts, Boston.

Technology, Activism, and
Social Justice in a Digital Age

Introduction and Plan of the Book

JOHN G. McNUTT ■

Be ashamed to die until you have won a victory for humanity.
—HORACE MANN

We live in a time of wonder and horror. Our growing knowledge, evolving tech-nology, and societal growth allows instant communications, miraculous cures, and a wide range of goods and services to address our every need. While we don't always use our capabilities wisely, new and exciting things are afoot. At the same time, terrorism, international pandemics, political instability and a host of other horrible developments are a product of the developments that we create. Add to this the traditional threats to well-being such as poverty, inequality, and violence, and we have a very negative environment for social justice and human potential.

To protect well-being and social justice, new techniques and strategies are needed to supplement those that have always been used by social change advocates. These strategies involve both traditional and emergent methods that use technology to build relationships, gather information, and address threats to social justice. This book will explore these traditional and emerging tools. We will look at traditional social change techniques such as lobbying, organizing, administrative advocacy, and so forth. Many of these techniques have been influenced by technology. We will also look at new and emerging strategies. While we say that technology in advocacy is new, we are really talking about a practice that cut its teeth in the 1980s and now represents a mature component of social change.

WHAT THIS BOOK IS ABOUT

This book is about social change in a digital world. As we move toward a global information society, we will need our traditional tools, sometimes reenvisioned with new capability and emerging approaches based on new and exciting technology. This book looks at how traditional approaches to lobbying and community work are aided by technology. It also explores how new approaches will continue to offer advocates and activists new capabilities.

Technology is a core part of advocating for social change in today's world (Hick & McNutt, 2002). It is not an adjunct or an also-ran. There are few social change movements that do not make liberal use of technology. Political campaigns of all sizes use technology tools extensively. It is also not new. Technology was used in social change during the 1980s and by the late 1990s was an accepted part of most organizations advocating for change (Downing, 1989; Downing et al., 1991; Wittig, & Schmitz, 1996). This reality hasn't gone down well with some advocates who have an investment in traditional pretechnology advocacy. Epitaphs like "Real Change Happens Offline" (Kohn, 2008) are bandied about without enough real evidence to support them. Whether something is harder or easier to do is not a reasonable test of effectiveness nor is whether the relationships that were developed online are somehow different from the face-to-face relationships that some people prefer.

On balance, others applaud the positive impact that even basic technologies can have on traditional practice. Tools like e-mail, smart phones, and texting are very helpful to lobbyists and organizers. The information that open data and the beginnings of big data provide gives policy researchers the ability to make what they have always done much more effective.

Technology is also a part of a changing society. The rise of the information society, the impact of globalization, and the declining state of the resource base have created a new reality that advocates must address (McNutt & Hoefer, 2016). These forces create new and unparalleled opportunities and potentially horrific threats. At a lower level, technology and the changes that it supports have altered our personal lives, work organizations, and future potential. Most people have come to expect the speed and ease of use that technology typically provides.

Technology has also changed how decision makers get information and how they justify their decisions (see McNutt, 2010; McNutt et al., 2016). Elaborate citizen participation systems that have been created to facilitate constituent involvement aren't always responsive to many of the techniques that were used in the past. Paper is difficult and expensive to process, and getting letters, petitions, and other artifacts of older social change practice to work in today's systems geared for a digital age can be difficult. At the same time, political leaders have turned to social media to promote their ideas with the public, sometimes ignoring traditional outlets such as the news media.

In the chapters that follow, we give you a look at the cutting edge of technology and social change. Developments like social media, civic technology, leaderless organizations, and so forth are not only discussed but also are more traditional approaches to social change. We also look at the changing nature of social change organizations and the issues that they face.

This is not a technology book per se. It will not teach you how to use various applications. What it will do you is help you think about advocacy and social change today and how technology will make a difference.

WHY THE BOOK IS SPECIAL

This book brings together a rich variety of perspectives to the issue of technology and social change. The authors are academics, pracademics, and practitioners. They share a common devotion to a future that is just and fair and that supports human potential as well as an understanding that we can achieve that goal. They come from social work, public administration, journalism, law, philanthropy, urban affairs, planning, and education. The chapter authors represent new voices and experienced researchers. It builds on 30-plus years of research and a network of people who contributed to the development of new and exciting ideas. Many of the contributors have been involved in traditional practice. This is a conversation that you can be a part of that will change how we look at changing the world.

WHO SHOULD READ THIS BOOK

This book is for anyone who is concerned about social justice and social betterment in today's world. This book will be useful to students, researchers, and practitioners in social work, nonprofit studies, community planning, public policy, and urban affairs. It will also be interesting to anyone who wants to better understand how society is changing and what could be done to make it different.

This is a great book for advocates and activists who want to stay current with their peers or who want to learn about other areas of advocacy practice. It is designed to help you be part of the excitement that we feel about these new developments and the hope we have for the future.

PLAN OF THE BOOK

The book is divided into five parts. The first part is titled Advocacy, Social Change, and Activism. In examining what social change and technology look like in our current world, we will talk about online and traditional social change techniques— lobbying, organizing, advocacy, and political action, and so on. An introductory chapter provides an overview of the lay of the land dealing with changing society in a wired world afire and the advocacy landscape. The first section also includes a chapter on advocacy as a moral imperative by Patricia Libby and a chapter on advocacy in the contract process by Lauren Miltenberger. The Libby chapter presents a highly organized framework for advocacy practice. Making use of her long years of experience as a scholar and practitioner, Miltenberger looks at the often-overlooked work of administrative advocates.

The next section, Advocacy, Social Change, Activism and Technology: Community Level, includes David Carter's study of online and offline advocacy in a community controversy, Karen Zgoda and Kryss Shane's analysis of the use of Twitter in social change efforts, and Jonathan Justice and his colleagues' analysis of civic technology and the nonprofit sector. These are all cutting-edge developments.

The third section explores advocacy, social change, and activism at the policy level. Chapters include Lori Brainard and Justine Augeri's analysis of efforts to save the Internet from the Stop Online Privacy Act/Protect Intellectual Property Act (SOPA/PIPA); Lori Goldkind and Suzanne Marmo Roman's discussion of technology and community action; and McNutt, Barlow, and Carter's study of social media usage in state-level child advocacy organizations.

Next, in the fourth section, we explore advocacy, social change, and activism at the global level. This section deals with global social movements and nongovernmental organizations (NGOs) and explores both how technology is facilitating global change in ways that are evolutionary (e.g., NGOs, human rights) and revolutionary (e.g., Arab Spring and other technology-led revolutions) and how technology facilitates development and change. Chapters include Warren and Zeng's work on social media and protest in China; Steve Kleinschmit's exanimation of technology and digital sanctuaries; and Brainard, Boland, and McNutt's look at technology-enhanced leaderless social movements and transnational advocacy.

In many ways, the divisions between these levels of analysis are artificial. Actors at higher levels influence action at the community level. While this has always been true, the ready availability of global telecommunications has moved the process forward at an accelerated pace.

The final section deals with the future of technology and social change. This section explores how the newest technology developments combined with cutting-edge social science will affect advocacy and activism. These developments include the Internet of things, big data and data science, the growth of experimental social science, and other important trends.

The book represents a substantial contribution in terms of cutting-edge scholarship and practice knowledge. We hope that it will inspire you to go further in the work and frame you own contribution.

REFERENCES

Downing, J. D. (1989). Computers for political change: PeaceNet and public data access. *Journal of Communication, 39*, 154–162.

Downing, J., Fasano, R., Friedland, P., McCollough, M., Mizrahi, T., & Shapiro, J. (Eds.). (1991). *Computers for social change and community organization.* New York: Haworth.

Hick, S., & McNutt, J. G. (Eds.). (2002). *Advocacy and activism on the Internet: Perspectives from community organization and social policy.* Chicago: Lyceum.

Kohn, S. (2008, June 30). Real change happens off-line: Millennials need to be activists face to face. *Christian Science Monitor.* Retrieved from http://www.csmonitor.com/Commentary/Opinion/2008/0630/p09s01-coop.html

McNutt, J. G. (2010, October). *Social networking and constituent relationships at the state level: Connecting government to citizens in a time of crisis.* Paper presented at the Northeast Conference on Public Administration (NECoPA), Newark, NJ.

McNutt, J. G., & Hoefer, R. (2016). *Social welfare policy: Responding to a changing world.* Chicago: Lyceum.

McNutt, J. G., Justice, J. B., Melitski, M. J, Ahn, M. J., Siddiqui, S., Carter, D. T., & Kline, A. D. (2016). The diffusion of civic technology and open government in the United States. *Information Polity, 21,* 153–170.

Wittig, M. A., & Schmitz, J. (1996). Electronic grassroots organizing. *Journal of Social Issues, 52,* 53–69.

Advocacy, Social Change, and Activism

Advocacy, Social Change, and Activism

Perspectives on Traditional and Electronic Practice in a Digital World

JOHN G. MCNUTT ■

The struggle for social change, social justice, and human well-being has engaged the human spirit for eons. Many dedicated people have devoted their lives to this quest. The methods that they use vary between disciplines, problem areas, and time periods. Making change is hard. It often takes a long time, and it is almost never what has been planned. Success is never guaranteed. On balance, without the work of advocates and activists, this would be a world that few will want to live in. As new challenges emerge, we will need innovative efforts to address them.

This chapter will provide an overview of the changing nature of social change efforts in a digital age. We will look at how methods are different and how many are the same. Technology-based advocacy is not new. In the 1980s and early 1990s, advocates and activists were using technology in their work (Dowling, 1989; Dowling et al., 1991). As time progresses, however, the case for technology-based advocacy becomes stronger. While traditional techniques continue to soldier on, new methodologies will be more and more useful.

WHY CHANGE IS INEVITABLE

Traditional methods of social change continue to be viable in a digital age, either in their original state or with the addition of technology. At the same time, new techniques are emerging on a regular basis. Some of these techniques will replace or complement existing traditional techniques. Others will prove ineffective and will be discarded. In the end, the practice of creating social change will be improved. While it is an either–or decision in the minds of some, the practical advocate looks at what works.

Changes in decision-making arenas will make technology-based advocacy methods attractive. Technology will also potentially change the way that technology is organized. While tools are important, the change of perspective that technology brings to the social change enterprise is also a substantial factor in examining the future of social transformation.

CHANGE IN DECISION-MAKING ARENAS

The forums that advocate work within are changing. The world economy and globalization mean that local control of economic affairs is often limited. This means that power projection strategies that target local decision makers might be aimed at the wrong power structure. Reaching the appropriate level of power structure might be beyond the capacity of much of the traditional arsenal. Technology allows for greater reach. What this means for community activists is that technology-based advocacy allows them to apply pressure directly to a remote power structure. It also creates the opportunity to network with similarly affected communities in other geographic areas.

The rise of e-government has led to changes in decision-making systems at the local, state, and national level. Over the past two decades, e-government efforts have altered the way that people participate in their government (Desouza & Bhagwatwar, 2014, 2012; West, 2005). Citizen participation systems often structure input in a variety of ways. Part of this is done to deal with the volume of participation that has inundated state and national offices, but it changes the mechanisms that people use to petition their government. This means that groups that do not use technology might find their options reduced or modified in important ways.

Legislatures, including Congress, have developed sophisticated legislative management systems that change how citizens and others interact with lawmakers (Congressional Management Foundation, 2005, 2008). Part of this is to keep up with the huge volume of participation that is received. Many of the paper-based approaches (e.g., letters, faxes, and petitions) are often difficult to incorporate into these systems. Many decision makers often use social media to inform the public and justify their decisions (Ahn, McNutt, Mossey, & Mundt, 2016, November; Germany, 2006; Newsome, 2013).

One factor driving these changes in the decision-making arena is that technology has become a part of the lives of most Americans. According to the Pew Internet and American Life Project (Smith, 2017), a substantial portion of the American public owns a smartphone, has home access to broadband, and uses social media. Pew reports, "Nearly nine-in-ten Americans today are online, up from about half in the early 2000s." The availability of technology has changed the way that we work, the way that family life is conducted, and the way that we participate in our communities.

HOW ADVOCACY IS ORGANIZED

Interest and advocacy groups, membership organizations, and political groups mount most advocacy efforts. Other types of organizations occasionally join them. The way that all of this works together has consequences for what issues are considered, what tactics are used, and what outcomes are possible.

Many of the organizations that undertake social change activities are traditional nonprofit advocacy, interest group, and social movement organizations. While some of the work is performed by unincorporated associations or traditional non-profit service organizations (Bass, Arons, Guinane, Carter, & Rees, 2007; Berry & Arons, 2002; Mosley, 2010), such arrangements are not typical. These organizations tend to be formally incorporated, have an Internal Revenue Service tax status—typically 501(c)3 or 501(c)4—and have a physical location. They tend to engage in substantial amounts of fundraising to support their activities. The role of members in many of these organizations has changed over the years, which has raised concern among some scholars (Putnam, 2000; Skocpol, 2003). Fundraising is important to most of these organizations and represents a major use of re-sources. It can also be a constraint on certain types of political activity.

We see the potential for changes in how advocacy and activism are organized in society. The rise of leaderless organizations (see chapter 13), virtual organizations, and sole practitioner activism are part of the current advocacy scene. Technology, to an extent, makes these developments possible. Consider that any traditional campaign requires a great deal of effort (Earl & Kimport, 2011). Creating a march or demonstration, a letter-writing campaign, or even a lobbying effort has huge transaction costs. A lot of effort is involved in creating these interventions, and they require many people who are committed to making them work. This means that an organization is necessary to coordinate all the parts and provide the ca-pacity for heavy lifting. Things then start to change. An organization with staff and facilities requires money. The next step is the capacity to raise funds. This means additional staff and controls on the way money is managed. This begins to limit the organization's freedom as fundraising becomes a criterion in taking action. It is hard to raise money from people who you are attacking. This seems to square with Saul Alinsky's (1971) observation that after five years organizations start working for themselves and stop working for their constituents. A more pos-itive way of looking at this is that goal displacement is the result of doing the things necessary to support traditional advocacy. It is a consequence of the work-load requirement for these methods. The demands of having a physical presence (i.e., bricks and mortar) and using tactics that require considerable transaction costs mean that organizations must engage in substantial fundraising and related activities, at the cost of other functions (Earl & Kimport, 2011).

Virtual organizations have far less need for staff, physical venues, and fund-raising. They can support the lower demands of technology-powered advocacy methods. In fact, some online advocacy efforts are conducted by individuals or small groups. These organizations could potential scale if the efforts became too large. What all this means is that change in the way that we do advocacy practice is probably inevitable. Some traditional methods will stay the same while others will change very little. Then there will be the techniques that will either be replaced by newer tools or will no longer function as they once did.

A difficult question is the difference between legitimate virtual advocacy organizations and illegitimate efforts to simulate advocacy commonly referred to as AstroTurf (McNutt & Boland, 2007). These efforts are created (often by a commercial firm) to sway public sentiment. While this is a problem in the face-to-face world, more sophisticated virtual AstroTurf can be indistinguishable from genuine efforts.

HOW CHANGE MIGHT OCCUR

It is useful to view this transition as points on a continuum. At one extreme we have those traditional techniques that are unlikely to change. Inside lobbying is likely to operate that way as is high-value fundraising. Almost every other part of traditional practice will use technology to some extent. Smart phones and e-mail for example, have added to the effectiveness of lobbyist, organizers, and others. Finally, there are the technology-led methods such as e-mail campaigns, e-petitions, data-based campaigns, and so forth.

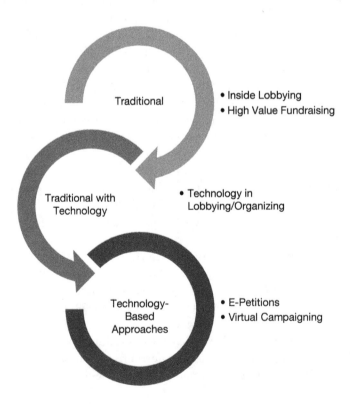

TRADITIONAL CHANGE TECHNIQUES

What we like to call the traditional social change techniques include lobbying, organizing, creating political action committees, political fundraising, legal and judicial intervention, administrative advocacy, public interest research, economic boycotts, and get-out-the-vote efforts (Ezell, 2000; Haynes & Mickelson, 2005; Hoefer, 2006). Many of these methodologies are used together or in sequence with each other (for a classic example, see Rothman, 1970). These traditional techniques are often helped by technology tools.

These techniques are useful across a range of problems and challenges. Some policy areas tend to specialize in certain techniques. For example, the environmental area is more likely to use legal action than some other areas. The reasons include tradition, resource availability, and other considerations. This doesn't mean that other tactics will not be used.

THE TRADITIONAL METHODS

The traditional methodologies developed over decades of practice. While they are presented here as distinct entities, there are large areas of overlap.

Lobbying

Lobbying means attempting to influence decision makers on an issue or piece of legislation (Libby, 2011, 2017; Smucker, 1999; also see chapters 3 and 4). While this usually means legislative or administrative decisions, it could include other forms of decision-making as well. Lobbyists represent an organization or cause before a decision-making body. They might be a volunteer or citizen lobbyist, a contract lobbyist who represents many organizations, or a government affairs professional who represents a single organization. The techniques that lobbyist use include individual contact with decision makers, legislative and policy research, testifying, letter-writing campaigns, constituent days, and so forth.

Community Organizing

Organizing means getting people to work together for social change (Kahn, 1991). This could be anything from consensus-based organizing to confrontational social action. Organizers work to shape an organization that can achieve the desired results. They may work for a local organization or some group external to the area. The techniques that organizers use include contacting stakeholders, power and issue research, organizing meetings and demonstrations, and building organizations. Some of the newer structures of crowdfunding and crowdsourcing can fit in here, as well as the creation of civic competition (McNutt et al., 2016; Newson, 2013).

Political Action Committees and Political Fundraising

Money is important in political action, and fundraising is critical to both lobbyists and organizers. At one end of the fundraising spectrum is community-based fundraising (e.g., special events, bake sales, soliciting small donations, fundraiser events) at the other is individual solicitation of high-worth donors. Internet-based fundraising has become important to social action organizations in the past few decades. Political action committees are organized to fund the electoral campaigns of political decision makers. They not only raise money but also issue political report cards and engage in other types of interventions. Traditional fund-raising makes substantial time demands on organizations. This means that it isn't feasible to raise funds from small donors.

Legal and Judicial Intervention

Legal action is used to change policies or address problematic issues through the courts or the administrative law system. This means that the organization hires a law firm or uses internal counsel to challenge a decision or prevent some action. Since litigation is expensive, many organizations are reluctant to use it, and others find it disempowering to the community.

Administrative Advocacy

While administrative advocacy (Ezell, 2001) generally means advocating within the process for creating regulations, it can also apply to lobbying within the bu-reaucracy. When a law is passed, an agency is tasked with creating regulations to implement the law. This is generally done through a process known as rule-making. Rule-making requires a period during which public comments are solicited and considered. This presents advocates with the possibility of changing or influencing rules before they become formal regulations. This is generally done electronically by e-rule-making platforms.

Public Interest Research

Public interest research is an important although often unheralded part of advo-cacy. This means conducting research that deals with a pending issue or problem. Organizing and lobbying depend on this type of information, as do other parts of the social change arsenal. In a study conducted by McNutt, Justice, and Carter (2014) of interest groups in Delaware, 63.3% reported doing original research where they collect or compile raw data, and 75.6% reported doing original research using data collected or compiled by others. The emergence of data science and open data should accelerate this process.

The growth of the data justice, data philanthropy, and open data movements have added substantially to this area of traditional methodology. The rise of data science and big data make the creation of policy research potentially more effective. Providing vast amounts of data from a variety of sources can be very convincing. In addition, techniques such as microtargeting can make organizing and lobbying more effective (McNutt & Goldkind, 2018).

Economic Boycotts

Boycotts use the power of consumer choice to pressure economic actors to change behavior. This is a time-honored social change tactic. Simply put, a boycott occurs when supporters decline to purchase from a company or other entity. This puts pressure on the economic entity to change its behavior or pressure some other organization to change its behavior.

Traditional Media Campaigns

The traditional media is still a potent player in American politics. While well-heeled causes can purchase coverage on television and in newspapers and magazines, most organizations have to content themselves with earned media coverage. This generally means doing something considered newsworthy such as holding a press conference for a report or research finding. Demonstrations also are occasionally considered newsworthy.

Electoral Efforts

Involvement in partisan elections is often difficult for many community-based organizations but represents a distinct opportunity for others. This can include candidate forums; get-out-the-vote campaigns, and other interventions. There are many legal rules that govern organizations, particularly nonprofit organizations, as they deal with political campaigns.

Civil Disobedience

Civil disobedience has a long history in the United States, and it is part of social change practice today. Demonstrations occasionally lead to violence, and some activists decide that illegal actions are needed. Sit-ins are one example of this activity, but there are many others.

The traditional methodologies represent the arsenal of social change that many advocates cut their teeth on. Most have been enhanced by technology and practical advocates have added newer modalities to their arsenal. Many of these techniques continue to evolve as needs dictate.

TECHNOLOGY-BASED ADVOCACY TECHNIQUES

Starting in the late 1980s and early 1990s (Downing, 1989; Downing et al., 1991; Wittig & Schmitz, 1996), activists and advocates began using technology in their work. The advent of the personal computer and the beginnings of computer networks provided the push for this, along with the development of community computer movements and community technology centers (Schuler, 1996). As the Internet developed, we began to see more activity. Activists were finding that technology could help them in their traditional work. Technology could help organize demonstration (such as the *Battle in Seattle* over globalization) and facilitate many other activities. Political campaigns started using technology, most of the pre-Web and Web 1.0 variety. In the early 2000s, there were a number of developments that moved online advocacy forward. These included the growth of online advocacy groups like MoveOn, the large-scale adoption of Web 2.0/social media, and the introduction of new modes of political campaigning, most notably the primary campaign of Howard Dean. This was a sea change for online advocacy. It represented a changing of direction from older forms of advocacy— new tools, new organizational models, and new ways to engage the public. All of this can be seen against the backdrop of a rising tide of technology in the world today. The growth of e-government began to change the nature of engagement and participation. Movements like civic technology promise additional change to communities throughout the world.

Against this backdrop, technology has evolved a set of tools for the activist and advocate. Again, there is a good deal of overlap among these methods and some overlap with traditional methods.

E-Mail and Text Campaigns

Electronic mail predates the popular Internet. In fact, discussion list software is also older than many realize (the Listserv software is a product of the early 1980s). E-mail campaigns are popular and are well within the capacity of even the least text-savvy organization. They can be used to mobilize other types of action or to directly pressure decision makers. Text-based campaigns have emerged as an alternative to e-mail and can do many of the same things. Smart phones will continue to accelerate the use of text as an advocacy and fundraising technique.

Website Strategies

Websites provide organizations with a place on the Internet. They can be used to present the organization's public face, provide information to the public, and may provide a central linkage for the organization's other technologies. Many websites today use a content management system such as Drupal. The content management system allows users to have a more personalized experience than is possible with static websites. Some organizations are beginning to use social networking sites (e.g., Facebook) as their primary organizational websites.

E-Petitions

E-petitions are websites that allow users to sign a statement or letter about an issue or action. These petitions have been in use for at least two decades. Move On was originally an e-petition site.

Advocacy Suites

These are comprehensive systems that provide an organization with a set of tools to power their online advocacy effort. They typically include a facility to allow users to e-mail their representatives, sign up for an online newsletter, and so forth. These systems are particularly good for organizations that have a small staff and need professional help to maintain their online advocacy program.

Social Media Campaigns

The rise of Web 2.0 techniques in political practice has led to a rush to use social media, particularly Facebook and Twitter, to advocate for causes (Germany, 2006; Guo & Saxton, 2013). When used properly, they introduce a relationship-building element into the equation and allow organizing online. While Facebook is clearly the commercial front runner, much of the dedicated political campaign software also has this capacity. Other Web 2.0 tools that have been useful to advocates include blogs, wikis, social bookmarking, image (Instagram), videosharing (YouTube), and podcasting. Meetup has been a robust contributor to this group of technologies. The Dean campaign made extensive use of its ability to organize face-to-face meetings via an online space (Trippi, 2004).

Mapping

Mapping technology and geographic information systems have been useful to advocates for both analyzing the problem and building public awareness and support (Budhathoki & Haythornthwaite, 2013; Goldstein & Rotich, 2008; Hall, Chipeniuk, Feick, Leahy, & Deparday, 2010). Providing a map that shows that a superfund site is right next to your home or your child's elementary school sends a powerful message. Open source mapping software such as OpenStreetMap has been useful in examining inequality and social problems throughout the world (Goldstein & Rotich, 2008). Technology can allow users to build their own maps with preloaded data. Combined with the movement toward data science for advocacy (McNutt & Goldkind, 2018), exciting developments are possible.

Online Fundraising

Money is critically important for social action, and the Internet provides the means to raise funds without the transaction costs that other fundraising methods entail. Simple e-mail fundraising is used by many organizations and consists of a solicitation letter sent by e-mail. Many organizations have a Web-based, secure donation system that might be used in concert with e-mail appeals. Organizations also use charity malls and "shop for a cause" systems. Social media provides another excellent platform for online fundraising, and the relationship-building capacity that helps them work for advocacy also helps them work for fundraising. Crowdfunding and crowdsourcing systems that have been useful in many venues can also be useful here (Davies, 2015). Finally, the rise of mobile technology has made text-based and mobile giving possible and productive.

One of the advantages of Internet-based fundraising is the potential for expanding the donor base. The cost of securing a donation is sometimes too high to make small donations feasible. The technology reverses that dynamic, which could have important consequences for organizational independence.

Online Marches and Demonstrations

Online demonstrations are comparatively rare. Perhaps the two best known are Move On's Million Mouse March against the invasion of Iraq and the Internet Goes Dark Campaign against the Stop Online Piracy Act and the PROTECT IP Act (see chapter 10).

Radical Techniques and Civil Disobedience

Like its face-to-face counterpart, civil disobedience involves breaking the law for social change. Some of these efforts include hacking websites, communications, and databases; distributed denial of service attacks; and intentional refusal to comply with intellectual property and other types of laws. This, as in the face-to-face world, walks the line between criminal activity and legitimate protest. It also comes uncomfortable close to terrorism and a host of related things such as cyberwar. Evidence that a political party's electronic communications were hacked, possibly by a foreign government should be of concern to all advocates. Terrorists groups have made good use of the Internet and particularly social media to support their work. Surveillance of legitimate political activity is not new but can take on a host of unpleasant connotations on the online world.

Taken together, the technology-based tools that have emerged over the past three decades provide advocates with a vast array of techniques that address many challenges in the work of social change. Combined with the traditional toolset, the arsenal is relatively vast, and, with our growing knowledge of how advocacy works, improved organizations and other capacities might lead to more effective practice.

CONCLUSIONS

The struggle for social and economic justice is a long and hard journey. The forces that oppose us are often powerful and well funded. Building the capacity to create effective change efforts is an important quest.

We have traditional tools that advocates have always depended upon. Add to that new and exciting tools, and we have something to bring to the table. Changes in the population and form of advocacy organizations promises to make them more effective and less dependent.

What we have seen is that advocacy and activism are different. We face different challenges, our organizations are different, our targets are also different, and our tools are different. We can't address today's challenges without some appreciation that the world has changed.

We have an opportunity to use the new tools that we have been offered to achieve things that were never possible. It would clearly be a pity if we threw them all away for nostalgia and fear of the future.

REFERENCES

Ahn, M., McNutt, J. G., Mossey, S., & Mundt, M. (2016, November). *Patterns of social media usage for networking and constituent relationships at the state level: The impact of legislator characteristics.* Paper presented at the Sixth Northeast Conference on Public Administration, Pennsylvania State University, Harrisburg.

Alinsky, S. D. (1971). *Rules for radicals: A realistic primer for realistic radicals.* New York: Random House.

Bass, G. D., Arons, D. F., Guinane, K., Carter, M. F., & Rees, S. (2007). *Seen but not heard: Strengthening nonprofit advocacy.* Washington, DC: Aspen Institute.

Berry, J. M., & Arons, D. (2002). *A voice for nonprofits*. Washington, DC: Brookings Institution.

Budhathoki, N. R., & Haythornthwaite, C. (2013). Motivation for open collaboration crowd and community models and the case of OpenStreetMap. *American Behavioral Scientist, 57*, 548–575.

Congressional Management Foundation. (2005). *Communicating with Congress: How Capitol Hill is coping with the surge in citizen advocacy*. Washington, DC: Author.

Congressional Management Foundation. (2008). *Communicating with Congress: Recommendations for improving the democratic dialog*. Washington, DC: Author.

Davies, R. (2015). Three provocations for civic crowdfunding. *Information, Communication & Society, 18*, 342–355.

Desouza, K. C., & Bhagwatwar, A. (2012). Citizen apps to solve complex urban problems. *Journal of Urban Technology, 19*, 107–136.

Desouza, K. C., & Bhagwatwar, A. (2014). Technology-enabled participatory platforms for civic engagement: The case of US cities. *Journal of Urban Technology, 21*, 25–50.

Downing, J. D. (1989). Computers for political change: PeaceNet and public data access. *Journal of Communication, 39*, 154–162.

Downing, J., Fasano, R., Friedland, P., McCollough, M., Mizrahi, T., & Shapiro, J. (Eds.). (1991). *Computers for social change and community organization*. New York: Haworth.

Earl, J., & Kimport, K. (2011). *Digitally enabled social change: Activism in the internet age*. Cambridge, MA: MIT Press.

Ezell, M. (2000). *Advocacy in the human services*. Belmont, CA: Brooks/Cole-Wadsworth.

Germany, J. B. (Ed.). (2006). *Person to person to person: Harnessing the political power of on-line social networks and user generated content*. Washington, DC: Institute for Politics, Democracy and the Internet, George Washington University.

Goldstein, J., & Rotich, J. (2008). *Digitally networked technology in Kenya's 2007–2008 post-election crisis*. Berkman Center Research Publication 9.

Guo, C., & Saxton, G. (2013). Tweeting social change: How social media are changing nonprofit advocacy. *Nonprofit and Voluntary Sector Quarterly, 43*, 57–79.

Hall, G. B., Chipeniuk, R., Feick, R. D., Leahy, M. G., & Deparday, V. (2010). Community-based production of geographic information using open source software and Web 2.0. *International Journal of Geographical Information Science, 24*, 761–781.

Haynes, K. S., & Mickelson, J. S. (2005). *Affecting change: Social workers in the political arena*. Boston: Allyn & Bacon.

Hoefer, R. (2006). *Advocacy practice for social justice*. Lyceum Books, Incorporated.

Kahn, S. (1991). *Organizing: A guide for grassroots leaders*. Washington, DC: National Association of Social Workers Press.

Libby, P. (2011). *The Lobbying strategy handbook*. Thousand Oak: Sage Publications.

Libby, P., Deitrick, L., & Mano, R. (2017). Exploring Lobbying Practices in Israel's Nonprofit Advocacy Organizations: An Application of the Libby Lobbying Model. *Administrative Sciences, 7*(4), 37.

McNutt, J. G., & Goldkind, L. (2018). E-activism development and growth. In M. Khosrow-Pour (Ed.), *Encyclopedia of information science and technology* (4th ed., pp. 3569–3578). Hershey, PA: IGI Global.

McNutt, J. G., Justice, J. B., Melitski, M. J, Ahn, M. J., Siddiqui, S, Carter, D. T., & Kline, A. D. (2016). The diffusion of civic technology and open government in the United States. *Information Polity, 21*, 153–170.

McNutt, J. G., Justice, J., & Carter, D. (2014, April). *Examining intersections between open government and nonprofit advocacy: Theoretical and empirical perspectives about an emerging relationship.* Paper presented at International Research Society for Public Management Conference, Ottawa.

McNutt, J. G., & Boland, K. M. (2007). Astroturf, technology and the Future of Community Mobilization: Implications for Nonprofit Theory. *Journal of Sociology and Social Welfare, 34*(3), 165–179.

Mosley, J. E. (2010). Organizational resources and environmental incentives: Understanding the policy advocacy involvement of human service nonprofits. *Social Service Review, 84*, 57–76.

Putnam, R. D. (2000). *Bowling alone: The collapse and revival of American community.* New York: Simon & Schuster.

Rothman, J. (1970). Three models of community organization practice. In J. Rothman, J. L. Erlich, & J. E. Tropman (Eds.), *Strategies of community organization: Macro practice* (pp. 20–35). Itasca, IL: Peacock.

Schuler, D. (1996). *New community networks: Wired for change.* ACM Press/Addison-Wesley Publishing Co.

Skocpol, T. (2003). *Diminished democracy: From membership to management in American civic life.* Oklahoma City: University of Oklahoma Press.

Smith, A. (2017). *Record shares of Americans now own smartphones, have home broadband.* Washington, DC: Pew Internet and American Life Project.

Smucker, R. (1999). *The nonprofit lobbying guide* (2nd ed.). Washington, DC: Independent Sector.

Trippi, J. (2004). *The revolution will not be televised: Democracy, the Internet and the overthrow of everything.* New York: Reagan/Harper Collins.

West, D. M. (2005). *Digital government: Technology and public sector performance.* Princeton, NJ: Princeton University Press.

Wittig, M. A., & Schmitz, J. (1996). Electronic grassroots organizing. *Journal of Social Issues, 52*, 53–69.

3

Advocacy as a Moral Imperative

PATRICIA LIBBY ■

You don't need a textbook to tell you why you decided to become a social work student or a student of nonprofit management. Nor, for that matter, do you need a textbook to tell you why you decided to take a course on advocacy. My guess is that just as Csikai and Rozensky (1997) found during their 1997 study of MSW and BSW students, you're idealistic and might even say, as most students they studied did, that altruism, rather than professionalism, is why you chose this career path.

Helping the poor, fighting unjust working conditions, easing the transition of immigrants, aiding people with mental illness, counseling substance abusers—these are among the many challenges that have consumed the lives of social workers since the earliest days of the profession and even before it was considered a profession (Weil, Reisch, & Ohmer, 2013). And although social workers choose to apply their craft in different ways with some concentrating on direct practice and others dedicating themselves to community engagement, the principles of the profession embody a commitment to "ethical responsibilities to the broader society" (National Association of Social Workers, 2014). The Code of Ethics of the National Association of Social Workers (2014) states:

> Social workers should engage in social and political action that seeks to en-
> sure that all people have equal access to the resources, employment, serv-
> ices, and opportunities they require to meet their basic human needs and to
> develop fully. Social workers should be aware of the impact of the political
> arena on practice and should *advocate for changes in policy and legislation* to
> improve social conditions in order to meet basic human needs and promote
> social justice. (Emphasis added)

Yet, despite this call to action, despite this moral imperative that is felt not only by social workers but also by many who choose a nonprofit career, the reality is that few nonprofit professionals actively engage in advocacy. There are many reasons for this lack of engagement that will be discussed throughout this chapter, but, first, let's define what we mean by the term.

DEFINING ADVOCACY AND LOBBYING

In the social service arena, client advocacy means intervening on behalf of an individual to represent and advance his or her interests within a particular system or a variety of systems. This might, for example, involve helping someone secure benefits or support services. The focus of this book is on policy and legislative advocacy, which Jenkins (1987) describes as "any attempt to influence the decisions of an institutional elite on behalf of a collective interest" (p. 297). Another way to think about it is that advocacy involves influencing both public opinion and public policy, as one tends to follow the other (Libby, 2012, p. 14). In other words, if the public is clamoring for some type of change, then, quite often, legislative bodies (i.e., any governing body that is capable of making law) will respond. You might therefore engage in advocacy by promoting your issue in the media, online, and through grassroots organizing as a way of influencing and rallying the public whose action, in turn, will hopefully put pressure on the legislature to act.

Lobbying is one slice of advocacy. It is the act of directly expressing your views to legislators (i.e., lawmakers) on proposed or pending legislation (legislation is a proposed law) with the goal of influencing their actions. As a lobbyist, you interact with legislators in an attempt to get them to understand your position on an issue and, ideally, to represent your interests by actively working to pass a law that reflects your needs and concerns. The lawmakers you are lobbying might be members of Congress, state legislators, elected county government officials, or city council members. In the event that you are lobbying in favor of or opposed to a ballot measure, the general public are the legislators since what the public decides by popular vote during that process becomes law. Interestingly, school boards are not law-making institutions even though they make policy. Therefore, when a nonprofit has policy discussions with members of a school board urging them to do one thing or another, that is technically not considered lobbying (even though the actions might feel exactly the same). Similarly, when nonprofits engage in voter registration and voter education, those activities are not considered lobbying.

There are legal parameters that dictate how much lobbying nonprofit organizations can do, what kinds of activities constitute lobbying, and how much money nonprofits can spend on lobbying. For purposes of this chapter, when the term *nonprofit* is used, it signifies public charities that are commonly referred to by their Internal Revenue Service (IRS) designation as 501(c)(3) organizations. 501(c)(3) organizations are what most people think about when they hear the word *nonprofit* and include, for example, human service agencies, health services organizations, scientific research centers, environmental organizations, arts and cultural institutions, international organizations, and other types of entities whose mission is dedicated to charitable purposes. According to the National Center for Charitable Statistics (2013), in 2012 there were 961,718 public charities in the United States registered with the IRS. This figure does not include 96,600 private foundation registered that same year and also listed as 501(c)(3) organizations. Other types of nonprofits exist in the United States as well; the IRS lists more than 30 different categories of nonprofit organizations, including labor unions, state-chartered credit unions, cemetery companies, farmer's cooperatives, and business associations, to name a handful (IRS, 2017).

LOBBYING RULES FOR 501(C)(3) ORGANIZATIONS

The most important thing you need to know about the lobbying rules for nonprofits organizations is this: Lobbying is 100 percent legal for public charities that are registered as 501(c)(3) organizations. Although there has been no formal research done on exactly why many nonprofits don't engage in lobbying, anecdotally, nonprofits will readily admit they don't understand the law, don't take time to learn the rules, are afraid they will lose their tax-exempt status for violating the law, and/or are governed by a board of directors that is fearful about all of the previously noted reasons or, perhaps, doesn't see participation in the legislative process as being core to the mission of the organization. Since the objective of this book is to teach you how to engage in advocacy and lobbying, providing you with a basic understanding of the rules is important.

Even though the IRS classifies both public charities and private foundations as 501(c)(3) organizations, each type of entity is subject to separate although fairly similar rules on lobbying activity. In addition, religious organizations have the option to file as 501(c)(3) organizations but are not required to by law. Perhaps for this reason religious organizations have narrower restrictions on lobbying than public charities in general. To simplify matters here, the focus of the explanation that follows will be on the legal parameters for lobbying by public charities that are not private foundations.

Public charities have two options for legally lobbying. First, as soon as any public charity is legally incorporated, it is entitled to dedicate an insubstantial portion of its resources (time and money) on lobbying. That rule is known as the "substantial part test" (IRS, 2017a). Nonprofits who meet with their legislators infrequently would be covered under this rule. The problem with the substantial part test is that, strangely, the IRS does not specify exactly what it means by either "substantial" or "lobbying." Therefore, organizations become concerned about whether they are violating an unseen rule by—for example, lobbying their elected officials five times a year versus twice a year.

The second option for public charities is to opt for what is called the "expenditure test," also known as the 501(h) election (IRS, 2017b). This requires filing out a one-line form with the IRS that only needs to be filed once during the life of your organization. Submitting the form does not require IRS approval; it is simply a notification to the agency that your organization has decided to incorporate this classification as part of its activities.

Filing the 501(h) form provides significant clarity and latitude to charities that wish to engage in lobbying. The rules governing the expenditure test, which were passed in 1976, define lobbying to be either "direct lobbying," which is when an organization "states its position on specific legislation to legislators (and/or their staff)" (Libby, 2012, p. 21), or engages in what is called "grassroots lobbying," which involves making an appeal to the general public to contact their elected officials to support that position. There is a technical term involved—"call to action"—that means your organization provides specific information to the public about the legislation you want them to lobby on. The easiest way to remember that term is to think about asking the public to call, write, send an e-mail, and so on to lobby legislators about a specific issue.

In addition to defining the terms *direct lobbying* and *grassroots lobbying*, the expenditure test also sets clear guidelines about how much money an organization can spend on each of these types of lobbying activities—and it is quite a bit of money. One hundred percent of a nonprofit's lobbying expenses can be directed to direct lobbying efforts whereas only 25 percent can be used for grassroots lobbying. Since most of your efforts are likely to involve direct lobbying, this should not impose any real impediment to your nonprofit's lobbying campaign activities.

Also noted in the chart, when the IRS refers to "exempt purpose expenditures" (IRS, 2017b), it means those costs associated with what the nonprofit spends to accomplish its mission including administrative overhead (but, interestingly, not including fundraising operations or consultants as well as a few other outside costs). Nonprofits can use the revenue they receive from dues and donations, special events, and grants for general operating support for their lobbying efforts. Community foundations can also earmark grants to nonprofits for lobbying campaigns. It is simply common sense (as well as the law) that government funds cannot be used by nonprofits to lobby; however, organizations often get confused by this regulation because they mistakenly believe that if they receive any government money, they cannot lobby. You cannot use government funding to lobby, even if you proposed taking money from one branch of government to lobby another, although you may use private funds (as previously stated) to lobby any branch of government.

PERMITTED LOBBYING EXPENDITURES FOR 501 (C) 3 NONPROFITS THAT HAVE TAKEN
THE 501H ELECTIONS

Total Exempt Expenditures	Direct Lobbying Communications (Direct Lobbying Expenditures)	Grassroots Lobbying Communications (Grassroots Lobbying Expenditures)	Total Lobbying Expenditures
$0–$500,000	20% up to $100,000	25% of Direct Lobbying Expenses	20% of the exempt purpose expenditures
Over $500,00–1,000,000	$100,000+15% of the surplus over $500,000	$25,000+3.75% of the surplus over $500,000	$100,000 plus 15% of the excess of exempt purpose expenditures over $500,000
Over $1,000,00–1,500,000	$175,000+10% of the surplus over $1,500,000	$43,750+2.75% of the surplus over $1,000,000	$175,000 plus 10% of the excess of exempt purpose expenditures over $1,000,000
Over $1,500,001–$17,000,000	$225,000+5% of the surplus over $1,500,000	$56,250+1.25% of the surplus over $1,500,000	$225,000 plus 5% of the exempt purpose expenditures over $1,500,000
More than $17,000,000	$1,000,000	$250,000	$1,000,000

In addition—and perhaps even more important than the generous financial limits pertaining to the 501(h) regulations—the rules also give nonprofits generous exemptions on the types of activities that are not considered to be lobbying. In other words, under the more general insubstantial test, these activities would be considered lobbying and would have to be reported by your nonprofit on its tax return (commonly known as the Form 990). Ironically, selecting to file the 501(h) makes it simpler to comply with the law and less complicated for your accountant. The following activities under 501(h) are exempt from lobbying limits:

Communicating with members. A nonprofit does not have to track the time and money it spends communicating with its members about specific legislation as long it does not ask its members to lobby. The organization can post something on its website that says, "Our staff and many of our members are meeting regularly with legislators throughout the state to talk about SB 143 the Affordable Housing Act, which will provide desperately needed funding for affordable housing." Since that post didn't contain a call to action urging members to do something like call, write, e-mail, or visit their legislator, that communication is not considered lobbying under 501(h) rules.

Nonpartisan research. Your organization should dedicate a substantial amount of time to documenting the issue you want to promote to legislators. As long as that research is presented as a fair analysis of the situation, the time you spend researching, writing, and producing the report is not counted toward your lobbying limits. The research can and should take a stand on a position—it does not have to be neutral. The idea is that someone reading your material should be able to form an independent opinion on the matter.

Influencing regulations. Once a law has passed, regulations are made that determine how the law will be implemented. The time you spend meeting with legislators or employees of the executive branch (i.e., the governor's office, mayor's office, etc.) to lobby on the shape of those regulations take does not count as lobbying.

Lobbying by volunteers. All of the time your volunteers dedicate to lobbying on your behalf—including board member time—does not need to be counted if your organization has the 501(h) designation whereas it does if you have not filed for the (h) with the IRS. The only expenses your organization needs to report are those pertaining to the time it takes staff to organize the volunteers and expenses relating to those activities.

Testifying. Often nonprofit employees are experts in a particular subject matter. You may have worked with victims of domestic violence for many years and might therefore be considered an authority in that area. Sometimes when that is the case, a legislative committee will request that you testify on a bill that you support (this could be at the city, county, state, or federal level). In those circumstances, the time you dedicate to preparing your testimony and to testifying does not count toward your lobbying limit.

Discussing the issue broadly. If your organization hosts a public forum on a particular issue or if you are asked to give a speech on a particular issue, those activities are not considered lobbying even if legislation is pending on the topic, as long as you don't mention the legislation by name. For example, at the annual meeting of your nonprofit, your executive director could give a talk about the importance of preventing elder abuse as long as she didn't refer to a specific piece of legislation.

Self-defense. Sometimes the government will propose a law—such as eliminating or reducing the charitable taxdeduction—that threatens the larger nonprofit sector. The time you and your organization spend to defeat this type of legislation is not considered lobbying.

Before you and your organization engage in any type of lobbying activity, be sure to contact the city or state where you plan to lobby to learn if there are any special registration requirements. Some state and local governments have requirements, and others do not; when they do, the requirements differ from place to place. In addition, it is important to ensure that the board and senior staff—whoever is involved in setting the legislative agenda and carrying it out—be familiar with the lobbying rules for nonprofits. Alliance for Justice is a terrific resource for this purpose. They are a nonprofit whose mission is to help other nonprofits understand the rules. They have a series of publications that can provide you with a more in-depth explanation of the rules than what has been presented here. You can find them at https://www.AFJ.org.

One thing that a public charity cannot do under any circumstances is endorse a candidate for political office. Other types of nonprofits with a designation known as 501(c)(4) may endorse candidates for office. These organizations are known as social welfare organizations and are established, in principle, to dedicate most of their resources to promoting a particular cause such as, for example, the National Rifle Association, which is focused on gun-owners' rights, or the Sierra Club, which is dedicated to environmental protection. During the spring of 2013, the IRS cracked down on many Tea Party-inspired social welfare groups that seemed to be spending the lion's share of their resources on getting candidates elected to office rather than on promoting a particular cause such as smaller government spending. This resulted in a congressional investigation of the IRS for partisan treatment of tax-exempt organizations (Confessore, 2013).

Even though partisan politics is prohibited for 501(c)(3) organizations, there is a lot an organization can do when campaigning is underway. Organizations can, for example, host a candidate debate, offer candidates the opportunity to tour their organization, and provide information to each campaign about the great work it does.

THE SAD TRUTH ABOUT NONPROFIT LOBBYING

Despite all the rich opportunities that are available to nonprofits, the sad truth is that a very small number engage in legislative advocacy. For example, a 2014 study of California nonprofits that found only 4 percent "report to the IRS that they engage in lobbying activities or take the 501 (h) election" (California Association of Nonprofits, 2014, p. 53). In addition, the report states that only 15 percent of California nonprofits reported registering or educating voters while 28 percent reported taking a public stand on a ballot initiative or piece of legislation. When nonprofits in California advocate, they do so predominately at the city and county level where laws impact a much smaller percentage of the population than those passed at the state and federal level. You can argue that California is only one state in our great nation; however, it holds 12 percent of the population. Based on similar national research conducted previously (addressed in the following discussion), it is very likely that the practices of the nonprofits that operate within

California mirror those of nonprofits throughout the country. The report reveals that 53 percent of the nonprofits surveyed reported belonging to "an association or coalition that lobbies on their behalf" although, depending upon the extent of each organization's involvement in a particular campaign, that could be like asking someone to go to the gym to do your exercises for you (California Association of Nonprofits, 2014, p. 9).

Previous national studies reinforce these points. In *Seen but Not Heard*, Bass, Arons, Guinane, Carter, and Rees (2007) report on a multiyear study of the lobbying practices of 1,700 nonprofits throughout the nation. They find that while nonprofits said "public policy is essential to . . . their mission," those same organizations didn't walk the talk; instead, they reported lobbying "at the lowest level" measured by the study (p. 17). For example, 63 percent said they either "never" or "infrequently" encouraged others to write, call fax, or email policymakers" (p. 17). A few years later, in 2009, Salamon, Geller, and Lorenz (2009) found similar results, reporting that most nonprofits engaging in advocacy "rely on the least demanding forms of engagement (e.g., signing a correspondence to a government official, endorsing or opposing a particular piece of legislation or budget proposal)" (p. i).

On the surface, it doesn't make a lot of sense: If policy advocacy is so core to the basic principles of social work and of nonprofit management, if changing the world and making an impact is what brought people to this work in the first place, then why is it that as a rule nonprofits don't engage in lobbying? Where is the sense of moral imperative?

WHY MORE NONPROFITS DON'T LOBBY

There is scant literature documenting why nonprofits don't engage more fully in legislative advocacy. However, practitioners and pracademics (the latter being those people who cross both worlds of academia and practice) will tell you that based on their interactions with nonprofits, there are four primary reasons why these morally motivated people aren't more active with lobbying. They are as follows:

1. **People don't know the rules.** Some have no idea that the option to file the 501(h) election exists. Some believe the rules for lobbying are more complex than they are in reality (hint: if you are ever confused about a provision in the nonprofit lobbying regulations, contact Alliance for Justice by telephone or e-mail, and they will provide you will free technical assistance). Some believe they might jeopardize the tax-exempt status of their organization if they engage in lobbying. Some believe, mistakenly, that their audit costs will increase and/or the IRS will be more likely to audit their organization. As already discussed, some mistakenly believe that if they receive government grants, they cannot lobby the government. In addition, many foundations are confused

about the rules and don't understand that they can legally make grants (without having to pay tax on them) directly to nonprofits for lobbying campaigns.

Unfortunately, the language used on the IRS website does nothing to dispel many of these notions. If you were unfamiliar with nonprofit lobbying rights, you could easily misinterpret what is posted:

In general, no organization may qualify for section 501(c)(3) status if a substantial part of its activities is attempting to influence legislation (commonly known as *lobbying*). A 501(c)(3) organization may engage in some lobbying, but too much lobbying activity risks loss of tax-exempt status.

Legislation includes action by Congress, any state legislature, any local council, or similar governing body, with respect to acts, bills, resolutions, or similar items (such as legislative confirmation of appointive office), or by the public in referendum, ballot initiative, constitutional amendment, or similar procedure. It does not include actions by executive, judicial, or administrative bodies.

An organization will be regarded as attempting to influence legislation if it contacts, or urges the public to contact, members or employees of a legislative body for the purpose of proposing, supporting, or opposing legislation, or if the organization advocates the adoption or rejection of legislation.

Organizations may, however, involve themselves in issues of public policy without the activity being considered as lobbying. For example, organizations may conduct educational meetings, prepare and distribute educational materials, or otherwise consider public policy issues in an educational manner without jeopardizing their tax-exempt status. (IRS, 2018)

You have to dig deeper on the website to find information about the expenditure test—501(h) election—for further clarification.

2. **Organizations don't make it a priority at the strategic level.**
   A common refrain is, "Where will we find the time to lobby?" when a better question to be asked might be, "What is the best way to meet the objectives that are stated in our mission?"

If an organization is dedicated to providing after-school support for low-income children but does not involve itself in advocacy efforts to expand school lunch and breakfast programs, is it meeting its mission of serving at-risk kids? If a theater company is so involved in its own productions that it fails to rally when the National Endowment for the Arts is threatened with elimination, is it meeting its mission of providing access to the arts? If a nonprofit is devoted to providing employment opportunities for low-income individuals through education, training, mentoring, placement, and so on, then should it be involved in advocating for a higher minimum wage or for a living wage? These types of philosophical discussions must take place at the board and senior staff level.

3. **An outcomes-driven culture skews the thinking of its leaders.** Hasenfeld and Garrow (2012) have written eloquently about the dynamics and challenges nonprofits face working within a system of New Public Management. New Public Management connotes a system in which the emphasis is on the accountability an organization has to the funder (a government agency) to produce results as well as increased competition between the private and nonprofit sectors for providing services. As government shrinks and outsources the provision of services to the local level, a move to measure success in terms of benchmarks becomes paramount, and nonprofits become concerned about keeping their contracts or losing them to the competition. According to Hasenfeld and Garrow, this pressure on nonprofits to produce results can lead to clients being seen as customers, rather than as citizens with rights and needs that extend beyond the scope of the services the nonprofits provide through these contracts (or could provide if the contracts were written differently). Nonprofits are reluctant to lobby for fear of biting the hand that feeds them. Predominately, larger organizations lobby as they have the bureaucracy to handle the application and reporting requirements. Innovation diminishes.

4. **People don't know how to lobby.** When most people hear the word *lobbyist*, they envision someone wearing an expensive suit who has a cozy relationship with an elected official. The idea of doing what that person does, or figuring out how to do it, seems far-fetched. In addition, on a much more basic level, many people simply have no idea how the legislative process works and are embarrassed to admit the truth. They may vote consistently in elections, campaign for a candidate, or even send money to a candidate. Yet when it comes to how laws get made, the system seems like a mysterious Rube Goldberg contraption that has no owners' manual. The truth is,

You don't have to understand all of the intricacies of the legislative process to be a good lobbyist, just like you don't have to be a veterinarian to own a dog. In fact, you probably already have what you need: a passion for your cause and good, hard facts about "it"—the "it" being the thing that needs to be funded or changed to make things better. (Libby, 2012, p. 1)

A MODEL FOR A NONPROFIT-LED LOBBYING CAMPAIGN

While the focus of this book is on advocacy, activism, and the Internet, the model described here uses both an on-the-ground and electronic approach. It is not the only nonprofit advocacy model in existence. In fact, many academics and pracademics have written about effective advocacy models, including Arons (1999), Coulby (2008), Flynn and Verma (2008), Hoefer (2006), Moore and Johnson (2002), and Srikantiah and Koh (2010), to name a few esteemed authors. This model was selected to share with you because it has been used successfully by practitioners who are also formally studying nonprofit management to pass many important state and local laws. None of these student-practitioners had previous experience with the legislative process. If the following brief description sparks your interest, you can read about the model in detail in *The Lobbying Strategy Handbook* (Libby, 2012).

The first thing to know before reading through the 10 steps that are described in the following discussion is that each step is not necessarily "done" when you have completed it and that the sequence is therefore not neat and tidy. If you carry out an advocacy campaign using the model, you will find yourself completing a step and then perhaps revisiting or updating that step as you progress through the model. The best way to think about it is like dance steps rather than walking a straight line.

1. **Identify an issue.** Sometimes the issue your organization wants to address is obvious because it is something you observe happening to the clients you serve or to people in your community, it is a hot topic on Twitter, or it is an issue that is a frequent topic of conversation among your colleagues who work at nonprofits that do similar types of work. Before settling on an issue though, it is important to talk directly with the people who will ultimately be affected by your actions to make sure that they view the situation as you do and believe it is important for you and your organization to expend energy on a fix. Do not gloss over this step by assuming you already know how others are thinking about or reacting to an issue.

2. **Research the issue.** Dedicating time to documenting the dimensions of your issue is critically important to being a good lobbyist. You will want to find information from individuals and organizations that are considered to be expert sources such as research organizations, academics, and public officials who have been studying the issue. Research might also include surveys you conduct of people you believe have been or are affected by the problem. The research will explain the issue, the proposed solution, and, ideally, if possible, how legislative bodies in other areas have addressed this issue. Remember, according to the lobbying rules, your task is to create a document that expresses your opinion while providing a fair analysis of the situation such that the reader could form an independent judgment. Ultimately, you will want to compile this research into a white paper or position paper that you will distribute to legislators who are interested in your issue.

3. **Create a fact sheet.** The fact sheet will distill your research into a single, double-sided page of information. It will also contain the name of your campaign (see step 4), contact information, and a list of your coalition members/supporters (see step 5).

4. **"Brand" the issue.** The brand you develop is the name you give your campaign. It should be easy to remember and, if thought through

carefully, might even present your idea in such a way that the opposition is neutralized (see step 5).

5. **Map out possible supporters and detractors.** Mapping is a multifaceted step. You will want to ascertain what kinds of people and organizations will be likely to join or oppose your campaign and, with regard to the opponents, to analyze why, exactly, you believe they may be in opposition. Those you think might join you should be approached to become members of your coalition (see step 6). You can use the arguments of those who might oppose you to help you craft the wording and branding for your campaign. In addition, you will need to map out the voting history and interests of the legislators you plan to lobby. This will enable you to understand who among them will be most likely to support your cause and who might oppose you and for what reason.

6. **Form a coalition.** The mapping that you have done in step 5 will enable you to figure out which people and organizations to approach to be members of your campaign coalition. You will also need to determine the role and expectation of coalition members. Coalitions that are broad-based and diverse in terms of the types of people and organizations represented are the most powerful.

7. **Develop educational materials.** The purpose of these materials will be to familiarize coalition members (and the members of those organizations) with the fundamentals of your issue, which will, in turn, enable those folks to call, write, or otherwise contact their legislators. This is a key Internet organizing strategy that will be discussed in detail elsewhere in this book.

8. **Launch a media campaign.** Electronic, print, radio, and TV can all be deployed to get the word out about your campaign, to encourage the public to become involved, and to put pressure on legislators.

9. **Approach elected officials and/or other appropriate policy makers.** In this step, you will present your case directly and professionally to the legislators you wish to influence using the materials you have developed (see steps 2, 3, and 4). In some instances, you will be lobbying their aides, but do not be discouraged if this should occur as the aids are a proxy for the legislators they serve.

10. **Monitor progress on the issue.** If you follow the previous steps, you will have a good chance of finding a legislator to champion your issue—most often in the form of a bill (i.e., legislation). Once that happens, you will work closely with that legislator's office to track the bill and to engage in advocacy and lobbying activities that move the legislation forward. For instance, you might testify at a hearing, organize a protest at the lobbying site (e.g., city or state offices), organize an e-mail campaign to generate signatures on a petition or phone calls into legislators, secure media coverage, and so on. When your bill becomes law, you will also need to be diligent about making sure that the regulations governing the law are designed according to what you had in mind.

This framework provides one way for you to think about organizing your legislative campaign. Nonprofits organizations have done successful lobbying for years using a variety of strategies and techniques. After reading this book, you will have lots of ideas and tools to use for advancing the causes you care about.

ONWARD!

Advocacy is a moral imperative. Every generation faces a crossroads where it sees the enormity of what needs to be changed to make society better. Whether it's fighting for income equality, social justice, environmental protection, immigrant rights, access to arts and culture—whatever your cause—learn to be an advocate for change.

REFERENCES

Arons, D. (1999). *Teaching nonprofit advocacy: A resource guide.* Washington, DC: Independent Sector.

Bass, G., Arons, D., Guinane, K., Carter, M., & Rees, S. (2007). *Seen but not heard: Strengthening nonprofit advocacy.* Washington, DC: Aspen Institute.

California Association of Nonprofits. (2014). *Causes counts: The economic power of California's nonprofit sector.* San Diego, CA: Caster Family Center for Nonprofit and Philanthropic Research, University of San Diego.

Confessore, N. (2013, May 13). Uneven IRS scrutiny seen in political spending by big tax-exempt groups. *New York Times.*

Coulby, H. (2008, January). INTRAC (International NGO Training and Research Centre) https://www.intrac.org/?s=advocacy+toolkit

Csikai, E. L., & Rozensky, C. (1997). "Social work idealism" and students' perceived reasons for entering social work. *Journal of Social Work Education, 33,* 529–538.

Flynn, L., & Verma, S. (2008). Fundamental components of a curriculum for residents in health advocacy. *Med Teach, 30*(7), 178–183.

Hasenfeld, Y., & Garrow, Eve E. (2012). Nonprofit human-service organizations, social rights and advocacy in a neo-liberal welfare state. *Social Service Review, 86,* 295–322.

Hoefer, R. (2006). *Advocacy practice for social justice.* Chicago: Lyceum.

Internal Revenue Service. (2017a). Measuring lobbying activity: Expenditure test. Retrieved from https://www.irs.gov/charities-non-profits/measuring-lobbying-activity-expenditure-test

Internal Revenue Service. (2017b). Other tax-exempt organizations. Retrieved from http://www.irs.gov/Charities-&-Non-Profits/Other-Tax-Exempt-Organizations

Internal Revenue Service. (2018). Lobbying. Retrieved from https://www.irs.gov/charities-non-profits/lobbying

Jenkins, J. (1987). Nonprofit organizations and policy advocacy. In W. Powell (Ed.), *The nonprofit sector: A research handbook* (pp. 296–320). New Haven, CT: Yale University Press.

Libby, P. (2012). *The lobbying strategy handbook.* Thousand Oaks, CA: SAGE.

Moore, L. S., & Johnston, L B. (2002). Involving students in political advocacy and social change. *Journal of Community Practice, 10*(2), 89–101.

National Association of Social Workers. (2014). NASW code of ethics. Retrieved from http://www.socialworksearch.com/html/nasw.shtml#NASW

National Center for Charitable Statistics. (2013). Quick facts about nonprofits. Retrieved from http://nccs.urban.org/statistics/quickfacts.cfm

Salamon, L., Geller, S., & Lorenz, S. (2009, November). *Nonprofit America: A force for democracy?* Paper delivered at the 2009 Conference of the Association for Research on Nonprofit Organizations and Voluntary Action, Cleveland, OH.

Srikantiah, J., & Koh, J. L. (2010). Teaching individual representation alongside institutional advocacy: Pedagogical implication of a combined advocacy clinic. *Clinical Law Review, 16*, 451–488.

Weil, M., Reisch, M., & Ohmer, M. (Eds.). (2013). *The handbook of community practice.* Thousand Oaks, CA: SAGE.

4

Collaborative Contracting
as Advocacy

LAUREN MILTENBERGER ■

This chapter discusses advocacy within human services through the contracting process. Staff of human service nonprofits can advocate for new public policies through a collaborative approach to contracting. The contracting environment has effectively transformed human service nonprofit organizations into routine, core, front-line agents carrying out a diverse array of critical public human services for those in need (Hasenfeld & Garrow, 2012). The contracting environment has also transformed the system of human services delivery, and contracts have effectively become part of the public policies that guide human service delivery in the United States. This focus of this chapter is on how nonprofit organizations can advocate for contract changes—that is, changes to public policies—via "back-door" discussions with their government contract manager.

Constituents of human service organizations are disproportionately reliant on and affected by the design, funding, and implementation of contracts, as delivered by nonprofit organizations but as designed by government agencies. Therefore, staff of human service organizations are often in a unique position to make connections between policymakers and the constituents they serve. Nonprofit human services can use their relationships with their government contract managers to advocate or lobby for changes informally, as opposed to the more dominant and formal view of lobbying to elected officials. Also, this type of "lobbying" could eventually lead to a more collaborative model of advocacy and lobbying for public policy changes, where nonprofit human service professionals and government contract managers work together to create new policies. There has been discussion in the literature that nonprofit organizations are reluctant to lobby government for changes, for fear of losing funding from the government (Gronjberg, 1993; Salamon, 1995). There has also been considerable discussion in the literature on collaborative governance in the management of public programs (Ansell & Gash, 2008; Donahue &

Zeckhauser, 2011; Emerson, Nabatchi, & Balogh, 2011). This chapter will discuss this new "advocacy" approach, which positions nonprofits human services staff (both managerial and program) and government contract managers not in adversarial relationships but in more collaborative ones whereby they can work together to uncover the problems, create new ways to set the agenda, gain access to decision-making arenas, and understand opportunities and challenges (e.g., federal block grant requirements) that exist in the human services policy domain. A collaborative contracting relationship allows for nonprofits to advocate for changes to programs during the process itself.

Local and state governments craft some of their social policy through the development of contracts. Nonprofits deliver social services by responding to the contracts, yet they are not systematically involved in their production. This creates a dysfunctional cycle in policymaking, where the state is not close enough to always recognize the problems that exist, yet they craft the solutions. Nonprofits have to stand by and watch this and not participate in the formulations of solutions, and this is very frustrating for them. Some state employees are far removed from the service population and do not interact with clients much at all. Through contracting, the state has distanced itself from the needs of the population, yet they are still in control of the planning and decisions about contract requirements. They are twice removed from the needs of the disadvantaged population. They are required by federal law and block grant regulations to provide services, yet they are at arm's length from the needs. The nonprofits fill that role.

Contracting out has sometimes created a policy framework where the state is very far away from the populations that it serves. "New modes of control have emerged under neoliberalism which have been characterized as the paradox of centralized decentralization. Nonprofit organizations that deliver various kinds of publicly supported social and human service are particularly affected" (Evans, Richmond, & Shields, 2005, p. 74). The state mandates the contract language but isn't close enough to clients to understand full needs, service levels, and so on. It is not the usual practice to consult nonprofits when drafting the contracts. In a very real sense, the language of the contracts written by the state is the social policy being implemented. These programs are designed to solve social problems, yet the agents designing these programs are not directly involved with the service populations nor fully understand the needs.

Street-level nonprofit staff are crafting public policy solutions, even though they aren't included in the state level development of contracts. This means that there are two worlds of policymaking in practice: (a) Nonprofits develop "street-level" policy as the implementers of social services, and (b) the state develops "state-level" social policy, which is expressed in the contracting language. However, there is a major disconnect in the crafting of state-level policy because the state is so far removed from the problems that exist; therefore, it is difficult for the state to develop effective policy formulations that respond directly to the emergent problems facing the disadvantaged communities. Anderson (2010) provides an extensive analysis of the public policymaking process. He articulates that the full cycle of policymaking occurs when there is a problem definition stage, followed by the formulation of programs/solutions to the problem, and then the adoption and implementation of the policy.

There is an inherent twofold paradox in the system that results from contracting, whereby (a) the state is formulating policy solutions, yet they are not completely cognizant of what the problems are, and (b) nonprofits are responding to state-level policies in the form of contracted services, yet they are also responding and developing street-level policies that address the emergent needs of their service populations. This complex, dysfunctional, and fragmented policymaking system is completely different from the traditional bureaucratic model of program and policy development within government institutions.

A policy conundrum exists within the advocacy efforts of nonprofits. Many nonprofits view their advocacy work as their ability to influence the state legislature and politicians and their ability to fund their services. In this sense, the nonprofits are advocating to the incorrect body. The state legislature controls the funding amounts, but contract managers in the state agencies make the decisions about the contracts, including what types of programs are selected and thus who is selected to receive the contracts. All of these nonprofits lobby and advocate for their service populations—expressing the collective interests of their communities—to their elected officials; however, there is an underlying tension in the advocacy cycle. This tension is due to the fact that often the nonprofits are not only advocating about spending; they are also advocating for changes in the delivery of programs. But there is not a specific route for the type of advocacy that makes programmatic changes to the system. For example, what type of communication would allow for the feedback of ideas from nonprofits to government? How would these be coordinated?

A new contracting system for human service delivery can be viewed through the lens of community building and collaboration and not just competition and market forces (Alexander & Nank, 2009). This new collaborative viewpoint allows for government to see nonprofits as partners in the delivery of social services and as central to the fulfillment of the policy's goals (Berry, Krutz, Langner, & Budetti, 2008). Likewise for nonprofits, if they operate in a vacuum away from the goals of public policies, it is likely that these goals will not be addressed in the provision of services. Collaboration can link nonprofits and government in effective ways to improve how the human service system is structured.

HOW TO ADVOCATE WITHIN THE SYSTEM OF CONTRACTING?

Collaboration in practice is a difficult undertaking (Hibbert & Huxham, 2010; Lowndes & Skelcher, 1998). Therefore, the practical implementation of combining contracting with collaboration is very complex. However, the overall goal of this chapter is to identify how collaboration can merge with elements of contracting as a form of advocacy. This can provide insight into how to overcome the some of the challenges that exist within the system.

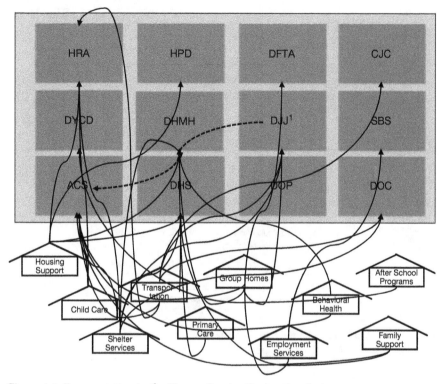

Figure 4.1 Fragmentation in the Human Service Contracting System
Created by the Office of Deputy Mayor of Health and Human Services, New York City.
Used with permission.

The model of collaboration used is Ansell and Gash's (2008) model of collaborative governance, which uses a contingency approach, based on a review of 137 studies on collaboration from the literature. This model is particularly useful to apply to contracting because it defines specific conditions, design and structures of successful collaborative governance systems, and the importance of leadership (see Figures 4.1 and 4.2; Ansell & Gash, 2008). Certainly there are certain aspects of Ansell and Gash's model that are difficult to align with the contracting environment—for example, consensus-style decision-making. However, the overall benefit of using a model as complete as this one to explain the complex collaborative environment overcomes any potential drawbacks. The main factors in Ansell and Gash's collaborative governance model, as in most models of collaboration, are trust, shared vision, and reciprocity. How can these work at the same time as the model of contracting, which focuses on the market, a request for proposal (RFP) process, and specific reporting requirements? Can we incorporate collaboration and contracting at the same time? One way to assess how the principles of collaborative governance can be transferred to contracting is to identify each step in the collaborative governance model (Ansell & Gash, 2008) and analyze these steps using the lens of contracting. Ansell and Gash's model is

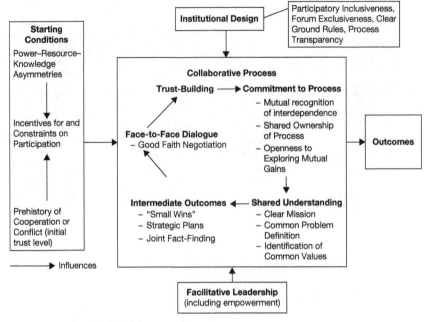

Figure 4.2 A Model of Collaborative Governance
Ansell and Gash (2008). Used with permission.

particularly useful because it compartmentalizes the process of collaboration into different elements. Then, each element can be compared to the contracting model to identify ways to overcome obstacles.

In addition to using Ansell and Gash's (2008) collaborative governance model to suggest ways to advocate for service changes through the contracting environment, an example from practice is also used to highlight a model to increase collaboration in the system of contracting. New York City is a pioneer in collaborative contracting, and many lessons can be learned from their experience integrating collaboration and contracting. New York City is offered here as a case for illustrative purposes only; it is not a test of the framework, and this technique has been used in the literature in other collaborative settings (Crosby & Bryson, 2010). New York City's experience helped to provide specific examples related to the conceptual framework of collaborative governance.

APPLYING LESSONS FROM NEW YORK CITY

Advocacy and Collaborative Contracting

Is it possible to introduce advocacy via collaborative working arrangements into the human service-contracting environment? In human services, collaboration is necessary because of the nature of providing human services. In addition, the contracting environment has certain components that are not necessarily going to help build collaborative working arrangements. Therefore, certain changes must be made to how this type of collaboration is best practiced. Building upon Ansell and Gash's (2008) collaborative governance framework and infusing examples from New York City's experience, a model of collaborative contracting can incorporate collaborative methods into the competitive contracting process. New management skills are required for today's public manager—and collaboration is a major knowledge competency (Berry & Brower, 2005; Getha-Taylor, 2008; O'Leary, Choi, & Gerard, 2012; Smith, 2008). Therefore, it is helpful to provide specific, practical guidance on how to successfully merge contracting and collaboration. The following discussion addresses how to develop this, using the approach from Ansell and Gash and updating it as a method of programmatic advocacy within human service contracting.

Starting Conditions

The first step in using collaboration as a way to advocate is to assess the starting conditions between the nonprofit organization and the government agency. The starting conditions can either make or break the collaboration. However, it is not necessary for the collaborative partners to be on good terms with each other when the partnership begins (Ansell & Gash, 2008). Ansell and Gash (2008) describe the counterintuitive process of antagonistic stakeholders who are highly dependent on each other also being able to create successful collaborations. Adversarial relationships between nonprofit and government employees can be common in human service contracting. This is due to sector differences, misconceptions, and fragmentation related to the contracting process. These problems do not mean that collaboration will be unsuccessful in contracting relationships. The high level of interdependence between the two parties creates strong incentives for collaboration and, once discussed, can reduce preconceived and misconstrued adversarial beliefs. Therefore, adversarial or negative perceptions of potential collaborators do not predict failure for the collaborative initiative. They do however, predict different ways to design the starting conditions than if the partners begin in a more congenial manner. The imbalance of power between stakeholders is a common problem in collaborative governance structures. This is good news for the creation of collaborative contracting because power can often be skewed toward government having more power in the relationship than nonprofits because they provide the funding. However, nonprofit organizations have the knowledge of program design and the institutional knowledge of the communities they serve. Described in this way, the power between nonprofits and government can be viewed as a shared power relationship. In addition, the recognition of the mutual dependence of each partner on the other can balance out the power dynamics. The explicit recognition of how much New York City needed the nonprofits was a key component in the city's experience of moving toward a collaborative model of contracting.

Participation and inclusion by organizations early in the collaborative process is an important strategy in the design of the collaboration (Auer, Nan, Hicks, & Johnston, 2010; Guo & Acar, 2005). A participatory process with significant input from nonprofits into the design of standards can diminish problems and contribute to a trusting and collaborative relationship in which both parties work together smoothly to fulfill the common mission of providing services (Brown & Troutt, 2004; Van Slyke, 2007). There are also suggestions that a partnership approach (Denhardt, 2003) to contracting and procurement or strong relationships (Amirkhanyan, Kim, & Lambright, 2012) can influence the levels of performance. Including nonprofits and encouraging their participation in the process can decrease coordination challenges and complexity within the application, or RFP, process. In addition, collaboration and formal performance measurement do not appear to be a zero-sum game. Instead, they coexist, and trust and joint decision-making can validate and enhance the existing contract monitoring procedures (Amirkhanyan, 2010). Lastly, because human services are a unique type of service, requiring human intervention-based services that are tailored to each program and recipient, collaborative exchanges are necessary to keep pace with updates in evidence-based practices in the field.

Certain conditions of contracting can work in opposition to perfect collaboration. For example, forces of the anonymous market and the notion of principal-agent theory can push the contracting relationship toward government on one side and nonprofits on the other. However, having a discussion on power and knowledge asymmetries can be used as a way to restructure the relationship and cultivate collaboration. In the design of a new collaborative contracting environment, power, resource, and knowledge asymmetries can and should be honestly discussed. In New York City, the Mayor's Office began the Nonprofit Initiative with an open and honest dialogue that described nonprofits as being key to the city's successful human service delivery system.

Collaborative governance models are based on voluntary participation; therefore, it is necessary to articulate incentives and constraints on participation. In addition to government incentives for the collaboration is the need for a streamlined system to reduce costs and make delivery of programs more efficient. The incentive for nonprofits is the steady funding revenue stream that government contracts provide.

The contracting environment is unique, and the application of collaboration to contracting can certainly be a constraint to the overall collaboration. For example, government contract managers can be constrained by federal regulations and requirements that are not understood by nonprofits. In addition, a constraint for both government and nonprofits is the RFP process and how this type of interaction affects the initial levels of participation. Through the creation of the Strengthening Nonprofit Task Force, the Nonprofit Initiative in New York City began with honest discussions on the positive incentives for collaboration and how these collaborative benefits could improve the human service system. There were also discussions about the many constraints that could derail the process.

However, having an open dialogue created a level playing field and helped start the collaboration in a productive way.

The last component of starting conditions from Ansell and Gash's (2008) model is trust. Trust is a complex issue in any collaborative endeavor but can be even more complicated in a contracting environment. Identifying the levels of trust as an antecedent in the collaborative relationship is key to moving forward successfully (Chin, 2010; Gardner, 1999). Even if there is a lack of trust, this must be acknowledged and discussed. The decision to hire Marla Gibson, who had come from the nonprofit sector, to co-lead the city's Nonprofit Initiative had a large impact on the initial trust levels for both sides. To encourage the development of trust, there was a focus on the need for each sector to empathetically view issues and constraints from each sector's perspective. For example, when using empathy, the time-consuming process of completing RFPs by nonprofits can be viewed as an outcome of the requirements of multiple government funding sources. As the solutions to the problems are identified, an empathetic view on why the problems exist can help to create a supportive environment. Gibson was able to see the issues and constraints from the perspectives of both the government and nonprofits, and this empathetic view influenced how the initiative took shape and helped to generate trust across the sector borders.

Institutional Design

Ansell and Gash's (2008) model points to the creation of an effective institutional design for the collaboration. This design creates the necessary protocols and procedures needed to provide the legitimate foundation for the collaboration. The main components of their model can conflict with a typical contracting arrangement. However, certain modifications can be made to introduce a more collaborative design that can include the voice of nonprofits into the design of the contract and provide the opportunity for them to advocate for change.

The best way to facilitate a collaborative governance approach is to create a transparent process. In the design of contracts, there is often a fundamental lack of transparency, with government agencies solely making the decision on which agency to select as a contractor. Using ideas from agency theory, government agencies argue that a closed process of developing the contract is needed to reduce contractor bias. However, the process can be made more transparent, with government contract managers discussing the origination of the contract content and funding from federal block grant funding, state funding, and the guidelines that are attached to those resources. Government contract managers can demystify the RFP and contracting process and can openly discuss where the funding comes from and how and why certain accountability measures must be enforced.

Participatory inclusiveness and forum exclusiveness are two other components of Ansell and Gash's (2008) model. The issue of forum exclusiveness is an interesting element when applying this approach to contracting because it opens up the discussion on the dyadic nature of the contract. This is unique to the contracting arrangement, as all other collaborations include multiple parties. However, even though the exclusive relationship between nonprofit organizations and government agencies is dyadic, or between two organizations, there are multiple levels of coordination among the two sectors. Forum exclusiveness within the contract is both an interorganizational process, which includes the collaborative exchange between the nonprofits and the government. It is also an intraorganizational process, which describes the collaborative exchange among different government agencies. In New York City, there are 11 city human service agencies involved with contracting to nonprofit human service providers. Their initiative included collaboration and participatory inclusiveness among these agencies inside government to create standard protocols and practices, while at the same time working with nonprofits to coordinate, streamline, and connect.

The last component of the institutional design is having clear ground rules. In the contracting environment this is key as both partners need clear rules to govern the coordination of the system. Since fragmentation can occur within contracting, coordination and communication is key to successful collaborative initiatives. Ground rules govern how decisions are communicated at the different stages of the contracting process. For example, before the Nonprofit Initiative, many city agencies would not even speak with nonprofit organizations before or during a contract because of the fear of contractor bias. This is an outcome of the powerful forces of competition and how it dictates the need for an anonymous market to operate at all times. However, once the Nonprofit Initiative began discussing this issue, it became clear that a new set of ground rules needed to be in place to allow for cross-sector communication and coordination about RFPs, contract goals, service recipients, program outcomes, and so on. Without this, city contract managers were in the dark about the realities of human service delivery programs and the issues facing New York City residents who are recipients of human services.

Advocacy via a Collaborative Process

Ansell and Gash's (2008) collaborative governance model describes the collaborative process as the most important phase, yet it can also be described as the most complex and intricate to implement (Thomson & Perry, 2006). A collaborative viewpoint allows for government managers to recognize nonprofit leaders as partners in the delivery of human services and to include them in making decisions that impact the communities they serve. This collaborative process in contracting can include systematic strategies using the RFP process, performance monitoring, and reporting (characteristics of the formal or competitive type of contract) but can also concentrate on building relationships and trust (characteristics of the relational or collaborative type of contract). One of the most important components of the collaborative governance process is face-to-face dialogue. However, in the contracting environment, this is often viewed as having a very high transaction cost and can skew the impartiality of contracting managers in the selection of contractors during the RFP process and therefore is less likely to occur. The overall benefit of face-to-face dialogue between contract managers and nonprofit service providers should outweigh the potential costs. Contract managers should have scheduled meetings with their nonprofit service providers to enhance effective communication and coordination. Also, system level/community level meetings can be convened to share best practices, communicate programmatic and service updates, and generally stay connected. In New York City, the creation of the Strengthening Nonprofits Task Force provided the opportunity for face-to-face dialogue and the chance to make the human connections necessary. It is also important for the process to include opportunities for both sides to create a shared understanding of each partners' mutual dependence. This shared understanding should also recognize that the social and relational factors in the collaboration could be the most important determinants of a successful relationship (Shaw, 2003) and reiterate the need for facilitative leadership throughout the process.

In addition, the contracting process can include the programmatic perspective and knowledge of the nonprofit in the design of the contract and the RFP. A collaborative dialogue between government contract managers and nonprofit service providers can discuss how those specific programs may be delivered. In New York City, this was accomplished via the use of concept papers, where the city invited nonprofit service providers to complete concept papers on the programmatic content of contracts before the RFP was issued. In this way, the city could receive information from the nonprofit community on emerging evidence-based practices, trends, and quality outcomes prior to the issuance of the RFP.

CONCLUSION

One of the important functions of nonprofit organizations in the United States has traditionally been advocacy, particularly for increased government funding for services to individuals, although service provision and other roles are also important (Kramer, 1981). However, findings from the literature examining the effect of high dependence on government funding also indicate that nonprofit human service organizations are reluctant to initiate political activity, because they are afraid that it will harm their greatest revenue stream, which largely comes from government sources (Gronjberg, 1993; Salamon, 1995). Researchers look at how civil society is affected by contracting and find that turning nonprofit organizations into little service delivery businesses dissipates their political potential. Many have noticed this trend and called this the "chilling" effect of government funding on advocacy efforts. In a study examining the impact of welfare reform in Delaware, Curtis and Copeland (2003) find that the majority of interview participants were hesitant to engage in advocacy and lobbying efforts.

However, Kramer (1981) found that nonprofits' reliance on public funds to deliver services did not necessarily constrain their advocacy activity. Legislative advocacy includes efforts to influence processes of legislation on social issues. In terms of the way advocacy is connected to community, there is a close relationship between the two as an organization's advocacy activities can be a critical way that they express the will of the communities that they serve. Nonprofit social service providers can be the voice of their communities and express the needs and concerns of these communities to their elected officials. The elected officials are in control of the state budgets and control the decisions around how much money is allocated to provide the social services.

Another advocacy function that nonprofits may use is programmatic advocacy where nonprofits advocate for changes to the guidelines affecting the program operations. This type of advocacy is communicated not to the legislature, but to the government contract managers who make decisions regarding contracts. Without activating their programmatic advocacy function and only activating the legislative advocacy function, nonprofits are depicting themselves as critical and combative agents in the policymaking process. The usage of programmatic advocacy might be beneficial by improving the street-level knowledge of state employees, by bringing the state and nonprofit together in collaborative arrangements, and by persuading bureaucratic contract managers to advocate to the legislature on behalf of their nonprofit partners.

REFERENCES

Alexander, J., & Nank, R. (2009). Public–nonprofit partnership: Realizing the new public service. *Administration & Society, 41*, 364–386.

Amirkhanyan, A. (2010). Monitoring across sectors: Examining the effect of nonprofit and for-profit contractor ownership on performance monitoring in state and local government contracts. *Public Administration Review, 70*, 742–775.

Amirkhanyan, A., Kim, H. J., & Lambright, K. (2012). Closer than "arms length": Understanding the factors associated with collaborative contracting. *American Review of Public Administration, 42*, 341–366.

Anderson, J. E. (2014). *Public policymaking.* Seventh Edition. Stamford: Cengage Learning.

Ansell, C., & Gash, A. (2008). Collaborative governance in theory and practice. *Journal of Public Administration Research and Theory, 18*, 543–571.

Auer, J., Nan, N., Hicks, D., & Johnston, E. (2010). Managing the inclusion process in collaborative governance. *Journal of Public Administration Research and Theory, 21*, 699–721.

Berry, F. S., & Brower, R. S. (2005). Intergovernmental and intersectoral management: Weaving networking, contracting out, and management roles into third-party government. *Public Performance and Management Review, 29*, 7–17.

Berry, C., Krutz, G., Langner, B., & Budetti, P. (2008). Jump-starting collaboration: The ABCD Initiative and the provision of child development services through Medicaid and collaborators. *Public Administration Review, 68*, 480–490.

Brown, L. K., & Troutt, E. (2004). Funding relationships between nonprofits and government: A positive example. *Nonprofit and Voluntary Sector Quarterly, 33*, 5–27.

Chin, B. (2010). Antecedents or processes? Determinants of perceived effectiveness of interorganizational collaborations for public service delivery. *International Public Management Journal, 13*, 381–407.

Crosby, B. C., & Bryson, J. M. (2010). Integrative leadership and the creation and main-
tenance of cross-sector collaborations. *The Leadership Quarterly, 21*(2), 211–230.

Curtis, K., & Copeland, I. (2003). The Impact of Welfare Reform on Nonprofits and
the People They Serve in Delaware. Report to the Aspen Institute Nonprofit Sector
Research Fund Grant # 2001-NSRF-08

Denhardt, K. (2003). *The procurement partnership model: Moving to a team-based
approach.* IBM Center for the Business of Government Paper Series.

Donahue, J. D., & Zeckhauser, R. (2011). *Collaborative governance: Private roles for
public goals in turbulent times.* Princeton, NJ: Princeton University Press.

Emerson, K., Nabatchi, T., & Balogh, S. (2011). An integrative framework for collaborative governance. *Journal of Public Administration Research and Theory, 22,* 1–29.

Evans, B., Richmond, T., & Shields, J. (2005). Structuring neoliberal governance: The
nonprofit sector, emerging new modes of control and the marketisation of service
delivery. *Policy and Society, 24*(1), 73–97.

Gardner, S. (1999). *Beyond collaboration to results: Hard choice in the future of service to
children and families.* Tempe: Arizona Prevention Resource Center.

Getha-Taylor, H. (2008). Identifying collaborative competencies. *Review of Public
Personnel Administration, 28,* 103–119.

Grønbjerg, K. A. (1993). *Understanding nonprofit funding: Managing revenues in social
services and community development organizations.* Jossey-Bass Inc Pub.

Guo, C., & Acar, M. (2005). Understanding collaboration among nonprofit organizations: Combining resource dependency, institutional, and network perspectives.
Nonprofit and Voluntary Sector Quarterly, 34, 340–361.

Hasenfeld, Y., & Garrow, E. (2012). Nonprofit human-service organizations, social
rights, and advocacy in a neoliberal welfare state. *Social Service Review, 86,* 295–322.

Hibbert, P., & Huxham, C. (2010). The past in play: Tradition in the structures of collaboration. *Organization Studies, 31,* 525–554.

Kramer, F. A. (1981). *Dynamics of public bureaucracy: an introduction to public management.* Cambridge, Mass.: Winthrop Publishers.

Lowndes, V., & Skelcher, C. (1998). The dynamics of multi-organizational
partnerships: An analysis of changing modes of governance. *Public Administration,
76,* 313–333.

Salamon, L. M. (1995). *Partners in public service: Government–nonprofit relations in the
modern welfare state.* Baltimore, MD: Johns Hopkins University Press.

Shaw, M. M. (2003). Successful collaboration between the nonprofit and public sectors.
Nonprofit Management & Leadership, 14, 107–120.

Smith, S. R. (2008). The challenge of strengthening nonprofits and civil society. *Public
Administration Review, 68*(Suppl), 132–145.

Thomson, A. M., & Perry, J. L. (2006). Collaboration process: Inside the black box. *Public
Administration Review, 66,* 20–32.

Van Slyke, D. M. (2007). Agents or stewards: Using theory to understand the government–
nonprofit social services contracting relationship. *Journal of Public Administration
Research and Theory, 17,* 157–187.

Advocacy, Social Change, Activism, and Technology

Community Level

5

The Energizing Citizen Action with the Power of Digital Technology

The Amplified Effort of the Newark Residents against the Power Plant

DAVID B. CARTER ■

The emerging ascendency of Internet-based advocacy tools have raised important questions about how these technologies are replacing traditional policy advocacy and the associated social ties that have long been a staple of collective
action (Bimber, Flanagin, & Stohl, 2012; Earl & Kimport, 2011; Shirky, 2008). It
has been recognized that for digital technology to be an ally of advocacy groups,
the organizations must have the resources and ability to make use of the technology, including both access to it and human talent to use it (McNutt, 2008).
While it is accepted that digital technology is increasingly being used in advocacy, it is less clear whether its use is leading to the development of new forms
of advocacy or simply enhancing established approaches and repertoires of contention (Earl & Kimport, 2011). There is also considerable debate about whether
digitally enabled activism can form the important social ties for collective
action that have traditionally developed through face-to-face interaction (Ganz,
2014; Gladwell, 2010; Morozov, 2009; Shirkey, 2008). Despite this debate, there
is a substantial literature on the prospects and existence of online social capital (Justice & McNutt, 2013; Kobayashi, Ikeda, & Miyata, 2006; McNutt, 2008;
Skoric, Ying, & Ng, 2009; Steinfield, DiMicco, Ellison, & Lampe, 2009; Wellman,
Haase, Witte, & Hampton, 2001). Questions have also emerged about the role of
organizations in a digital age, particularly whether their role in bringing people
together for collective actions has diminished (Bimber et al., 2012).

Digital advocacy tools have emerged in recent decades, post establishment of many of the community organizing tactics associated with the social action model. The traditional social action community organization model is based on resource-intensive face-to-face interaction that empowers community members and seeks social change (Kahn, 1970, 2010; McNutt & Borland, 2007; Putman & Feldstein, 2003).

Recent studies have focused on the need to integrate online and offline relationships, rather than focusing on the virtues or limits of digital technology (Castells, 2012; Earl & Kimport, 2011; Han, 2014). Earl and Kimport (2011) compare theories that digital technologies are changing the underlying processes of advocacy versus having a supersizing effect that enhances, amplifies, and expedites traditional advocacy, noting that the debate is not yet settled. Also, these studies are based on large geographic scales, often at the national or international level. Much of the research remains focused on the Internet's ability to connect people globally in a manner that has neglected its use locally at the smaller place-based community geographic scale (Hampton & Wellman, 2003). More data rich empirical studies are needed to understand the influence of new digital technology on collective action and advocacy, particularly at the local scale (Ackland & O'Neil, 2011; Earl & Kimport, 2011; Hampton & Wellman, 2003; Han, 2014; Obar, Zube, & Lampe, 2012).

This study of digital advocacy as part of a community action event contributes to our understanding of advocacy in the digital age. It provides a data-rich empirical evaluation of online and offline participation as part of a local community-organizing event. I also consider how this effort compares with a traditional social action organizing model, a hybrid of traditional and online organizing, and the new model of online only organizing.

THE DATA CENTERS PROJECT

This study analyzes the Newark Residents against the Power Plant (NRAPP), a community organization that emerged in opposition to the proposed data center and its associated 279-megawatt power plant.

Support for the project among Delaware's elite was bolstered by the promise of economic development and job creation, as impacts of the 2008 financial crisis had been particularly severe in Delaware (Boyer & Ratlege, 2016). Delaware had recently suffered the loss of 2,100 jobs at the Newark Chrysler Plant, 550 jobs at a General Motors Plant, 400 jobs at the Invista Nylon Plant, and several thousand jobs lost due to the acquisition of MBNA Bank by Bank of America (Goss, 2015). The state had also experienced significant job cuts by Hercules, Avon, Merck, Astra Zeneca, and the Dupont Company and an estimated loss of over 10,000 construction industry jobs (Boyer & Ratlege, 2016). This created a political and economic environment in which the governor, the general assembly, Delaware's congressional delegation, and most other state leaders placed job creation at the top of their policy agenda. The Data Centers LLC (TDC) project was estimated to be a

$1.1 billion project creating hundreds of jobs. The State of Delaware had already committed a $7.5 million grant to the project for infrastructure improvements as an incentive to the developer (Kemp, 2013).

TDC incorporated in Delaware in 2011 and had already secured support from the governor, members of Delaware's legislature, union representatives, the University of Delaware (owner of development site), the City of Newark, the Delaware State Chamber of Commerce, and other influential groups that had been engaged in the decision-making process for nearly two years. Thus, their political support prior to the public disclosure of the project seemed, to many, unstoppable.

EMERGENCE OF NRAPP

On June 6, 2013, executives from TDC contacted a member of the Delaware chapter of the Sierra Club seeking their support for a proposed data center and its associated 279-megawatt power plant. The combined-cycle, natural gas-fired power plant was being marketed by TDC as a "clean energy" project and was presented with an expectation of support from the environmental community.

Contrary to the TDC expectations, both the environmental and local community raised concerns. In response, NRAPP formed in opposition to the project soon after this first public disclosure about the TDC project. The community action was a surprise in the Delaware, which experiences limited organized contention on issues that reverse corporate and economic development interests. Delaware has long been recognized as having weak and inactive public interest and social issues groups and as a state dominated by strong corporate history and decidedly pro-business culture (Johnson & Pika, 1993; Peterson, 1999). Changing the power projection in a small state with intimate political relationships among business interest and elected leaders is a formidable challenge.

DIGITALLY ENABLED ADVOCACY AND SOCIAL BONDS

The rapid emergence of digital communication tools and media beginning in the 1980s and growing to maturity in the 1990s have raised important questions about how these technologies are altering policy advocacy and the associated social ties that have long been a staple of collective action and advocacy (Bimber et al., 2012; Earl & Kimport, 2011; Shirky, 2008). While the important social ties for collective action have traditionally developed through face-to-face interaction, some authors argue that these important relationships can be developed online. In his book *Here Comes Everyone*, Shirky (2008) represents those who believe that relevant social connections not only can be but also are being developed using Internet technology. Others, including Ganz (2014), Gladwell (2010), and Morozov (2009), challenge this idea that strong enough social ties can be formed

electronically despite the lack of research evidence to rebut the substantial literature on the development of online social capital.

Tarrow (2011) argues that social movements still require organizations that
work out of an identifiable, physical space because the Internet can only produce
weak, diffuse ties. It may be that digitally enabled collective actions function more
as a transactional activism than transformational actions (Bennett, 2005; Keck &
Sikkink, 1998). Much of this research on transactional activism was focused on
large geographic scales and broader movements, rather than local community-
based actions. These transactional activities emerging from new technology may
create space and opportunities for more personalized transformational actions
when integrated with traditional face-to-face advocacy that is well documented as
producing the important ties of trust, credibility, loyalty, and mutual dependence
at many scales (Bimber et al., 2012).

Wellman (2002) argues that in the Internet age, social relationships are based
on network ties of individuals and are no longer geographically place based.
Recent research has indicated that digital technology can improve participation
in civic organizations (Valenzuela, Park, & Kee, 2009). Earl and Kimport (2011)
argue, "Truly meaningful collaboration—the power of collective action—can be
created and facilitated without copresence for protest" (p. 126).

INTEGRATION OF ONLINE AND OFFLINE ACTIVITY

A recent focus of research has been on the need to integrate online and offline
relationships as part of collective actions (Castells, 2012; Earl & Kimport, 2011;
Han, 2014). It is well established that the Internet is now "deeply embedded in
group and organizational life in America," with the Internet now as important for
holding groups together and keeping members informed of group activities as the
phone and in-person meetings (Raine, Purcell, & Smith, 2011, p. 1). For advocacy,
it is also an important tool for mobilization and recruitment. Digital technology
like social media is now a prominent feature of political activity and civic engagement (Raine, Smith, Schlotzman, Bardy, & Verba, 2012). However, the nuances
of this social phenomenon—in particular, the importance of integration of traditional face-to-face interaction versus online activity alone for building social
ties, trust, and mutual dependence—are not fully understood. Han (2014) points
out that to be effective at achieving social change organizations must go beyond
focusing just on mobilizing people and organize them for sustained action. This
may require going beyond the mobilizing power of the Internet communication
technologies and require integration with significant face-to-face activities and
actions.

This integration of online and offline organization and advocacy efforts provides
opportunities for more diffuse and emerging online advocacy groups to build legitimacy and grounding. It can also provide more agility to established traditional
organizations, which, prior to the emergence of digital technology, depended
upon resource-intensive tools like phone trees, flyers, posters, billboards, and

door-to-door canvasing. The effective use of technology can lower participation thresholds by significantly reducing the cost of the start-up and sustaining of advocacy efforts and movements (Earl & Kimport, 2011; Garrett, 2006; Hick & McNutt, 2002; McNutt, 2008; Shirky, 2008; Van Laer & Van Aelst, 2010).

Research indicates that online collective action relates closely to offline collective action and that those who participate online are typically the same people that participate offline (Brunsting & Postmes, 2002; Han, 2014; Wojceiszak, 2009). Technology-enabled advocacy has been a considerable transition in advocacy practice, and its use is an outgrowth of the influence of local groups and community problems that contributed to its recent position as a well-respected method (Han, 2014; Hick & McNutt, 2002). As digital advocacy use evolves, it may serve as an automation tool for well-established traditional social action practices, may re-engineer some of the social action practices to improve them, and/or may re-invent social action practices with new processes.

TRADITIONAL SOCIAL ACTION MODELS OF COMMUNITY ORGANIZING

Some of the collective action at the community level is rooted in the social action model of community organizing. Cnaan and Rothman (1968) described this model as one in which the less-advantaged part of the community needs to be organized to make demands on the larger community with a focus on power redistribution. This is particularly true for community contestation that targets a local problem. The social action model of organizing seeks to change the projection of power in a way that empowers an oppressed group or community. It is a "vehicle for social change and local empowerment" (Fisher & Shragge, 2000, p. 2). It seeks to reallocate social and political power to disenfranchised citizens, especially underserved and/or oppressed citizens. (Kahn, 1970; Rothman & Tropman, 1987). The model guides leaders, often social workers, on ways to empower communities to seek and achieve their community goals. It is based on building collaboration, partnerships, and alliances and often utilizes confrontational tactics.

The social action community organizing model predates the emergence of digitally enabled advocacy. Understanding how the technology tools that have emerged in the past two decades are affecting community-level advocacy is of considerable interest. The technology now has ubiquitous distribution and use in society with the capacity to significantly change practice models of community-based collective action. In short, does the community social action model still accurately describe community collective action that now occurs both online as well as offline?

Most of the literature on online and offline activities strongly supports a relationship between the level of online and offline engagement. However, very little of this scholarship is based on smaller local community action efforts. It is primarily derived from analysis of Internet sources or perception survey data over larger geographic or virtual community scales, rather than actual online and off-line participation rates at a community scale of geography. One such case is that of the community opposition to the TDC project proposed to be constructed in Newark, Delaware.

TECHNOLOGY-ENABLED ADVOCACY

To evaluate the significance of the form of advocacy that impeded the development of the TDC project and its associated 279-megawatt power plant, we need to clarify what we mean by advocacy. A useful and expansive definition we will use here is that advocacy is "fundamentally about speaking out and making a case for something important" (Bass, Abramson, & Dewey, 2014, p. 255). Advocacy can be done by an individual but is considered more effective when a collection of individuals organize together to have a stronger voice. This type of collective behavior has a long tradition in the United States. The understanding of collective action has also been rooted in resource mobilization theory that posits that organizations must form and get control over resources for collective actions to occur (Jenkins, 1983). Due to resource requirements, organizations are at the center of collective action and social movements.

The effective use of technology can significantly reduce the cost of starting and sustaining of movements (Earl & Kimport, 2011; Shirky, 2008). It has been clearly established that the availability of resources is one of the most critical obstacles to successful collective action and that it is a prerequisite for collective action (Jenkins, 1983; Johnson, Agnone, & McCarthy, 2010; Mosley, 2010; Zald & McCarthy, 1987). In the fight of NRAPP, the effective use of technology was utilized in a way that reduced fiscal resource needs and allowed control over other resources such as mobilization of volunteers, organizing of protest, and control of messaging.

While there is a long tradition of civic engagement, the methods and sophistication have changed over time and may now be rapidly evolving into new forms that are emerging due to digital technologies that may be reducing or changing the central role of organizations (Bimber et al., 2012; Earl & Kimport, 2011; Shirky, 2008).

DIGITAL TECHNOLOGY AND COMMUNITY ORGANIZING

Digital technologies may be helping to address concerns about the declining trend of organizational participation such as those articulated in *Bowling Alone* (Putman, 2000). It has been extensively reported that in postindustrial society, citizens have become increasingly disengaged from political participation (Dalton 2006; Scocpol & Fiorina, 1999). If society is more disengaged, digital technology has been identified as a tool that could help rekindle political engagement by making once-impossible forms of group interaction possible (Shirky, 2008).

Digitally enabled advocacy significantly reduces costs and shortens the timeframe for organizing (Earl & Kimport, 2012; McNutt, 2008). In the case of the Newark Power Plant, many individuals with a common claim joined together to form a sustained effort to press their collective interest of opposition to the proposed power plant project. The group overcame formidable opposition from powerful interests well endowed with fiscal and staff resources in a short span of about a year. What the community group lacked in fiscal resources to support their efforts may have been overcome through the effective use of new digitally enabled advocacy tactics. Yet the question remains as to whether the NRAPP community action can be understood through the lens of the literature that dominantly considers larger social movements that play out across large geographic areas and likely leverage the affordances of digital technologies differently than at the local geographically bound scale.

AFFORDANCES OF DIGITAL TOOLS

Consideration of the affordances provided by technology for collective actions at different scales is an important consideration. Affordance theory holds that the world is perceived not only in terms of object shapes and special relationships but also in terms of the object possibilities for actions, or affordances (Gibson, 1977). This theory is now applied to the use of digital technology, recognizing that it is more than simply the availability of the technology that determines its use but also the perception of how it can be utilized better than existing actions that leads to its utilization. The more it is perceived to be a useful tactic for advocacy, the more it will be used. This leveraging of affordances leads to these digital tools being combined with evolving advocacy practice models that guide practitioner utilization and decision-making (Earl & Kimport, 2011; McNutt, 2008). There are several basic processes of how digital technology is used, including issue research, information dissemination/awareness, coordination/organizing, and influence (McNutt, 2008). As such, digital technology will be used to the extent that it is perceived and acted upon as a better tactic for community action. This has the potential to replace, update, add new, or merge digitally enabled advocacy approaches with traditional tactics commonly associated with the community social action organizing.

RESEARCH OBJECTIVES

Considering the available literature and theoretical approaches, I offer the following research objectives:

1. To identify any distinct patterns in the online and offline activities by level of engagement in a local collective action due to affordances in a local context.

2. To evaluate the level of participant recruitment using digital technologies versus face-to-face activities.
3. To identify advocacy conditions in which digitally enabled advocacy is closely related to traditional social action models of advocacy using new technology and conditions where it represents new forms or models of advocacy.
4. To identify evidence indicating that the digitally enabled advocacy approach of NRAPP was a factor affecting the decision not to construct the TDC project.

DATA SOURCES

This is a study of the use of digital technology as part of a community collective action event. The study uses a mixed methods approach with both quantitative and qualitative elements as described in the following discussion (Patton, 2002). An overview of the NRAPP case precedes discussion of the data sources and analysis of results.

I obtained the NRAPP participation and other records. I then organized, processed, and analyzed the extensive data and documents. The data cover the period from July 2013 through August 2014. These data include all original records of individual participants as documented on event sign-up sheets in both online and offline activities by specific activity, type of activity, online/offline, and date. A total of 6,916 participation events occurred. The earliest date of each participant is defined as the recruitment event and unique participant ($N = 3,722$). Additional data were collected from documents, letters, news articles, and other sources for qualitative analysis for the period from September 2011 through August 2014. The research was approved by the University of Delaware's Institutional Review Board.

In addition to participation events, I analyzed the complete export of all NRAPP Facebook analytics and utilization statistics and records of MailChimp activities.

Quantitative analysis of the NRAPP participation data was conducted to gain insights into the group's operation and extensive integration of online and offline advocacy. This analysis included detailed descriptive and comparative statistical analysis of online and offline participation, whether initial recruitment was online or offline, growth of participation over time, formal versus informal NRAPP membership, levels of online and offline participation by individuals, and the geographic distribution of participants. All quantitative analyses were conducted using SPSS Statistical Software.

Additional qualitative analysis was conducted including the review of documents and brief informal discussion with NRAPP participants during the action events in 2013–2014 and with three active participants during the fall of 2015. This information is primarily used to supplement quantitative findings, fill knowledge gaps, and validate findings. This included an analysis of pre-existing advocacy capacity and description of the NRAPP leadership structure.

ANALYSIS AND DISCUSSION

Analysis of the data related to the participation events and type of advocacy actions taken, group and type of participation, online and offline activity, fundraising, and other factors are summarized in the following sections. The analysis focuses on the use of online versus offline activities.

Repetoire of Advocacy Tactics Utilized

To address each of the research objectives, I first consider how leveraging of affordances of digital technology may interact with traditional social action advocacy tactics and strategies. I develop the major catagories of tactics utilized by NRAPP and code them as traditional/face-to-face tactics, digital-only tactics made possible due to new digital technologies, or as hybrid tactics that merges traditional and digitally enabled advocacy approaches.

Traditional tactics included the development of a formal membership, the recognition of various leadership roles (vs. truly distributed leadership), traditional information sharing with press releases and factsheets/information handouts, a variety of grassoots mobilizing tactics, legal actions, and fundraising.

The NRAPP group also utlized digital technology to leverage many of the traditional tactics. Several are only available due to the new communication technologies such as web pages, social media, and e-mail campaigns. Numerous tactics leveraged digital technologies to improve traditional approaches such as coordination of group activities, dissemination of information digitally, and fundraising. Digital technology was typically used as the primary communication mechanism for NRAPP actions, activities, and events. A summary of tactics used can be found in Table 5.1.

The analysis in the sections to follow will further analyze the use of this repetoire of traditional and digitally enabled tactics. It will evaluate the extent that tactics were used for initial recruitment, their use in validating and sustaining participation, their role in fundraising, and other analyses that better explains their utilization and significance to the NRAPP collective action efforts.

Patterns in Online and Offline Activities and Levels of Engagement

The participation rate for NRAPP activities shows a steady increase over the duration of the collective action. Records of individual participant's involvement in both online and off line activities document that the NRAPP action had at least 3,722 unique participants that were involved with 6,916 participation actions. Participation actions are defined as an individual having signed up either in person or online for any of the 48 documented activities associated with the

Table 5.1. NRAPP ADVOCACY TACTICS

Advocacy tactic	Traditional/ face-to-face tactic	Hybrid/ co-digital tactic	Digital- only tactic
Formal membership (NRAPP)	X		
Leadership actions			
Steering committee	X		
Coordination		X	
Information dissemination			
Web page			X
Social media			X
Press peleases		X	
Fact sheets/materials		X	
FOIA requests	X		
Grassroots activism			
Canvassing residents	X		
Community meeting/events	X		
Letter writing campaigns		X	
Email campaigns			X
Testify at public meeting	X		
Protests	X		
Advocacy training	X		
Petitions		X	
Yard sign	X		
Legal action	X		
Fund raising		X	
Number of tactics	10	6	3

NRAPP effort. All participation actions were obtained from the original digital and hardcopy sign-up records provided by NRAPP. The steady growth of NRAPP unique participants by month is summarized in Figure 5.1.

Of those unique individuals that participated in the NRAPP effort, 25.4% ($n = 933$) participated in more than one NRAPP activity. A summary of recruitment, defined by each individual's first involvement with the effort, and repeat involvement of individuals is depicted in Figure 5.2. Reduced recruitment occurred in the months of December and January as well as in June and July. These months correspond to University of Delaware semester session breaks when most students are away and may reflect less student activity and recruitment during these times.

There were also differences between participants and those formally joining as members of NRAPP. Only eight percent ($n = 299$) of the unique individuals ($N = 3,722$) that participated in NRAPP actions formally joined the group.

Online versus Offline Participation Recruitment

The NRAPP group had a very active online presence to support the traditional social action community organizing using a variety of online tools as part of the

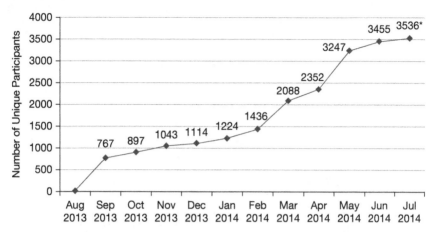

*186 Cases not included due to not having a specific date for Like of NRAPP Facebook Page (Actual N = 3,722).

Figure 5.1 Growth of Unique Participants in NRAPP Effort

advocacy campaign opposing the TDC project. I analyzed data for three of these tools including MailChimp, Facebook, and Change.org. As shown in Figure 5.3, each of these digital technologies experienced significant online participation by unique users over the span of the NRAPP effort. These three tools were used to reach 81% of the unique participants ($n = 3,014$) documented as being involved with NRAPP actions.

MailChimp is an e-mail marketing service. It enables the user to collect and mail a list of recipients, to design e-mail newsletters, and to integrate e-mail with social networks. NRAPPs MailChimp list grew steadily throughout the effort

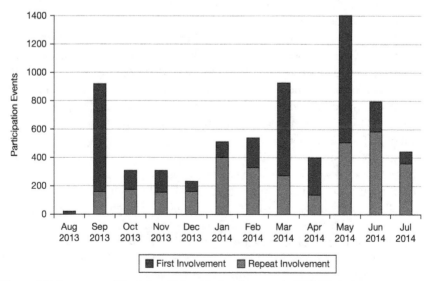

Figure 5.2 Summary of Participant Monthly Involvement in NRAPP Actions

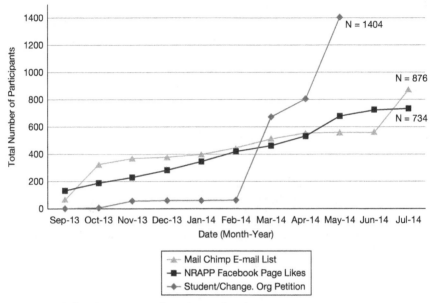

Figure 5.3 Online Participation Recruitment Levels

reaching a total of 876 recipients. The group sent 23 unique MailChimp e-mail messages and action requests, delivering 11,262 messages directly to the inboxes of their subscribers. The number of recipients ranged from a minimum of 61 early in the NRAPP effort to a maximum of 862 in the final stages. The electronic mailings also experienced relatively high rates of being checked or opened by recipients, with open rates of 49.9%, well above the average open rate of 23.45% for similar sized group mailings (MailChimp, 2017). The messages announced NRAPP meetings and events, called for participation in direct actions such as fundraising activities and protests, and were integrated with information posted to social media and a web page.

NRAPPs primary social media platform was Facebook. Throughout the duration of the advocacy effort, the group's Facebook page had 791 posts, an average of 2.36 posts per day that reached Facebook users 200,372 times. Analytics of the group's Facebook page show a steady and continuous increase of page likes, the clicking of a button showing support or interest by a person. The page reached a high of 734 likes over the 334 days from September 2013 through July 2014, a mean of 2.21 new likes per day.

A third technology utilized was a Change.org petition established by a group of University of Delaware students. The growth of participants utilizing this tool was quite different from that observed with either MailChimp or Facebook. The petition collected only 60 participants from September through February. However, it quickly surged in early 2014 with 612 participants in March, 124 in April, and 598 in May. This technology was less integrated with many of the other NRAPP activities. Forty-eight percent of those who participated only once did so using this technology ($n = 1,795$) as compared to the next highest types of one-time participation events including 11.2% (n = 419) who signed a petition in person, 7.8% (n = 292) who put out a yard sign, 6.9% (n = 260) who added their name to a sign on a letter, and 4.9% (n = 186) who used Facebook.

Relationship of Traditional Advocacy Actions and Digitally Enabled Actions

The steady growth of online activities of NRAPP were well integrated with and supportive of the group's offline activities including face-to-face meetings, participation in public meetings, fundraising events, and protests events. A simple comparison of online and offline activities of NRAPP participants show them to be similar, with offline actions comprising 55.5% of the participant actions (n = 3,834) and online activity comprising 44.5% of participant actions (n = 3,082). This analysis does not include the messages sent through MailChimp due to the inability to determine which individuals received the earlier messages versus later messages as the mailing database grew.

While the number of online participation events was similar to offline, the types of activities were very different. The vast majority of online events were associated with signing of online petitions (n = 2059) and Facebook activity (n = 897), both of which are helpful to disseminate information that have low transaction cost to participants. Offline events include a mix of low and high transaction cost activities. High transaction cost activities included physically participating in protest events or community canvasing efforts (n = 341), participating in legal challenges (n = 97), taking on leadership responsibility in the NRAPP organization (n = 59), providing comments at public meetings (n = 199), and writing a letter to the editor (n = 26). Low transaction cost offline actions included formally joining NRAPP and attending meetings (n = 817), displaying a "No Newark Power Plant" yard sign (n = 560), signing a letter to a decision maker (n = 1,095), and signing a petition (n = 486).

There were also significant differences in the online/offline participation among individuals with different participation rates. As depicted in Figure 5.4, those participating in one event were more likely to have done it online, while those participating in three or more events were more than twice as likely to have engaged in offline activities.

This relationship of online/offline activity by participation events is even more pronounced for the first activity, considered the recruitment entry point for each NRAPP participant (see Figure 5.5). Sixty-two percent of participants for one event did so online. Conversely, those most active were more than twice as likely to have their entry event be an offline activity, with 68% offline and 32% online.

Online and Offline Fundraising

NRAPP fundraising also utilized a hybrid tactic. Over the span of the NRAPP action, the group raised $28,686.25. NRAPP partnered with Delaware Audubon

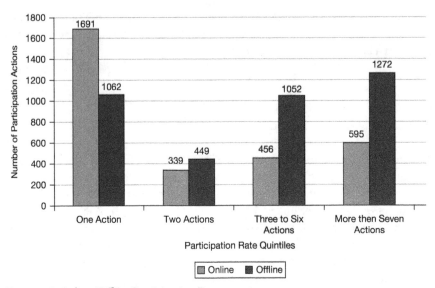

Figure 5.4 Online/Offline Participation Rates

Note: Observed variation is statistically significant (Pearson's chi square = 564.6, $p = 0.001$).

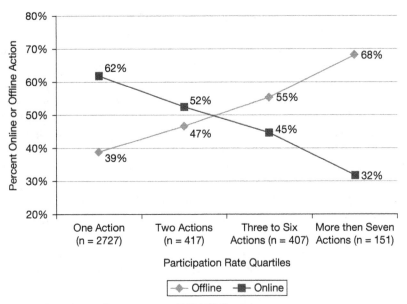

Figure 5.5 First Action/Recruitment of NRAPP Participants

Society, a 501(c)(3) charitable organization, which agreed to act as NRAPP's fiscal agent to allow tax deductible contributions and to utilize Audubon's established nonprofit accounting and auditing capacities, alleviating the need to formally incorporate NRAPP and providing fiscal oversight of charitable contributions to the community advocacy effort.

The majority of the funds were collected offline. Yet, online activity accounts for much of the fundraising, both through its use to communicate the needs for donations and by direct online collection of individual donations ($n = 352$). About 33.2% of donations ($n = 117$) were made online for a total of \$9,529.00. However, all donation requests were delivered to potential donors through online solicitations, distributed multiple times using social media and the e-mail marketing system. The remaining funds were collected from offline donations (59.8%) and through a one-time grant for \$2,000 from the Greenwatch Institute (6.9%).

Funding was utilized for activities including fees for Freedom of Information Act requests, printing, postage, transcription services, legal fees, a noise level study, and purchasing of yard signs.

Digitally Enabled Advocacy and Traditional Community Action Organizing

This study looks at the utilization of digital technology as part of a community movement or collective action effort. The analysis of the data indicates that online tools were an extensively utilized tool critical to the rapid mobilization and effective advocacy of the NRAPP. It also indicates that traditional face-to-face organization and advocacy techniques were also critical to NRAPP's success. The digital technologies essentially enhanced the community opposition efforts that were grounded in traditional social action-type advocacy tactics, providing a data rich example of the "amplifying" effect of technology on advocacy described by Earl and Kimport (2011).

Nearly half of the recorded participation events occurred digitally. Digitally enabled tactics were extensively used to quickly disseminate information, mobilize supporters for a range of action, raise funds, and recruit additional supporters and volunteers. Of particular interest was its high level of integration with traditional face-to-face organizing activities. The more involved participants were in the activities of the organization, the higher the percentage of their activities that were face to face. This strongly supports that the digital technology was used to enhance and "supersize" the traditional advocacy tactics and approaches.

Digital technology allowed for the rapid growth and development of the community collective actions that is highly unlikely to have been possible without these tools. It should be noted that although the organization was able to raise considerable funds in a short time period, they had extremely limited resources throughout most of the effort. The low cost of technology for mobilization is what made it possible to rapidly recruit and retain supporters.

The capacity to immediately distribute key information made possible by digital technology allowed NRAPP to frame the issue on its terms. The rapid dissemination of information provided first-strike capability limiting the ability of TDC, the decision-making authorities, or project supporters to control the message.

In considering the tactics and strategies utilized, the majority were traditional tactics that were enhanced and amplified by digital technology ($n = 10$), followed by hybrid tactics ($n = 6$) and digital only tactics ($n = 3$; see Table 5.1). These separations are, however, not always clear cut. For example, new digital-only tactics like social media were often used to communicate information about events using traditional tactics. Of interest is that the participation of digital technology tactics was highest among those individuals who also participated in face-to-face activities. This provides compelling evidence that the use of digital technology did not fundamentally change advocacy but enhanced it. The vast majority of those most active were engaged regardless of whether the actions were online or offline. Of the 186 most active NRAPP participants who participated in six or more events, 87.6% ($n = 156$) utilized both online and offline tactics. None of the most active people utilized online actions exclusively, and 13.4% participated only in face-to-face events. This indicates that the traditional social action organizing model of advocacy is enhanced by digital technology.

Expanded Traditional Organizational Membership Boundaries

Digital technology does appear to have expanded the boundaries of organizational membership, or at least conflated the concept of membership. This is different from the more bounded neighborhood focus of the traditional social action organizing model. Figure 5.6 shows that while the formal membership of NRAPP, or those

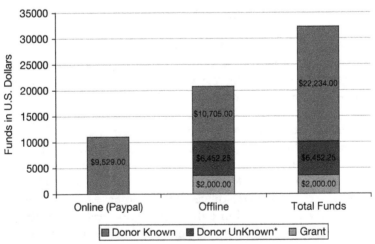

*Unknown donors include cash contributions such as those made at meetings and events.

Figure 5.6 Origins of NRAPP Funding

officially joining the organization, included 299 individuals, the unique number of participants was over an order of magnitude higher ($N = 3,722$). Are participants who work for social change also members? Additionally, a simple geocoding of the address information of participants show a drastic geographic expansion of participants, well beyond the neighborhood or Newark community map boundaries.

Increasingly, advocacy organizations are using the Internet and social media in different ways for advocacy (Bass et al., 2014). These digital tools are a boon for advocates, enabling them to communicate with large audiences in a rapid and inexpensive way (McNutt, 2008; Shirky, 2008). Of interest is that the technology has developed to a point of critical mass ensuring further adoption is much easier (Bimber et al., 2012). The NRAPP digitally enhanced action may simply be an example of the coming new normal for community advocacy actions.

Networked Leveraging of Digital Technology Affordances

The NRAPP Facebook page provided an outlet for the rapid dissemination of information, particularly regular updates to its members and others following the group's activities. It provides the best platform for analysis, since nearly every addition of information to the web page, press releases, digital copies of printed information, and information about NRAPP activities were posted to Facebook, which was also integrated with Twitter. It was a central platform for leveraging affordances.

As the group's efforts grew, the daily reach or number of Facebook users receiving the posts in their Facebook news feed increased. By January 2014, the Facebook page was experiencing daily reaches over 1,000. This daily reach level occurred 32 times during the period, with three days in excess of 2,000, one day at 7,510, and a high day of 20,543 users reached. The two posts with the most daily reach were at the announcement of the NRAPP victory and their announcement of a press release about the victory, respectively. Daily reaches over 2,000 per day were associated with a letter published regarding a Board of Adjustment Hearing in a state-wide newspaper, a protest event associated with the university's board of trustees, and a story about the community activism published in the *Chronical of Higher Education*. Daily reach above 1,000 was typically associated with protest events and articles published by local media sources. Mean daily reach was 493.85. Engagement, measured according to users that like or comment on a post, also increased over time with a mean of 54.87 engagements per day, which peaked at 2,241 in July 2014.

Complementary online activities occurred throughout the effort, including considerable redistribution of messages through e-mail by participants and people sympathetic of NRAPP claims, sharing of Facebook, other online petition for sign-on letters, the sharing of information using Google Docs, and a web page. Each event and post was also linked and shared through Twitter (@NNPP_UD), and all information was added, posted, and archived for easy access through the organization's web page (www.nonewarkpowerplant.org). These online activities were all utilized to mobilize members for offline actions related to the 48 key events and to share information about the project's factual records that conflicted with claims of those supporting the project.

Evidence on the Effectiveness of Digitally Enabled Advocacy Tools

Whether the use of digitally enabled advocacy was a factor affecting the decision not to construct the TDC project is difficult to answer with definitive data. Like most social phenomenon, measuring the influence of the NRAPP mobilization effort is challenging, but anecdotal records clearly indicate that the mobilization had an effect and that the use of digital technology was an important component of that effect. For example, business and data center trade magazines covered the issue and reported on how online technology was being effectively used by those opposing the project (Miller, 2014; Rainy, 2014). *The Chronicle of Higher Education*, an influential publication for academia, also reported on the campus controversy, providing additional evidence of the broader impact of the advocacy efforts (Troop, 2014).

It is important not to romanticize the role of digital technology as a mechanism of social change in communities. In the NRAPP case, it appears to have been the highly effective use of this technology to support traditional mobilizing and organizing efforts that made it so powerful for the grassroots effort. Digital tactics occurred seamlessly with the challenging, resource-intensive, and difficult traditional high-personal-contact organizing efforts. Digital technology was effectively used to expedite communication, crowd source information to improve its accuracy, rapidly disseminate the information, and bring people together face to face at public meetings, protests, community meetings, and other high-contact interactive gatherings that are largely held as necessary actions to solidify a collective identity and solidarity of groups. The integration of online and offline activity, as well as the use of digital technology to enhance mobilizing and organizing tactics, were critical factors for NRAPP's successful effort that stopped the power plant project. Miller (2014) states:

> The Data Centers was clearly taken by surprise by the fervent opposition of NRAPP and its skill in community organizing. Nothing like this had been seen before in the data center industry. . . . The group quickly deployed a web site and built a following through an e-newsletter, Facebook and Twitter. NRAPP tracked every development on its web site and social channels, posting 150 documents, hours of videos of local meetings and maps of the data center site and the surrounding neighborhood.

These finding are consistent with studies showing that the role of digital technology effectively used in movements is to increase the size, speed, and reach of activism, and in this case, it does not indicated that digital technology changed the underlying process of local community activism (Earl & Kimport, 2011; Gibson & Cantijoch, 2013; Han, 2014; Obar et al., 2012).

This distinction between the integration of technology and e-advocacy used alone merits attention, as online mobilizing and building of electronic lists is pursued by many organizations because it is an inexpensive and easily implemented form of advocacy. But reliance on technology for e-mobilization alone, without the associated benefit of the more difficult traditional organizing and face-to-face relationship building is argued to be far less effective, unsustainable, and deceiving in terms of its actual advocacy effectiveness (Han, 2014). The high level of one-time participants in the student-administered Change.Org petition provides some support that online actions used alone, at least as tactics for local contestations, have limited utility. More important, the extensive hybridization of traditional and digital tactics is now commonplace, making digital technology an important tool not only in mobilization but also in organizing in a way that builds social capital.

CONCLUSION

The speed and intensity of advocacy energized by digital tools will clearly place new strains on policymakers as they struggle to adapt to this new approach that can scrutinize their every action, reframe and redirect issues, slow decision-making, and undermine public confidence in our public agencies. Despite this concern, digital technology is here to stay, and its use will exponentially increase now that we have passed the critical threshold of availability and utilization throughout society. As observed in the NRAPP community action, the use and integration of technology is nearly ubiquitous in our communities and, like all major technology adoptions, will have profound social change impacts.

The practice of digitally enabled advocacy is continuing to evolve, powered by the extensive access to digital technology in the past decade and the collective innovation of advocates who are now developing new ways to use these tools. The NRAPP example indicates that digital technology was primarily used to innovatively improve traditional social action community organizing tactics. But the rate, speed, and reach of the efforts in such a short time frame were likely impossible just a decade ago. Community organizing is still evolving with technology, changing long-standing approaches, and will likely evolve to new models of action. Understanding the current changes and likely future developments requires revisiting some of our basis assumptions about social action processes and their evolution. One possible approach to consider in evaluating our theoretical models of community organizing in the digital age is an application of the theoretical concepts applied to business process re-engineering (Hammer & Champy, 2009). There is little question that digital technology gives rise to a need for advocacy organizations to re-evaluate their own processes. In this way, we can consider the key phases of the "re-engineering" of community organizing. As illustrated in figure 5.7, this re-engeering includes the automation of time- and

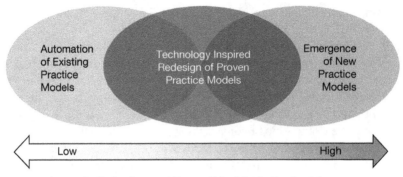

Figure 5.7 Phases of Technology Influenced Changes in Community Organizing Practice

labor-intensive traditional social action tactics, the re-engineering of these tactics with improvements in process that are leveraged with digitally technology, and perhaps eventually the emergence of completely new models of social action organizing.

The adoption of digital technology for social action organizing will continue to increase. This provides enormous promise for improved democratic involvement from a broader range of citizens through venues that go far beyond the traditional boundaries of organization memberships. It also provides powerful tools for social change. However, its impact during the transition and in the future is less clear, and our current models may not adequate describe the emerging digitally enabled practice or the impacts on policy and society.

It is time to rethink our traditional assumptions and models of social action organizing and the role of organizations in the digital age. Only then can we begin to understand the rapid changes taking place and bring our knowledge about an emerging practice of community action closer to reality.

REFERENCES

Ackland, R., & O'Neil, M. (2011). Online collective identity: The case of the environmental movement. *Social Networks, 33,* 177–190.

Bass, G., Abramson, A., & Dewey, E. (2014). Effective advocacy: Lessons for nonprofit leaders from research and practice. In R. Pekkanen, S. Rathgeb Smith, & Y. Tsujinaka (Eds.), *Nonprofits and advocacy: Engaging community and government in an era of retrenchment* (pp. 254–296). Baltimore, MD: John Hopkins University Press.

Bennett, W. L. (2005). Social movements beyond borders: Organization communication, and political capacity in two eras of transnational activism. In D. della Porta & S. Tarro (Eds.), *Transnational protest and global activism* (pp. 203–226). Lanham, MD: Rowman & Littlefield.

Bimber, B., Flanagin, A., & Stohl, C. (2012). *Collective action in organizations: Interaction and engagement and engagement in an era of technological change.* New York: Cambridge University Press.

Boyer, W., & Ratledge, E. (2016). *Growing Business in Delaware: The Politics of Job Creation in a Small State.* Newark, DE: University of Delaware Press.

Brunsting, S., & Postmes, T. (2002). Participation in the digital age: Predicting offline and online collective action. *Small Group Research, 33,* 525–554.

Castells, M. (2012). *Networks of Outrage and Hope.* Cambridge, UK: Polity Press.

Cnaan, R., & Rothman, J. (1968). Conceptualizing community intervention: An empirical test of "three models" of community organizing. *Administration in Social Work, 10*(3), 41–55.

Dalton, R. (2006). Social Modernization and the End of Ideology Debate: Patterns of Ideological Polarization. *Japanese Journal of Political Science, 7,* 1–22.

Earl, J., & Kimport, K. (2011). *Digitally enabled social change: Activism in the Internet age.* Cambridge, MA: MIT Press.

Fisher, R., & Shragge, E. (2000). Challenging Community Organizing: Facing the 21st Century. *Journal of Community Practice,* 8/3, 1–19.

Ganz, M. (2014, October 17). Why hasn't "big data" saved democracy? Review of *The big disconnect: Why the Internet hasn't transformed politics (yet),* by Micah Sifry. *The Nation.*

Garrett, R. K. (2006). Protest in an information society: A review of literature on social movements and new ICTs. *Information, Communication & Society, 9,* 202–224.

Gibson, J. J. (1977). The Theory of Affordances. In R. Shaw & J. Bransford (Eds.), *Perceiving, Acting, and Knowing. Toward an Ecological Psychology* (pp. 67–82). Hillsdale: NJ, Lawrence Erlbaum Associates.

Gibson, R., & Cantijoch, M. (2013). Conceptualizing and measuring participation in the age of the Internet: Is online political engagement really different to offline? *Journal of Politics, 75,* 701–716.

Gladwell, M. (2010, April 4). Small change: Why the revolution will not be tweeted. *The New Yorker.*

Goss, S. (2015, November 18). Layoffs could spur Delaware's bioscience industry. *The News Journal.*

Hammer, M., & Champy, J. (1993). *Reengineering the Corporation.* Harper Business, New York, NY.

Hampton, K., & Wellman, B. (2003). Neighboring in Netville: How the Internet Supports Community and Social Capital in a Wired Suburb. *City and Community, 2*(4), 277–311.

Han, H. (2014). *How organizations develop activists: Civic associations and leadership in the 21st century.* New York: Oxford University Press.

Hick, S., & McNutt, J. (Eds.). (2002). *Advocacy and activism on the Internet: Perspectives from community organization and social policy.* Chicago: Lyceum Press.

Jenkins, C. (1983). Resource mobilization theory and the study of social movements. *Annual Review of Sociology, 9,* 527–553.

Johnson, E., Agnone, J., & McCarthy, J. (2010). Movement organizations, synergistic tactics and environmental public policy. *Social Forces, 88,* 2267–2292.

Johnson, J., & Pika, J. (1993). Delaware: Friends and neighbours politics. In R. J. Hrebenar & C. S. Thomas (Eds.), *Interest group politics in the northeastern states* (pp 61–94). University Park: Pennsylvania State University Press.

Justice, J., & McNutt, J. (2014). Social capital, e-government and fiscal transparency in the states. *Public Integrity, 16*(1), 5–25.

Kahn, S. (2010). *Creative community organizing: A guide to rabble-rousers, activists, and quiet lovers of social justice.* San Francisco: Berret-Koehler.

Khan, S. (1970). *How people get power: Organizing oppressed communities for action.* New York: McGraw-Hill.

Keck, M., & Sikkink, K. (1998). *Activists beyond borders: Advocacy networks in international politics.* Ithaca, NY: Cornell University Press.

Kemp, A. (April 13, 2013). *Star data center project moves forward.* Newark Post.

Kobayashi, T., Ikeda, K., & Miyata, K. (2006). Social capital online: Collective use of the Internet and reciprocity as lubricants of democracy. *Information, Communication & Society, 9*(5), 582–611.

Mail Chimp. (2017). Mail Chimp research, email marketing benchmarks. Retrieved from http://mailchimp.com/resources/research/email-marketing-benchmarks

McNutt, J. (2008). Advocacy organizations and the organizational digital divide. *Currents: New Scholarship in the Human Services, 7*(2).

McNutt, J., & Boland, K. (2007). Astroturf, technology and the Future of Community Mobilization: Implications for Nonprofit Theory. *Journal of Sociology and Social Welfare, 34*(3), 165–179.

Miller, R. (2014, July 22). NIMBY and the data center: Lessons from the battle of Newark. Retrieved from http://www.datacenterknowledge.com/archives/2014/07/22/lessons-of-the-newark-data-center-cogeneration-project-fiasco

Morozov, E. (2009, May 19). The brave new world of slacktivism. Retrieved from http://foreignpolicy.com/2009/05/19/the-brave-new-world-of-slacktivism

Mosley, J. E. (2010). Organizational resources and environmental incentives: Understanding the policy advocacy involvement of human service non-profits. *Social Service Review, 84,* 57–76.

Obar, J., Zube, P., & Lampe, C. (2012). Advocacy 2.0: An analysis of how advocacy groups in the United States perceive and use social media as tools for facilitating civic engagement and collective action. *Journal of Information Policy, 2,* 1–25.

Patton, M. (2002). *Qualitative Research & Evaluation Methods* (3rd Ed.). Thousand Oaks, CA: Sage Publications.

Peterson, R. (1999). *Rebel with a conscience.* Newark, DE. University of Delaware Press.

Putnam R. D. (2000). Bowling Alone: America's Declining Social Capital. In L. Crothers & C. Lockhart (Eds.), *Culture and Politics.* Palgrave Macmillan, New York.

Putman, R., & Feldstein, L. (2003). *Better together.* New York, NY: Simon & Shuster.

Raine, L., Purcell, K., & Smith, A. (2011). *The social side of the Internet.* Washington, DC. PEW Internet and American Life Projects.

Raine, L., Smith, A. Schlotzman, K., Brady, H., & Verba, S. (2012). *Social media and political engagement.* Washington, DC: PEW Internet and American Life Projects.

Rainy, D. (2014, June 30). Data centers receives feelers as area awaits findings of UD working group. *Delaware Business Daily.* Retrieved from http://delawarebusinessdaily.com/2014/06/data-centers-receives-feelers-area-awaits-findings-u-working-group/

Rothman, J., & Tropman, J. E. (1987). Models of community organizing and macro practice perspectives: Their mixing and phasing. In F. M. Cox, J. L. Erlich, J. Rothman, & J. E. Tropman (Eds.), *Strategies of community organization: Macro practice* (pp. 3–25). Itasca, IL: Peacock.

Shirky, C. (2008). *Here Comes Everybody*. New York: Penguin Books.

Skocpol, T., & Fiorina, M. (1999). *Civic Engagement in American Democracy*. Washington DC: Brookings Institution Press and Russell Sage Foundation.

Skoric, M., Ying, D., & Ng, Y. (2009). Bowling Online, Not Alone: Online Social Capital and Political Participation in Singapore. *Journal of Computer-Mediated Communication, 14*(2), 414–433.

Steinfield, C., DiMicco, J. M., Ellison, N. B., & Lampe, C. (2009). Bowling online: Social networking and social capital within the organization. In Association for Computing Machinery (Ed.), *Proceedings of the fourth international conference on communities and technologies* (pp. 245–254). New York: ACM.

Tarrow, S. (2011). *Power in movement: Social movements and contentious politics*. Cambridge: Cambridge University Press.

Troop, D. (2014, July 11). U. of Delaware Pulls Plug on Controversial Power Plant and Data Center. *The Chronicle of Higher Education*.

Valenzuela, S., Park, N., & Kee, K F. (2009). Is there social capital in a social network site? Facebook use and college students' life satisfaction, trust, and participation. *Journal of Computer-Mediated Communication, 14*, 875–901.

Van Laer, J., & Van Aelst, P. (2010). Internet and social movement repertoires: Opportunities and limitations. *Information, Communication, and Society, 13*, 1146–1171.

Wellman, B. (2002). Little boxes, glocalization, and networked individualism. In M. Tanabe, P. van den Besselaar, & T. Ishida (Eds.), *Digital cities II: Computational and sociological approaches* (pp. 10–25). Berlin: Springer.

Wellman, B., Haase, A., Witte, J., & Hampton, K. (2001). Does the Internet Increase, Decrease, or Supplement Social Capital? Social Networks, Participation, and Community Commitment. *American Behavior Scientist, 45*(3), 436–455.

Zald, M. N., & McCarthy, J. D. (1987). *Social movements in an organizational society: Collected essays*. New Brunswick, NJ: Transaction Books.

6

Social Justice 280 Characters at a Time

The Role of Twitter in Social Action

KAREN ZGODA AND KRYSS SHANE ■

There is no shortage of articles warning us of the dangers posed by technology and social media. The mere sighting of a cell phone or laptop may cause those who prefer nontechnological communication to quickly wax poetic about how great the world was before so many became obsessed with technology and the use of social media. They may view Facebook, Twitter, and other social media platforms as ways to avoid social interaction, prevent people from knowing each other, seeing each other, and enjoying each other. What was once a place for people to trade photos and details about their personal lives has now become a place to share images of violence, discontent, and protest; heartfelt and hate-filled messages; and other aspects of society that may not be covered by traditional media. While technology and popular culture discussions were once rooted in online dating or weekend event planning, some of these conversations have shifted to coordinate social action, communicate protests to stop acts of violence, voice political opinions, social cause fundraising, and spread awareness for social causes.

To the detriment of the speed of textbooks, educational materials, and even traditional media organizations such as newspapers, current events can feel like old news by the time the information is published in hard copy and available to be read. This can make it difficult for social movements to utilize printed materials for the sharing of their messages, which can lead to outdated knowledge by readers who only utilize hard copies of information. This lag time (e.g., the National Association of Social Workers [NASW] Technology Standards were in the process of being updated in 2017 after over 10 years of stagnation) can account for some professionals relishing cultural incompetence and a fixed growth mindset with technology, a lack of resources such as adequate training, and an overall professional dependence on face-to-face communication (Berzin, Singer, & Chan, 2015; MacroSW, 2016; Smyth, 2010).

To that end, there are numerous opportunities and compelling reasons for social workers to develop technology literacy and competence at all educational and practical levels. Social media sites are increasingly being used by social workers for advocacy purposes (Brady, Young, & McLeod, 2015). Working professionals and clients alike are turning to social media for options to augment their industry knowledge and become more empowered in the process, and, as a result, the communication and philanthropic landscapes have shifted (Berzin et al., 2015; González-Bailón & Wang, 2016). When considering the direct impact within many professional fields, the impact of social media on networks may be vast, "given the proliferation of social media and technology-based communications, the boundaries of social workers may shift in their attempts to build networks of support, cultivate external support systems, and aggregate multiple support avenues." (Berzin et al., 2015, p. 13). Recognizing the need for these support systems between social work students, professors, and the NASW Code of Ethics guidance toward social and political action, social media can be a great way to further that professional path (Berzin et al., 2015). As social media becomes increasingly ubiquitous in social work practice, there is a notable attention and movement to use social media tools for social change and impact (Berzin et al., 2015; Hill & Ferguson, 2014). One of the most common tools for this is Twitter, one specific social media platform intended for communication among individuals, groups, and companies.

TWITTER BASICS

Twitter (http://twitter.com) is a real-time microblogging service freely available to anyone with Internet access. A post on Twitter is called a tweet. Each tweet contains no more than 280 characters and may include text, links, photos, videos, images, and hashtags. Twitter is one of the most popular forms of social media. Twitter (2016) claims the following in terms of service usage:

- 313 million monthly active users
- 1 billion unique visits monthly to sites
- 82% of Twitter users access the site on their mobile phones
- 79% of Twitter accounts are located outside of the United States
- 40+ supported languages

Greenwood, Perrin, and Duggan (2016) found that 21% of all US adults currently use Twitter; these users were more likely to be between the ages of 18 and 29 and more likely to have a college degree. In addition, they found that 42% of these users visit Twitter daily, 23% of whom visit multiple times per day.

To use Twitter, you create an account with a username and password and are then searchable by this username. For example, you can see all of NASW's tweets by looking at the @NASW username page on Twitter here: https://twitter.com/nasw. You can search Twitter without an account via the Twitter search page here: https://twitter.com/search-advanced?lang=en. One of the benefits of creating a Twitter account is the ability to follow others on Twitter (also called tweeters) and view the tweets of other people. If you create an account, you can also group different users together in a list to follow a particular subject more easily, for example social workers (https://twitter.com/karenzgoda/lists/social-workers) or social work educators (https://twitter.com/laurelhitchcock/lists/social-work-educators). Within the Twitter platform, users also now have the ability to create Moments, or a permanent link to a collection of tweets on a particular topic. For example, here are the most popular Twitter Moments from the year 2015: https://blog.twitter.com/official/en_us/a/2015/this-yearontwitter.html

A hashtag is a way to follow a conversation by putting a # sign in front of a word (e.g., #research) or collection of words (e.g., #socialwork). This allows people from all over the world to share a thought or opinion in a format that requires little time to create and equally little time to be read by others (Alias et al., 2013). By using hashtags, an individual tweet can go from a stand-alone message to a contribution to a conversation that is automatically archived and searchable. This particular feature of Twitter sets it apart from other social media in that the conversation piece is built in, intentional, and discoverable by a worldwide audience both synchronously (in real time) and asynchronously (archived). Additionally, one is not required to know the person he or she is following or responding to, and this can be a great way to network professionally; essentially, hashtags open Twitter discussion to anyone in the world. For example, Gleason (2013) found that hashtag #OccupyWallStreet (sometimes shortened to #OWS to save characters) opened dialogue to diverse perspectives and contained a wide range of content. For those looking to utilize hashtags, Saxton, Niyirora, Guo, and Waters (2015) recommend the following:

> First, it is necessary to use hashtags that are likely to advance the organization's cause. Although an organization can use generic hashtags, such as #cancer, organizational messaging becomes more memorable and serves for better brand recognition when a hashtag is more specific, such as #FindaCure or #CancerSucks. . . . Once an organization selects its hashtag, the next challenge is to grow a community around that hashtag. While regular usage of the hashtag may help increase the public's association of the hashtag with a specific organization, it is more important to have active social media consumers also using the hashtag in positive messaging surrounding the cause and organization. . . . Organizations should consider how they can use hashtags to get individuals involved with an advocacy effort by creating a personal user experience—not simply focusing on the organization. For example, the Red Cross could have simply used the hashtag #npm14 to promote its campaign for "National Preparedness Month" in September, 2014. However, #npm14 became a widely successful hashtag because users were encouraged to share how they were preparing for natural disasters. (pp. 166–167).

TWITTER AS SOCIAL CHANGE TECHNOLOGY

Twitter as Community

The concept of Twitter may seem, on the surface, indistinguishable from other forms of social media. This is because a new user may simply identify with the general idea of each person having an online persona and being able to post his or her thoughts and feelings on a website. However, Twitter is quite different from its social media peers in some very specific ways. For example, Facebook requires a person to use his or her actual name for his or her account and has a constantly changing array of privacy settings that limit the availability and access of posts. In addition, posts can be as long as a person chooses, which often means that a person posting his or her opinion may use hundreds or thousands of characters or words, which can lead to a reader skimming for sentiments. In addition, a reader must be the person's Facebook friend, someone the account holder has chosen to connect with. Privacy settings can be altered on Facebook, but many choose to allow only their own chosen connections to view their postings. Instagram allows for unique usernames; however, it is primarily rooted in images, meaning that most of the online postings of its users are photographs of celebrities, food, or other visual commentary, often with an image caption. This can be beneficial to those who prefer a more visual style; however, this limits the communication, conversation, and impact a post may have. Twitter incorporates the ideas of sharing one's thoughts similar to Facebook but in a more compact and efficient message, allowing a Twitter reader to quickly ascertain the poster's message in a format rooted in language but where succinct is priority (Alias et al., 2013). This creates a Twitter world in which a person can read one tweeter's entire set of posts for a month or a year in quick succession if he or she is seeking knowledge into one person's perspective, or it can allow for someone interested in a specific hashtag to quickly read the conversation, both previously written tweets and in situations where conversation is currently occurring. This gives the reader insight and some kind of context, as well as quick access to information both to learn from and to have opportunity to dialogue with others. That said, many choose to connect their social media accounts so that anything they post to one site simultaneously posts to the others, thus allowing their networks on each to view the same messages and images within the context of what the other sites allow. This may mean that an Instagram photo is also visible on someone's Facebook page or that someone's Twitter tweet is also on their Facebook page or individual website. However, depending on the Facebook settings, it is much less common for someone's Facebook post to be visible on their Instagram or Twitter pages.

Twitter as Social Presence and Participation

Although the concept of short spurts of thoughts was intended to help tweeters to think through their message and pare it down to its necessary components, this shortened form of expression is often beneficial for social messages and presence (Alias et al., 2013). Using Twitter allows a person to quickly share a thought or experience with the world without any major interruption to his or her life and to do so in a format that can be read by millions, if he or she so chooses (see the appendix for sample tweets). For example, if a celebrity is enjoying food at a restaurant during lunchtime, his or her tweet can simply be to list a few adjectives for the experience, followed by tagging the restaurant or city in the tweet. Almost instantly, the celebrity's followers know that he or she is eating lunch, where he or she is eating, where they can go to eat what the celebrity is eating, and they can decide to respond to that tweet with comments on that restaurant, on that city, or by sharing what they themselves are eating for lunch. The tweet has taken mere moments and not interrupted the celebrity's meal, yet the celebrity has created the opportunity for attention and for conversation among fans through the quick use of Twitter. In addition, celebrities may use this to let the paparazzi know where they are, which can lead to their image being used on gossip websites and magazines, only furthering their celebrity status (Guo & Saxton, 2014). For example, President Trump sparked much Twitter dialogue, fact-checking, and discussion during his presidential campaign by tweeting a selfie with a taco bowl using hashtag #CincoDeMayo from Trump Tower Grill (Tesfaye, 2016).

Noncelebrities may utilize the same tactics to create their own community "buzz" or influence High school kids may use the same tactics to show their importance to their classmates while publicizing their great seats at a concert or an expensive gift bought for them for their birthday. Others use Twitter to try to show a different side of themselves. College professors, for example, may seem stuffy or boring during class, but a peek at their Twitter handles may show them to be the bass player in a local band, someone who enjoys specialty coffees, a world traveler, or a motorcycle enthusiast. In each of these cases, people are choosing to include pieces of their personality and of their experiences on a social platform to create an image of themselves that they want others to include mentally when thinking of them. Some nonprofits try to use what they call "celebrity poking" or "celebrity fishing." If a nonprofit can capture the attention of an actual celebrity (someone with fame outside of the social media world) or an Internet celebrity (someone whose fame is captured largely or solely based on his or her online persona), the payoff in terms of geometrically increasing the diffusion of an organizational message or call to action is enticing (Guo & Saxton, 2014). Not only is this based on the potential to attract attention from the celebrity's fans to the organization or its cause, it is also a financially efficient way to create conversations about the topic at hand, draw attention to the need for the organization's support, and to bring eyes and minds to situations that might be ignored by more traditional forms of media (Guo & Saxton, 2014). For those with political goals, Facebook and Twitter can be vital for sharing a message or bringing new signatures to petitions quickly (Brady et al., 2015). Some Twitter users simply participate through viewing or passively clicking to support a cause, whereas others become enlightened to the possibilities of using social participation as an active way to promote new content with a purpose amid a sea of silliness or mindless drivel (Gleason, 2013).

Twitter and Periscope as Live Event, Social Action Broadcasting

Since 2015, Periscope is part of Twitter and enables a Twitter user to distribute live, location-based broadcasting to followers (Weil, 2015). A Twitter user downloads the separate Periscope app onto their mobile device and connects their Twitter account to share broadcasts with followers. It is possible to follow a user on Periscope but not Twitter, and vice versa, although a user will be prompted to follow users with both accounts to make it easier to find friends. Periscope has often been used to broadcast protests, current news items (e.g., accidents, snowstorms, terrorist events), and entertainment (e.g., live fireworks, concerts, running commentary during live television show broadcasts or presidential debates, etc.).

Most notably for social action purposes, Periscope was used as a tool of congressional defiance. There has long been power and control issues with broadcasting Congress live, with both Democrats and Republicans controlling what is broadcast on C-SPAN and with much political posturing alternately keeping cameras running and shutting them off. However, after Republicans cut C-SPAN's live feed during a debate on gun control measures in the wake of the Pulse Orlando shooting, members of Congress downloaded the Periscope app and became the cameras broadcasting to the world, "but in a move that would not have been possible even five years ago, C-SPAN picked up a live video feed from a lawmaker recording the sit-in from inside the chamber—doing an end-run around House leaders" (Gold, 2016). The first congressperson to livestream in this manner was Representative Scott Peters (Hamblin, 2016).

Twitter as Portal for Empowered, User-Generated Content

One of the most interesting evolutions in the growth of Twitter over time is the creation of user-generated content. Much like the empowered Congress broadcasting congressional protests live, Twitter tools allow other forms of user-generated content to be created, distributed worldwide, and archived with a permanent hyperlink. This is another way in which Twitter users can bypass mainstream or corporate media content, typically in the form of videos or blogs (Gleason, 2013). Within the context of the Occupy Wall Street (#OWS) movement, Gleason (2013) found this important for two reasons:

> First, it provides many additional voices to the conversation about #OWS than are available using only traditional media (newspapers, television, and radio). Indeed, the low barriers to participation in a social movement seem to be spurring many citizen journalists to publish and distribute their work. Second, user-generated media opens up multiple opportunities for participation in a social movement; although participation of content is important, equally important is the act of passing on information. Gruzd et al. (2011) discussed how coauthor Barry Wellman's network could be

called an information neighborhood because of user practices geared toward contributing and sharing information. Similarly, participation in the Occupy movement takes many different forms, including the work of citizen journalists who record social protest and the many activists who locate this content, tag it with an appropriate hashtag, and share it with the community. What will be seen is that this issue—Occupy Wall Street—quickly "spun out" into multiple, related issues involving campaign finance reform, mass transit, credit unions, and civil rights in the United States. (pp. 973–974)

Applications of Twitter to Promote Social Justice and Social Action

There are a variety of ways in which Twitter can be used to engage in social action for social justice purposes (Guo & Saxton, 2014). This section will summarize and provide examples of some of the major ways in which tweeters have engaged in social action. Gleason (2013) found that social media coverage both informed protest movements and educated those who wanted to learn more about the movements. González-Bailón and Wang (2016) found that the connections developed over social media were well suited for diffusion of information that lead to political mobilization and decision to protest. In fact, Fromm (2016) found that politicians are now more likely to engage with constituents in ongoing, real-time conversations over social media. Xenos, Vromen, and Loader (2014) as cited in Boulianne (2015), found that social media use predicted political engagement among youth:

> Their single measure of social media use explains more variance than all their demographic variables combined. They conclude, "If one were seeking an efficient single indicator of political engagement among young people in the countries studied here, social media use would appear to be as good as, or better than, SES" (p. 163). (p. 534)

Macro social work practice has incorporated elements of social media into advocacy practice with positive results for equalized power (Hill & Ferguson, 2014; Hitchcock & Battista, 2013). Guo and Saxton (2014) developed a model of social media-based advocacy that involved message awareness and outreach, constituency building, and then mobilization of that constituency to social action. This has been shown to be quite effective as a tool for politicians. Some use Twitter to reach out to constituents to ask their position on a subject before an upcoming vote, others use their Twitter account to provide information about new policies or programs within their local communities, and some see Twitter as a way to reach out to voters in a way that is more efficient and cost-effective than through campaigning alone (Ahn, McNutt, Mossey, & Mundt, 2016).

Much research has noted the similarity of successful offline and online so-cial action efforts albeit with some differences (Chakradhar, Raj, & Raj, 2009). González-Bailón and Wang (2016) noted that the scope of social media has had a major impact on advocacy efforts:

> Digital technologies have not changed the basic social processes that un-derlie communication and the flow of information [or] the mechanisms that encourage people to join a collective action effort. What technologies have changed is the speed and the reach of communication. (p. 103)

They further add that such social media efforts are grounded in the larger social context. Similarly, Buettner and Buettner (2016) caution that Twitter connects people to each other and is not in and of itself a revolution. Both Brady et al. (2015) and Chiluwa and Ifukor (2015) recommend that organizing efforts require both online and offline tactics to be most successful.

There are a variety of ways in which people engage in Twitter conversations. In general, a particular topic can be followed via conversations, hashtags, following and interacting with people involved in the cause, sharing resources, and connecting with others. This allows for conversation with anyone, without requiring people to already know each other, to speak the same language, to be in the same time zone, or to have ever interacted previously. This format is different from other social media platforms and often encourages a much more inclusive conversation than would occur if the discussion was open only to those in one's friendship group, one's community, one's geographical neighbors, or any other homogeneous group.

The most common way that individuals follow or join a discussion is through the hashtag approach. For example, the #BringBackOurGirls social media cam-paign started in Nigeria and reached social media users worldwide via shared photographs of protesters and schoolgirls on Twitter and Facebook (Chiluwa & Ifukor, 2015). This led to the ability for viewers to recognize the faces of the girls impacted and to see their humanity. This changed them from a concept to a group of humans, which changed the conversation from something abstract to some-thing heartbreakingly horrific. This emotional connection turned people vocal and that outrage sparked mass media attention to a situation that might have oth-erwise gone unnoticed.

One of the most widely known hashtag approaches is #BlackLivesMatter. In 2013, after the acquittal of George Zimmerman for the killing of African American teen Treyvon Martin, Black Lives Matter was born. Initially, the intent was to begin a dialogue among those who were feeling isolated and confused by the verdict. The hashtag was picked up quickly by tweeters, and the conversation ranged from personal feelings and the sharing of personal stories of racism to discussions about systemic racism and what should be done to prevent future deaths of African Americans and Blacks (McKesson, 2015). Although Martin died in Florida, the hashtag went viral, and its popularity led those in other nations to join in the conversation. Some simply expressed solidarity or remorse, others shared stories of racism in their countries, and the rest seemed keen to provide awareness that millions were listening to the tweets of those who were posting their own fears.

Over the next few years, there were numerous killings of Black men and boys by non-Black people throughout the United States, including 560 Black men who were killed by members of the police in 2016 alone (Gay, 2016). With every new incident, the hashtag became reinvigorated. This allowed for a much lengthier discussion than in many typical hashtags, since this was not rooted in one event that quickly faded as new media replaced it but by a continued resurgence of outrage and the need for outcry with each reported death.

In 2014, the Black Lives Matter movement participated in its first protest in Ferguson, Missouri, in response to the death of Michael Brown, where more than 500 gathered. This became an indication of just how strong the Black Lives Matter social movement had become, as protesters came together peacefully and were clearly unified, though they had come from all over the nation and many had only previously interacted through Twitter. Since, there have been thousands of protests, both in the United States and in other nations, all organized primarily through Twitter using #BlackLivesMatter to continue the conversation and planning. The hashtag has been estimated to have been tweeted over 30 million times (Wortham, 2016). In addition to any one individual's experience, the movement became so strong that US presidential candidates were asked about the topic during debates and town hall meetings, which were nationally and internationally televised, furthering the message and bolstering its importance within the world. A t-shirt for Black Lives Matter hangs in the National Museum of African American Culture and History, alongside artifacts of slavery, an article of clothing from slave leader Harriet Tubman, and an invitation to the inauguration of America's first Black president, Barack Obama (Kennicott & McGlone, 2016).

Often when a social action or breaking news event occurs, teachers and professors may want to add this information into their coursework. In situations where a news story results in backlash in the form of a protest or the uprising of an oppressed people, the opportunity to turn the situation into a teachable moment is even more compelling to many educators. In these situations, Twitter has now become a place for teachers and other educators to gather their knowledge and share their lessons with others so that the message can be taught in classrooms throughout the world. For professionals to find these resources, they can follow the conversation via a specific hashtag and the word "syllabus." For example, for those looking for lesson planning help after the death of young Black Michael Brown by a White police officer in Ferguson, Missouri, Chatelain (2014) created hashtag #FergusonSyllabus to collect and resources for educators. Additional information can be found via #FergusonSyllabus (Zgoda, 2014). Another example of educational assistance through Twitter is rooted in the Orlando Massacre at the LGBT nightclub Pulse in 2016. For this information, interested parties can follow #PulseOrlandoSyllabus or #OrlandoSyllabus, where educators, librarians, and other professionals contributed materials for those looking to educate others on the tragedy, LGBT history, LGBT people in Orlando, and the ways in which communities can come together after a horrific experience to grieve, heal, and support each other (http://bit.ly/orlandosyllabus). Other popular syllabi created in the wake of such events include NYC Stands with Standing Rock Collective (2016) (https://nycstandswithstandingrock.wordpress.com/standingrocksyllabus/) and the #CharlestonSyllabus created by the African American Intellectual History Society (AAIHS) (2015). In addition, the #MacroSW community has created a continually updated syllabus that contains educational materials and case studies for macro social work practice (http://bit.ly/macroswsyllabus).

For many hashtag conversations, the discussions occur when the event happens or when new information regarding the event is provided. For example, in the case of #Ferguson regarding the death of a Black man by a White police officer, the hashtag was used when the death first occurred, when the city decided whether to charge the police officer involved, when protests were being organized, when the protests occurred, and when the victim's name was included in the Black Lives Matter movement and subsequent protests. The hashtags followed the news and the situations. However, other hashtag situations intentionally keep the conversation going by having regularly scheduled hashtag-based conversations/chats.

In addition to using Twitter hashtags, another popular option is commonly called tweet-streaming, or sending numerous tweets for advocacy purposes to educate and advocate specific changes. Ricci (2016) describes the work of journalist Igor Volsky and how he publicly shamed the members of Congress who accepted money from the National Rifle Association in the wake of the Pulse Orlando shooting. Brady et al. (2015) describe a similar tactic called "guerilla tweeting" to agitate, raise awareness, and mobilize the Society for Social Work and Research conference around the Hyatt Hotel labor boycott.

ETHICAL CONSIDERATIONS

The use of social media such as Twitter for social action and advocacy purposes raises ethical dilemmas to be resolved. For example, the same technology that allows user-generated content to be distributed worldwide at the click of a button must be met with the precaution that not all will report facts accurately, describe context, and otherwise follow traditional journalistic standards. In other words, instant access to content allows a user to see news as it happens, but the context and accuracy often comes later. User-generated social media content must be verified, especially when presented with conflicting perspectives (Gleason, 2013). Another important consideration for both Twitter and the use of social media overall is the aspect of how easy it is for people to voice their opinions without realizing who may be impacted by their words. Since the writer of a tweet is typically alone at his or her keyboard or mobile device, it can be easy to feel a lack of connection to those reading his or her words. Often, this is how online bullying can begin. What may seem harmless or only slightly sarcastic to one can easily come across as horribly mean to a reader. When a person chooses to speak directly to or about a person, including his or her name and/or social media handle, this not only impacts him or her, it can also lead others to follow suit, tweeting agreement or additional insults at or to the targeted person. Preceding social media, bullying was typically confined to school or working hours, allowing the victim several hours away from his or her tormentors each day. However, the use of social media removes those emotional breaks. Instead, the victims often receive insults on their phones, laptops, computer tablets, and all other forms of technology. In addition, the bullying is not just heard by those walking by during the time of the insult; it is posted in a public forum to be seen, read, and easily repeated ("retweeted") by any viewer who so chooses. It is available in the present and remains for the indefinite future. While this ubiquity and permanence can be a benefit when using social media for activism and for documenting inequities in the world, it can prove to be overwhelming to those who are bullied. The resulting suicides have underscored the importance all so-cial media users should place on the words they choose to write on any social media platform (Lewinsky, 2015).

BEST PRACTICES

With the pros and cons acknowledged, the options are to either avoid using Twitter or to become more present and more aware of the benefits and detriments of Twitter and to become a responsible user of the social media site. In today's society, many pieces of news and many opportunities exist initially or even solely through Twitter, so deciding to avoid the site altogether may lead to missed information or a lack of opportunities to participate in personal and professional discussions. This means that a professional should be using Twitter, and thus, with this recommendation, there are required moments of awareness as well as responsibilities that are incumbent upon the user to recognize.

Before even considering using Twitter with one's own name, it is vital to un-derstand the information being presented to a reader via the website itself, as well as any time Twitter is shown as a source for news on any other website. First, it is important to recognize the immediacy of the website and the goal of this speed for many users. During a time of crisis, it is quite common for a person to tweet information as soon as he or she hears or thinks it, regardless of whether any effort has been made to verify the information. This means that a person can be reading incorrect news, either in that it is slightly different than the reality or in that it could be completely false information. In the best cases, the information is deleted or updated as new knowledge becomes known. In other cases, though, the person tweeting may be either unavailable to add updates or he or she may have ulterior motives regarding why misinformation was given. Thus, when reading Twitter, it is vital that the reader question the information, as well as the source providing the information. Before sharing the information on Twitter or in general, it is important to verify the information using additional and unbiased sources. This may mean that you are not the first to provide the knowledge to others, but it will mean that the information you provide is correct. This will help to stop the spread of misinformation, which can be crucial during times of trauma or chaos, especially when people's personal fears and prejudices may be stronger than ever.

If you are deciding to use Twitter to mobilize people to social action, either through discussion or behavior, one of the best ways to begin to gain traction is to craft a memorable name and hashtag that is not already being used for other purposes. This hashtag will allow people to follow the conversation and contribute to it. Twitter's main homepage shows which topics are most popular (called "trending"). When a hashtag appears on that list, it brings millions of viewers to the topic, and, if even a small percentage of those viewers click on the hashtag, the opportunity presents to bring new eyes, minds, and money to the cause.

Through the use of Twitter, viewers from around the world can come together to discuss their feelings, to express their outrage, and to create plans to mobilize to create real opportunities of change within the world. On a macro level, political rallies can occur simultaneously in major cities throughout the world, showing solidarity internationally, which can increase the likelihood of change, as well as encouraging all participants in knowing they are not alone in their actions. On a mezzo level, small groups can help to find each other and to merge, bringing a stronger united voice to the belief system and to the cause. On a micro level, which some may argue is most important, individuals can quickly be reassured that their concerns are valid, their feelings of loneliness, anger, fear, or isolation can be replaced with feelings of connection, and they can be guided toward options to act in ways that encourage positive impacts for the social issues they are experiencing and for the personal drive they are feeling within themselves.

REFERENCES

African American Intellecutal History Society. (2015). #CharlestonSyllabus. Retrieved from https://www.aaihs.org/resources/charlestonsyllabus/

Ahn, M., McNutt, J. G., Mossey, S., & Mundt, M. (2016, November). *Patterns of social media usage for networking and constituent relationships at the state level: The impact of legislator characteristics.* Paper presented at the Sixth Northeast Conference on Public Administration, Pennsylvania State University, Harrisburg.

Alias, N., Sabdan, M. S., Aziz, K. A., Mohammed, M., Hamidon, I. S., & Jomhari, N. (2013). Research trends and issues in the studies of twitter: A content analysis of publications in selected journals (2007–2012). *Procedia—Social and Behavioral Sciences, 103,* 773–780.

Berzin, S., Singer, J., & Chan, C. (2015). *Practice innovation through technology in the digital age: a grand challenge for social work* (Grand Challenge 9: Harness Technology for Social Good No. Working Paper No. 12). Retrieved from American Academy of Social Work and Social Welfare website: http://aaswsw.org/wp-content/uploads/2013/10/Practice-Innovation-through-Technology-in-the-Digital-Age-A-Grand-Challenge-for-Social-Work-GC-Working-Paper-No-12.pdf

Boulianne, S. (2015). Social media use and participation: A meta-analysis of current research. *Information, Communication & Society, 18*, 524–538.

Brady, S. R., Young, J., & McLeod, D. A. (2015). Utilizing digital advocacy in community organizing: Lessons learned from organizing in virtual spaces to promote worker rights and economic justice. *Journal of Community Practice, 23*, 255–273.

Buettner, R., & Buettner, K. (2016). A systematic literature review of twitter research from a socio-political revolution perspective. In T. X. Bui & R. H. Sprague Jr. (Eds.), *Proceedings of 49th Hawaii International Conference on System Sciences 5–8 January 2016, Kauai, Hawaii.* (pp. 2206–2215). Piscataway, NJ: IEEE.

Chakradhar, K., Raj, V., & Raj, A. (2009). Modern social support structures: Online social networks and their implications for social workers. *Advances in Social Work, 10*, 157–175.

Chatelain, M. (2014). How to teach kids about what's happening in Ferguson: A crowdsourced syllabus about race, African American history, civil rights, and policing. Retrieved from https://www.theatlantic.com/education/archive/2014/08/how-to-teach-kids-about-whats-happening-in-ferguson/379049/

Chiluwa, I., & Ifukor, P. (2015). "War against our children": Stance and evaluation in #BringBackOurGirls campaign discourse o Twitter and Facebook. *Discourse & Society, 26*, 267–296.

Fromm, J. (2016, June 22). New study finds social media shapes millennial political involvement and engagement [Web log post]. Retrieved from http://www.forbes.com/sites/jefffromm/2016/06/22/new-study-finds-social-media-shapes-millennial-political-involvement-and-engagement/#799d5cf415de

Gay, R. (2016, July 6). Alton Sterling and when black lives stop mattering. *New York Times*, p. A23.

Gleason, B. (2013). #Occupy wall street: Exploring informal learning about a social movement on Twitter. *American Behavioral Scientist, 57*, 966–982.

Gold, H. (2016, June 22). C-SPAN's viral video moment. *Politico.* Retrieved from http://www.politico.com/story/2016/06/cspan-house-sitin-democrats-224696

González-Bailón, S., & Wang, N. (2016). Networked discontent: The anatomy of protest campaigns in social media. *Social Networks, 44*, 95–104.

Greenwood, S., Perrin, A., & Duggan, M. (2016). Social media update 2016. *Pew Research Center, 11*, 83.

Gruzd, A., Wellman, B., & Takhteyev, Y. (2011). Imagining Twitter as an imagined commu- nity. *American Behavioral Scientist, 55*(10), 1294–1318.

Guo, C., & Saxton, G. D. (2014). Tweeting social change: How social media are changing nonprofit advocacy. *Nonprofit and Voluntary Sector Quarterly, 43*(1), 57–79.

Hamblin, A. (2016, June 22). Why Scott Peters live streamed House gun control sit-in. *San Diego Union-Tribune.* Retrieved from http://www.sandiegouniontribune.com/

opinion/the-conversation/sdut-scott-peters-periscopes-house-sit-in-2016jun22-htmlstory.html

Hill, K., & Ferguson, S. (2014). Web 2.0 in social work macro practice: Ethical considerations and questions. *Journal of Social Work Values and Ethics, 11,* 2–11.

Hitchcock, L., & Battista, A. (2013). Social media for professional practice: Integrating Twitter with social work pedagogy. *Journal of Baccalaureate Social Work, 18,* 33–45.

Kennicott, P., & McGlone, P. (2016, September 19). The top 36 must-see items at the African American museum. *Washington Post.* Retrieved from https://www.washingtonpost.com/graphics/lifestyle/national-museum-of-african-american-history-and-culture/must-see-exhibit-items/

Lewinsky, M. (2015, March). The price of shame [Video file]. *Ted Talks.* Retrieved from https://www.ted.com/talks/monica_lewinsky_the_price_of_shame

MacroSW. (2016). #MacroSW's feedback on NASW Draft Technology Standards in Social Work Practice. Retrieved from https://macrosw.files.wordpress.com/2016/08/macroswresponsetonaswtechstandards_final_7-20-16.pdf

MacroSW. (2018). #MacroSW Syllabus. Retrieved from http://bit.ly/macroswsyllabus

McKesson, D. (2015, August 9). Ferguson and beyond: How a new civil rights movement began—and won't end. *The Guardian.* Retrieved from https://www.theguardian.com/commentisfree/2015/aug/09/ferguson-civil-rights-movement-deray-mckesson-protest?CMP=share_btn_tw

Ricci, K. (2016, June 13). A journalist publicly shames all the politicians who accept money from the NRA. *Uproxx.* Retrieved from http://uproxx.com/news/igor-volsky-shame-politiican-nra-money/

Saxton, G. D., Niyirora, J. N., Guo, C., & Waters, R. D. (2015). #AdvocatingForChange: The strategic use of hashtags in social media advocacy. *Advances in Social Work, 16,* 154–169.

Smyth, N. (2010, September 10). When is cultural incompetence okay? [Web log post]. Retrieved from https://njsmyth.wordpress.com/2010/09/10/when-is-cultural-incompetence-okay/

Tesfaye, S. (2016, May 5). We are now fact-checking Donald Trump's lunch: Trump tweets patronizing Cinco de Mayo image, reporters rush to confirm if Trump Tower serves taco bowls. *Salon.* Retrieved from http://www.salon.com/2016/05/05/we_are_now_fact_checking_donald_trumps_lunch_trump_tweets_patronizing_cinco_de_mayo_image_reporters_rush_to_confirm_if_trump_towers_serves_taco_bowls/

Twitter. (2016). Our company. Retrieved from https://about.twitter.com/company

Weil, K. (2015, March 26). Introducing Periscope [Web log post]. Retrieved from https://blog.twitter.com/2015/introducing-periscope

Wortham, J. (2016). Black tweets matter. *Smithsonian Magazine.* Retrieved from http://www.smithsonianmag.com/arts-culture/black-tweets-matter-180960117/

Xenos, M., Vromen, A., & Loader, B. D. (2014). The great equalizer? Patterns of social media use and youth political engagement in three advanced democracies. *Information, Communication & Society, 17*(2), 151–167.

Zgoda, K. (2014, November 29). #FergusonSyllabus resources. Retrieved from https://karenzgoda.org/2014/11/29/fergusonsyllabus-resources/

APPENDIX

SAMPLE TWEETS

Description	Link to tweet
C-Span switching to Periscope after House cameras shut off	https://twitter.com/cspan/status/745691027701260290
Rep. Scott Peters broadcasting House sit-in	https://twitter.com/ScottPetersSD/status/745715863748251649
Rep. Scott Peters House sit-in Periscope feed	https://www.periscope.tv/ScottPetersSD/1OyKAlbWydexb
Rep. Maloney picture of Rep. Tammy Duckworth taking off her legs to sit on floor of Congress	https://twitter.com/spmaloney/status/745715623783604226
Deray McKesson, arrest photo and surrounded by #BlackLivesMatter hashtags	https://twitter.com/yamiche/status/752306958800125953
Michelle Obama, #BringBackOurGirls	https://twitter.com/FLOTUS/status/464148654354628608
Calling out politicians who take money from gun groups—Twitter moment	https://twitter.com/i/moments/742046002429841411
First call to contribute to #PulseOrlandoSyllabus crowdsourced document	https://twitter.com/muncielibrary/status/742384857867681796

7

The Civic Technology Movement

Implications for Nonprofit Theory and Practice

JONATHAN B. JUSTICE, JOHN G. McNUTT,
JAMES MELITSKI, MICHAEL AHN, NINA DAVID,
SHARIQ SIDDIQUI, AND JOHN C. RONQUILLO ∎

One of the most interesting threads in modern nonprofit theory has been the blurring of the boundaries between the business, nonprofit, and public sectors. At one point, these divisions were considered to be formidable, immutable, and powerful. Only in unusual circumstances would division lines be crossed. This, of course, was probably more evident in theory than in fact.

As privatization and other forces began to take hold in the 1960s, the understanding was that sector boundaries were more permeable. The move toward purchase of services contracting in health and human services created a recognition of the growing complexity of the relationship between the nonprofit sector and government. This led to a revisiting of nonprofit government theory and a renewed interest in nonprofit theory dealing with the role of government in the sector. This increased governmental involvement also led to a consideration of nonprofit advocacy and how advocacy might be related to funding as well as to the blossoming of government–nonprofit relations theory and the growth of scholarship about nonprofit advocacy.

We believe that the sector might be turning yet another corner. We think that civic technology and related forces might be bringing the sectors together in important ways that might have dramatic results.

CIVIC TECHNOLOGY

Civic technology is a technology-led social movement that promises to transform the relationships among technology, the nonprofit and commercial sectors, and government. It involves voluntary action (both online and offline) and nonprofits. It represents the nexus of several related trends (i.e., self-organization, leaderless organizations, social media/Web 2.0, open source software development, etc.) as well as a set of situations that have created the opportunity for collaboration among sectors facilitating the growth of new partnerships and perspectives.

Civic technology is an emerging area, and many of the concepts are tentative. Nonetheless, strides are being made to define civic technology and its major components. An early definition is provided by Living Cities (2012):

> Civic technology—the use of digital technologies and social media for service provision, civic engagement, and data analysis—has the potential to transform cities and the lives of their low income residents.

This approach addresses many of the major features of civic technology, although the general tide of civic-technology practice to date is for efforts that benefit wide swaths of urban populations, rather than low-income residents specifically. While much of the civic technology movement is aimed at evolutionary social change, there is a definite political spin to many efforts. It is not surprising that there a range of efforts can be found under the civic technology umbrella. The civic technology scan conducted by Living Cities (2012) found that civic technology tools have been used to pursue three broad objectives: (a) "improving quality of and accountability in public service delivery," (b) "facilitating resident-driven improvements to neighborhood quality-of-life," and (c) "deepening participation in public decision-making" (p. 3).

Civic technology brings together different partners in multiple sectors. One is usually government. Both nonprofit organizations and voluntary associations are commonly part of the mix, and for-profit organizations are frequently included. This, of course, is true of long-standing intersectoral relationships. What makes civic technology different is changes in the roles and relationships of the participants. The inclusion of voluntary associations as well as individual citizens adds complexity and richness to the government relations analysis because these actors are often given little attention.

Components of Civic Technology

Three major arenas support civic technology: open civic data, technology, and civic technology practices (David, McNutt, & Justice, 2018; McNutt et al., 2016). Each component is viable within itself, but they come together to create civic technology efforts. Open civic data make possible the other two processes. The larger context is the growth of online social interaction and the impact that technology has on organizational forms. The relationship between these three fields is depicted in Figure 7.1.

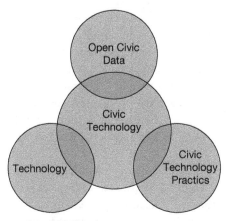

Figure 7.1 Components of Civic Technology

OPEN CIVIC DATA

Open data is the practice of making government data available to the public in a format that is easy to use and accessible (David et al., 2018; McNutt et al., 2016). The move toward open civic data is not only part of an international effort to promote open government and transparency (see Durose, Justice, & Skelcher, 2015; Justice & Dülger, 2009; Justice & McNutt, 2014; Justice, McNutt, & Smith, 2011; Justice & Tarimo, 2012; Lathrop & Ruma, 2010) but also reflects an even larger trend toward making research data and other information more accessible. Greater transparency is thought to engender greater trust in government and more support for government. It is one requisite for enhancing the accountability of public officials and organizations and has the potential for reducing corruption. Open civic data are a critical ingredient of civic technology that makes the partnerships and technology "work."

Governments possess an extensive amount of information about all aspects of society gathered through research and administrative record-keeping. National and subnational governments collect data on housing, taxation, voting, population, economic activity, air and water pollution, educational achievement, crime, poverty, disease incidence and prevalence, and so forth. This information is frequently important in identifying problems and documenting the need for community change and changes in the conduct of government affairs. Data sources vary to the extent that they are easily available and easy to use.

Public policy worldwide (although not everywhere) is moving to make more and more government information available, particularly through the use of contemporary information and communications technologies (ICT). Efforts in the United States, the European Union and its member states, and other nations have led to a situation where data are now being released in substantial quantities and in formats that facilitate analysis by interest parties.

An example is what the US Public Interest Research Groups has termed Transparency 2.0 (Baxandall & Wohlschlegel, 2010), an effort to make checkbook-level as well as aggregated financial government information available to every citizen via the Internet (see Justice & McNutt, 2014). This moves past the traditional provision of budget documents and financial reports to make available detailed information on government disbursements. It is very unlikely that this system would be feasible without technology.

Open Civic Data comes in a variety of forms. The Census of Open Data, a project of Code for America and other organizations, logs the type of Open Civic Data collected by Local Governments. McNutt et al. (2016) found that few of the local governments that they studied collected the entire range of possible civic data.

Open civic data are only useful if civic innovators are aware of the data, and they are provided in a format that it is useful. For example, a recent study of advocacy-group data use in Delaware (McNutt, Justice, Auger, & Carter, 2013; McNutt, Justice, & Carter, 2014) found that advocacy groups were often unaware of what data were available or couldn't use data that they were knowledgeable about. And while Transparency 2.0 efforts make new information available and searchable, online checkbooks often are not designed to make it easy for stakeholders outside of governments to download or perform extensive independent analysis of the underlying data (e.g., for a critique of Delaware's online checkbook, see Headd, 2009).

TECHNOLOGY

Civic technology is a technology-enhanced effort, but, strictly speaking, many aspects of civic technology are not technology dependent. Technology in the form of ICT hardware and software does not create civic technology but facilitates the process. At least some of the technology is very basic, but other technology represents some of the more sophisticated interventions represent the forefront of Web 3.0 developments (the Semantic Web; Hendler, 2009), applications of the Internet of things (Atzori, Iera, & Morabito, 2010), and pervasive technology (Cook & Das, 2012). Many of the technology tools used to support civic technology efforts come from social media/Web 2.0 and mobile technology applications, while others represent advanced data management and analysis and data visualization technologies. Some of the latter are characterized as big data, but most open civic data re not big data per se.

These technology-based tools track the range from applications that can be used on a smart phone to back-end technologies that manipulate billions of data points. Some of the leading-edge technology tools on the citizen side are service apps, public engagement or participation apps, civic mapping, and 311 and Open311.

Service applications (Desouza & Bhagwatwar, 2012) allow citizens to contact and be engaged in municipal services. Some are presented by government, but others are not. One of the earlier and better known of the latter type of service applications is Fix My Street (https://www.fixmystreet.com/), which allows participants to report road issues and makes the reports publicly available. This is an arrangement that began in the United Kingdom and spread worldwide. Fix My Street is operated by My Society, a project of the nonprofit UK Citizens Online

Democracy. This application not only identifies issues for local government but also pressures government to take action (King & Brown, 2007).

These apps, often using the Open 311 application program interface, interface with municipal call centers (typically referred to in the United States as 311 systems) to support making nonemergency service requests and queries through mobile apps and other type of contact in addition to traditional voice telephone calls. By extending the reach and ease of access to nonemergency call centers, these apps help to free emergency services for more pressing matters and build citizen support for government (Clark & Brudney, 2014; Clark, Brudney, & Jang, 2013; Offenhuber, 2015; Suri, 2013).

One notable US example is Boston 311. This platform allows citizens to provide real-time information to government about graffiti, sidewalk issues, potholes, damaged street lights, and missed trash removal over the phone, on social media, and through mobile applications. Government, in turn, can communicate directly with citizens when their reported problem is fixed. In addition to improving efficiencies, these platforms empower citizens and allow them control and influence over government (Aladalah, Cheung, & Lee 2015; Crawford & Walters, 2013).

Other technology includes neighborhood forums and peer-to-peer local applications, which allow residents to communicate with each other and with government and political participation apps that promote public involvement are a growing aspect of e-government and are used by a wide range of public interest groups as well as governments; for an excellent overview, see Desouza and Bhagwatwar (2014). Open and civic mapping allows communities to crowdsource geographic information and produce spatial collective intelligence (Budhathoki & Haythornthwaite, 2013). OpenStreetMap is an open source application that has enjoyed popularity in a large number of community efforts. Another system is provided by Ushahidi (www.ushahidi.com), which provides a set of crowdsourcing and crowdmapping applications that have been used to combat violence and deal with disease outbreaks and disasters (Goldstein & Rotich, 2008; Okolloh, 2009).

Crowdfunding is a developed strategy in the commercial sector but an emerging idea in both the nonprofit and governmental sectors (Davies, 2015). This type of system allows residents to support projects that they find interesting and useful and that government can't or won't provide. Funds are raised via a technology application that demonstrates what possibilities are available and permits residents to invest in a given service or program.

The management and visualization of both open civic data and data created by the use of the other technology applications, outputs from applications of the Internet of things, or provided voluntarily by participants is crucial to the civic technology process. This means the ability to manage, understand, and apply data to issues and concerns. Strictly speaking, most open civic data are not big data, which often come from social media and the Internet of things.

Social media and Web 2.0 technology are a bedrock of current civic technology. Much of this technology regime grew out of earlier developments in technology and evolved over a number of years (Germany, 2006). Both social media and Web

2.0 are more popularized and less exact terms and are often used inaccurately. The applications that are generally referred to as social media or Web 2.0 technologies are a set of stable and well-understood systems with some similar characteristics. While they are more interactive than most previous arrangements, interactivity alone does not qualify a technology for inclusion. All Web 2.0 technologies are based on the Internet—or "Web as platform," to use O'Reilly's (2007) term—allow the harnessing of collective knowledge or collective intelligence, and facilitate the creation of user-generated content and promote software as a service and so forth (O'Reilly, 2005, 2007).

Finally, there are several globally innovative examples of ICT-enabled civic engagement in governance that are currently operational. These systems use citizen collaboration to build governmental capacity; encourage citizens to become more active in their neighborhoods; build partnerships among business, academia, and government to provide access to data; allow citizens to directly invest in and monitor public projects; and engage citizens in budgeting and fiscal transparency (for examples, see David, 2018).

The most accepted definition of Web 2.0 is offered by technology thought leader O'Reilly (2005) who suggests the following definition:

Web 2.0 is the network as platform, spanning all connected devices; Web 2.0 applications are those that make the most of the intrinsic advantages of that platform: delivering software as a continually-updated service that gets better the more people use it, consuming and remixing data from multiple sources, including individual users, while providing their own data and services in a form that allows remixing by others, creating network effects through an "architecture of participation," and going beyond the page metaphor of Web 1.0 to deliver rich user experiences.

Existing Web 2.0 technologies can be combined with each other or additional types of applications to build new systems through a process known as a mash-up. This might include data from a social networking app and applying the data to a mapping program to create visual geospatial interpretations of the data. The mash-up process could yield an almost unlimited supply of Web 2.0 applications.

Collaborative Civic Technology Practices

The use of collaborations and social interventions are distinctive for civic technology. For present purposes, we will consider them under the rubric of civic technology practices. Some of these elements are unique to civic technology, while others are used more broadly. Civic technology depends on a wide-ranging set of relationships including commercial and nonprofit organizations, government, and citizens. It is this rich set of networked relationships that makes civic technology happen. Major types of civic technology practice include information crowdsourcing; local contests, civic hacking, and hackathons; and sponsored interventions to foster civic-technology innovations, such as Code for

America fellowships and Code for America brigades (Living Cities, 2012; McNutt et al., 2016).

Civic hacking and hackathons are a major component of the civic technology movement (Baraniuk, 2013; Hébert, 2014; Johnson & Robinson, 2014; McNutt & Justice, 2016; Popyack, 2014; Stepasiuk, 2014). Civic hackers work on technology tasks that are needed by some group or organization (often government). They have prosocial aims and contribute many hours of what is essentially episodic volunteering. While some hackers work on their own, hackathons provide a means for civic hackers to collaborate. These events often provide contests that provide an opportunity to compete against other civic hackers.

Code for America fellowships are perhaps the signature civic technology intervention. Modeled on programs like the Peace Corps and Teach for America, Code for America (www.codeforamerica.org) fellowships place technologists in communities to create technology solutions that meet local citizen and government needs. The fellow creates the technology for the local government. Code for America also sponsors local brigades that put local technologists in touch with governments that need assistance.

Code for America is a central organization in the civic technology space. A nonprofit founded in 2009 by Jennifer Pahlka, Code for America has been in the forefront of civic technology. Code for America (n.d.) states its mission on its homepage: "Code for America believes government can work for the people, by the people in the 21st century. We build open source technology and organize a network of people dedicated to making government services simple, effective, and easy to use." A relatively small organization, Code for America has had a substantial impact in a brief amount of time.

Civic technology, then, is composed of data, a set of technologies, and a set of generally nontechnological practices that bring the other two components together. This technology and that data with those particular practices make the civic technology mix.

ONLINE PARTICIPATION, CIVIC TECHNOLOGY, AND THE NONPROFIT SECTOR

One of the most persistent debates in nonprofit theory is the relationship between government and the nonprofit sector (Ott & Dicke, 2011). While much of this involves blurring of the sector boundaries, there is also discussion about how changes in government and government policy affect the nonprofit sector (usually negatively) and some consideration about how the sector can affect government. Much of this literature seems to have a propensity for seeing government as a fixed entity.

Regulation of the nonprofit sector and the corresponding nonprofit tax status is clearly a part of this discussion. State and federal (and sometime local) governments have a stake in the conduct of the sector and exercise considerable power over nonprofit organizations.

One of the most persistent discussions has been about purchase of services by governments through contracts with nonprofits. This includes discussions about contracting and its impact on a variety of sector issues, including advocacy and the relationship with community (Smith & Lipsky, 1993; Wolch, 1990). This parallels discussion in political science about the "hollow state" (Agranoff & McGuire, 1998; Fredericksen & London, 2000; Rhodes, 1997).

Many political actors are nonprofits. This includes political parties, political action committees, and other politically related groups. These nonprofits often have substantial sway over government and government operations but are rarely discussed as such.

Finally, there is discussion of how nonprofits can affect government policy via advocacy (Berry & Arons, 2002). Nonprofit advocacy is a fundamental but often controversial part of the sector. A lot of this analysis is tied to the literature on interest groups in political science and social movement theory in sociology. The rise of new, often leaderless technology-based advocacy efforts has yet to be incorporated in any serious way (Castells, 2012; Brainard, Boland, & McNutt, 2012).

While this might be an overgeneralization, the idea that government and nonprofits are partners is rarely advanced in any serious manner. Given that the two sectors constitute the two wings of the larger public-service enterprise, this is truly unfortunate. It is also an inaccurate representation of reality, since in practice this interaction is common and intersectoral working relationships are essential to the work of each sector. Moreover, nonprofit–government relations theory generally deals only with sets of organizations engaged in interaction. Rarely, if ever, does it consider the role of individual citizens.

These are all useful and important things to consider. They are worthy of study. As things develop, they may become part of a larger set of questions about the nature and meaning of sector boundaries. Civic technology may affect these debates, especially in the context of the changing nature of civic engagement. Civic engagement is a fundamental part of nonprofit theory and most conceptions of civil society and the nonprofit sector.

TECHNOLOGY AND THE EVOLVING NATURE OF POLITICAL ENGAGEMENT

Political civic engagement has traditionally meant a limited direct role for citizens to appeal to their government (such as petitions, letter writing, and voting) and a more powerful indirect method of membership organizations that advocated for their members (Putnam, 2000; Verba, Schlozman, & Brady, 1995). The development of public interest groups and managed participation (Berry, 1977) limited the possibilities for direct participation, but community organizations represented and continue to symbolize a robust force in many communities. In the past few decades there has been apprehension that public engagement is diminishing in America (Putnam, 2000). People are supposedly becoming less involved in their communities, in local government, and even with their neighbors. This would make having a viable democracy difficult.

While this might be the case with traditional technologies of political engagement, a number of observers have pointed to the growth of online forums for civic engagement and suggested that participation is simply going to other places (Norris, 2002). Succeeding research establishes that online participation is robust. Whether online participation is as effective for building community and affecting public policy as traditional efforts is open to argument, but advocacy groups, political parties, and local organizations have embraced technology with enthusiasm throughout the world.

Earlier technologies became part of politics and civic engagement in the late 1980s. Even before there was widespread Internet availability, there was technologically based community engagement through the Freenet/community networking movement. The worldwide advocacy movement MoveOn was founded in the late 1990s, years before social media were available. Web 2.0/social media probably developed as an important political technology in the United States with Howard Dean's unsuccessful run for the democratic nomination for president in 2004, which made use of many of these new tools in an innovative campaign. After that, it was an expected part of political organizing. A similar path occurred in much of the world. Probably the most dramatic application was the 2011 Arab Spring demonstrations in northern Africa and the Middle East.

While most modern approaches to e-government account for public participation, it is difficult to take into account the evolution of participation in the online work. Research suggests some considerable changes in the future of technology (Smith, Schlozman, Verba, & Brady, 2009; see also Gibson & Cantijoch, 2013; Gordon, Baldwin-Philippi, & Balestra, 2013; Guo & Saxton, 2013; Smith, 2008) as it relates to political participation.

The development of civic technology and related movements brings forward an additional set of challenges and opportunities. Not only can these movements potentially reinvent government from outside, they also hold forth the opportunity to ask whether sector boundaries are functional in a postindustrial world.

In essence, civic technology builds collaborative structures around, or sometimes parallel to, government technology and services. While at one level this might mean simply an incrementally new form of procurement, at another level it might evolve into real transformation of governance, in effect reinventing government from the outside in. When this is combined with substantial online activity that goes beyond the traditional approaches to government, nonprofits, and citizen action, it can engender major change.

CIVIC TECHNOLOGY AND TECHNOLOGY-LED SOCIAL MOVEMENTS

One aspect of voluntary action that is related to civic technology is social movements, especially those that make substantial use of technology (Omidyar

Table 7.1. Examples of Evolutionary and Confrontational
Social Movements

Evolutionary	Evolutionary/confrontational	Confrontational
Open source movement civic technology	Umbrella movement	Occupy Wall Street Arab Spring Tea Party

Network, 2016). The growth of online and partially online social movements has been a feature of the social movement landscape for the past few years (Earl & Kimport, 2011; Omidyar Network, 2016). The Omidyar Network (2016) argues that civic technology shares some of the characteristics of contemporary social movements and offers a case based largely on online data to support this conclusion. Some of the ideas are compelling, although traditional social movement scholars might not agree.

Many traditional social movements advocate for relatively slow, evolutionary societal change, while others are more confrontational in their pursuit of more rapid, significant transformation. Emerging, contemporary social movements follow a similar path, and some change strategy during the course of their development. Examples of selected contemporary social movements, most of which combine both online and offline components, follow. Table 7.1 lists the movements and groups them according to whether they are evolutionary, confrontational, or both in their goals and approaches.

The open source movement and civic technology tend to emphasize working within the system. The umbrella movement in Hong Kong tended to be more confrontational but still had elements of work within the system. Finally, Arab Spring, Occupy Wall Street, and the American Tea Party were the most confrontational. Another candidate for this category might be the movement for Brexit in the United Kingdom.

As social movements evolve, they often change. While civic technology is an evolutionary social movement at the present, it may change as a time goes forth. Applications of civic technology of the type represented by Fix My Street offer the beginnings of a confrontational dimension.

Another possibility is that the civic technology movement could combine with other movements to bring about greater change in government. The emerging leaderless movements (see chapter 13) are an example, because technology is a large part of their operating system.

DISCUSSION

We tend to regard the nonprofit sector in terms of the development of the sector within the industrial era. Occasional references to agrarian and horticultural periods aside, this industrial model is strongly reflected in our scholarship and public pronouncements about nonprofits and how they relate to other parts of the economic system. While there are occasional attempts to come to grips with what a postindustrial nonprofit sector (or for that matter, postindustrial government) will look like, there is not as yet a fully articulated consensus model. Nevertheless, it is clear that nonprofit organizations will be different, and the sector will evolve. If nonprofit theory is to remain relevant, change it will also have to change.

Our current models emphasize the primacy of traditional, physically located nonprofit organizations—what one might call brick-and-mortar nonprofits. While voluntary associations are acknowledged by theorists, they are often incorporated into our conceptual frameworks of the sector in a haphazard manner (for a critique of this situation, see Smith 1997). McNutt, Brainard, Zeng, and Kovacic (2016) have argued that, given the changes likely to occur on other parts of society, voluntary associations (many of them virtual) are likely to enjoy a resurgence. If this happens, it is likely to make our ideas about intersectoral relations more complex.

A similar argument can be made about public management theory. Early public management theory owed much to the model of routinized efficiency and standardized industrial management. Progressive reformers including Woodrow Wilson (1887) sought to adapt industrial firms' efficiency-oriented methods to government administration, formulate universal principles of administration (Gulick, 1925), and identify the one best way to perform each task (Taylor, 1911). By now, the limitations of simplistic prescriptions for how public-service arrangements and government jurisdictions are and should be configured (Ostrom, 1989; Ostrom, Tiebout, & Warren, 1961) and managed (Simon, 1946) are fairly widely recognized. This clears the field for scholars' and activists' increasing openness to recognizing innovative organizational forms and approaches, including boundary-blurring innovations such as civic technology, and analyzing them on their own terms (Warren, Rosentraub, & Harlow, 1984; Warren, Rosentraub, & Weschler, 1988).

An example of a comprehensive research program building upon these fundamental insights to generate advances in descriptive and explanatory research capable of providing sound support for normative conclusions is the extended program of Nobel laureate Elinor Ostrom (1990, 1998). There is also a potential application for elements of social capital theory as we look at the micro foundations of political and social life (Ostrom, 1995). While we have always seen the relationships in social capital as face to face, substantial research has documented that online social capital exists. The fact of the matter is that nonprofit theory needs to move away from its industrial motif. If we limit ourselves to what has been proposed in the past, we will miss what the future has to offer.

Civic technology, as a movement, offers the potential not only to reinvent government but also to change the relationship between the sectors in profound and important ways. This will happen, of course, in concert with other changes in technology, politics, social organizations, and economic institutions. David et al. (2018) argued that this would take the form of a three-step process over

Figure 7.2 The Evolution of Intersectoral Relations

time and that we are already in the midst of substantial changes in inter-sectoral relationships.

Early in the industrial period, the sectors developed into reasonably independent entities with occasional, but minor interactions. This "structure" stage began to transition to a "blurring" stage as changes in government policy, ideology, and economics began to converge in a push for devolution and privatization of the delivery of many public goods and services. This began to erode the boundaries. Nonprofit scholars, such as Steven R. Smith and Jennifer Wolch warned that the nonprofit sector was being changed by government contracting and privatization in ways that neither theorists nor the sector itself were fully engaging with in a strategic fashion (Smith, 1993; Wolch, 1990; also see Warren et al., 1988). Finally, we begin to see a more amorphous set of sector relationships that civic technology falls squarely in the middle of. The merging of online and offline movements is clearly a part of this as well as a move toward virtual organizations. This is what David et al. (2018) call the "soup" phase. This progression from structure to soup is portrayed in Figure 7.2.

This process should bring exciting change in the nonprofit sector and in communities, real and virtual.

CONCLUSIONS

For centuries, the nonprofit sector and the organizations that are part of it have served the interests of society and individual members, working independently and in concert with other social institutions to meet human needs. Over the years, these relationships have changed, but the evolution has often been unhurried and sometimes barely noticed.

Society has recently changed in important ways, however, which have already begun to accelerate the pace of change and potentially the scope of that change as well. The development of high technology and the emergence of the information society (McNutt & Hoefer, 2016) have created a new playing field that is only beginning to become apparent. We can expect greater changes within the sector as well as in the intersectoral assignment of social roles and functions and in the relationships between nonprofit organizations and governments.

Civic technology is one of the movements that can help redefine intersectoral relationships in many ways. It is currently a small but vibrant set of individuals, organizations, and institutions, and it is already having an impact on the dialogue about the future of government.

It also makes available a series of lenses to view nonprofit theory in general and nonprofit–government relations theory in particular in a new light.

It illuminates possibilities that have not been previously considered. It also provides a wonderful setting in which nonprofit theory can begin to explore the nuances of the emerging information society's implications for the sector. We should not miss the opportunity to capitalize on the possibilities that are available.

REFERENCES

Agranoff, R., & McGuire, M. (1998). Multinetwork management: Collaboration and the hollow state in local economic policy. *Journal of Public Administration Research and Theory, 8,* 67–91.

Aladalah, M., Cheung, Y., & Lee, V. (2015). Enabling citizen participation in Gov. 2.0: An empowerment perspective. *Electronic Journal of e-Government, 13,* 77–93.

Atzori, L., Iera, A., & Morabito, G. (2010). The Internet of things: A survey. *Computer networks, 54,* 2787–2805.

Baraniuk, C. (2013). The civic hackers reshaping your government. *New Scientist, 218*(2923), 36–39.

Baxandall, P., & Wohlschlegel, K. (2010, April 13). Following the money: How the 50 states rate in providing online access to government spending data). *U.S. PIRG Tax & Budget Reports.* Retrieved from http://www.uspirg.org/home/reports/report-archives/tax--budget-policy/tax--budget-policy--reports/following-the-money-how-the-50-states-rate-in-providing-online-access-to-government-spending-data

Berry, J. M. (1977). *Lobbying for the people.* Princeton, NJ: Princeton University Press.

Brainard, L., Boland, K., & McNutt, J. G. (2012, November). *The advent of technology enhanced leaderless transnational social movement organizations: implications for transnational advocacy.* Paper presented at the 2012 ARNOVA Meeting, Indianapolis.

Budhathoki, N. R., & Haythornthwaite, C. (2013). Motivation for open collaboration crowd and community models and the case of OpenStreetMap. *American Behavioral Scientist, 57,* 548–575.

Castells, M. (2012). *Networks of outrage and hope: Social movements in the Internet age.* New York: Polity.

Clark, B. Y., & Brudney, J. L. (2014). *Representation and beyond: Coproduction and the new information technology.* Working paper, SSRN no. 2473543. http://dx.doi.org/10.2139/ssrn.2473543

Clark, B. Y., Brudney, J. L., & Jang, S. G. (2013). Coproduction of government services and the new information technology: Investigating the distributional biases. *Public Administration Review, 73,* 687–701.

Code for America. (n.d.). About us. Retrieved from http://www.codeforamerica.org/about/

Cook, D. J., & Das, S. K. (2012). Pervasive computing at scale: Transforming the state of the art. *Pervasive and Mobile Computing, 8*(1), 22–35.

Crawford, S. P., & Walters, D. (August 7, 2013). *Citizen-centered governance: The Mayor's Office of New Urban Mechanics and the Evolution of CRM in Boston.* Berkman Center Research Publication No. 17. http://dx.doi.org/10.2139/ssrn.2307158

David, N. P. (2018). Democratizing government: What we know about e-government and civic engagement. In M P. Rodríguez Bolívar and L. Alcaide-Muñoz (Eds.),

International e-government development: Policy, implementation and best practices (pp. 73–96). Berlin: Springer.

David, N., McNutt, J. G., & Justice, J. B. (2018). Smart cities, transparency, civic technology and reinventing government. In Manuel Pedro Rodríguez Bolívar (Ed.), *Smart technologies for smart governments. Transparency, efficiency and organizational issues* (pp. 19–34). Berlin: Springer.

Davies, R. (2015). Three provocations for civic crowdfunding. *Information, Communication & Society, 18*, 342–355.

Desouza, K. C., & Bhagwatwar, A. (2012). Citizen apps to solve complex urban problems. *Journal of Urban Technology, 19*(3), 107–136.

Desouza, K. C., & Bhagwatwar, A. (2014). Technology-enabled participatory platforms for civic engagement: The case of US cities. *Journal of Urban Technology, 21*(4), 25–50.

Durose, C., Justice, J. B., & Skelcher, C. (2015). Governing at arm's length: Eroding or enhancing democracy? *Policy & Politics, 43*, 137–153.

Fredericksen, P., & London, R. (2000). Disconnect in the hollow state: The pivotal role of organizational capacity in community-based development organizations. *Public Administration Review, 60*, 230–239.

Germany, J. B. (Ed.). (2006). *Person to person to person: Harnessing the political power of on-line social networks and user generated content.* Washington, DC: Institute for Politics, Democracy and the Internet, George Washington University.

Gibson, R., & Cantijoch, M. (2013). Conceptualizing and measuring participation in the age of the Internet: Is online political engagement really different to offline? *Journal of Politics, 75*, 701–716.

Goldstein, J., & Rotich, J. (2008). *Digitally networked technology in Kenya's 2007–2008 post-election crisis.* Berkman Center Research Publication 9.

Gordon, E., Baldwin-Philippi, J., & Balestra, M. (2013). *Why we engage: How theories of human behavior contribute to our understanding of civic engagement in a digital era.* Berkman Center Research Publication 21.

Gulick, L. (1925). Principles of administration. *National Municipal Review, 14*, 400–403.

Guo, C., & Saxton, G. (2013). Tweeting social change: How social media are changing nonprofit advocacy. *Nonprofit and Voluntary Sector Quarterly, 43*, 57–79.

Harris, M. (2012). Nonprofits and business: Toward a subfield of nonprofit studies. *Nonprofit and Voluntary Sector Quarterly, 41*, 892–902.

Headd, M. (2009, December 14). Delaware checkbook a step backwards for transparency. Retrieved from http://www.voiceingov.org/blog/?p=1425

Hébert, M. K. (2014). Come hack with me: Adapting anthropological training to work in civic innovation. *Practicing Anthropology, 36*(2), 32–36.

Hendler, J. (2009). Web 3.0 emerging. *Computer, 42*, 111–113.

Johnson, P., & Robinson, P. (2014). Civic hackathons: Innovation, procurement, or civic engagement? *Review of Policy Research, 31*, 349–357.

Justice, J. B., & Dülger, C. (2009). Fiscal transparency and authentic citizen participation in public budgeting: The role of third-party intermediation. *Journal of Public Budgeting, Accounting & Financial Management, 21*, 254–288.

Justice, J. B., & McNutt, J. G. (2013–2014). Social capital, e-government and fiscal transparency in the states. *Public Integrity, 16*, 5–24.

Justice, J., McNutt, J., & Smith, E. (2011, May). *Holding state governments accountable for the public purse: What institutional, organizational and environmental factors promote fiscal transparency?* Paper presented at the First Global Conference on Transparency Research, Newark, NJ.

Justice, J. B., & Tarimo, F. (2012). NGOs holding governments accountable: Civil-society budget work. *Public Finance and Management, 21,* 204–236.

King, S. F., & Brown, P. (2007, December). Fix my street or else: using the Internet to voice local public service concerns. In Association for Computing Machinery (Ed.), *Proceedings of the 1st International Conference on Theory and Practice of Electronic Governance* (pp. 72–80). New York: ACM.

Lathrop, D., & Ruma, L. (Eds.). (2010). *Open government: Collaboration, transparency, and participation in practice.* Sevastopol, CA: O'Reilly.

Living Cities. (2012, November 26). Field scan for civic technology. Retrieved from https://www.livingcities.org/resources/131-field-scan-of-civic-technology/

McNutt, J. G., & Hoefer, R. (2016). *Social Welfare Policy: Responding to a Changing World.* Lyceum Books/Oxford University Press.

McNutt, J. G., Brainard, L., Zeng, Y., & Kovacic, P. (2016). Information and technology in and for associations and volunteering. In D. H. Smith, C. Rochester, R. Stebbins, & J. Grotz (Eds.), *Palgrave Handbook of volunteering and nonprofit associations* (pp. 1060-1073). Basingstoke, UK: Palgrave Macmillan.

McNutt, J. G., & Justice, J. B. (2016, June–July). *Predicting civic hackathons in local communities: Perspectives from social capital and creative class theory.* Paper presented at the 12th International Society for Third Sector Research Conference, Ersta Skondal University College, Stockholm, Sweden.

McNutt, J. G., Justice, J., Auger, D., & Carter, D. (2013, November). *Once they built it, who came? Nonprofit advocacy organizations and government transparency programs.* Paper presented at the 2013 ARNOVA Annual Conference, Hartford, CT.

McNutt, J. G., Justice, J., & Carter, D. (2014, April). *Examining intersections between open government and nonprofit advocacy: Theoretical and empirical perspectives about an emerging relationship.* Paper presented at International Research Society for Public Management Conference 2014, Ottawa.

McNutt, J. G., Justice, J. B., Melitski, M. J., Ahn, M. J., Siddiqui, S., Carter, D. T., & Kline, A. D. (2016). The diffusion of civic technology and open government in the United States. *Information Polity, 21,* 153–170.

Newsome, G. (2013). *Citizenville.* New York: Penguin.

Offenhuber, D. (2015). Infrastructure legibility: A comparative analysis of open311-based citizen feedback systems. *Cambridge Journal of Regions, Economy and Society, 8,* 93–112.

Okolloh, O. (2009). Ushahidi, or "testimony": Web 2.0 tools for crowdsourcing crisis information. *Participatory Learning and Action, 59,* 65–70.

Omidyar Network. (2016). Engines of change: What civic tech can learn from social movements. Retrieved from http:/www.enginesofchange.omidyar.com

O'Reilly, T. (2005, October 1). Web 2.0: Compact definition [Web log post]. Retrieved from http://radar.oreilly.com/2005/10/web-20-compact-definition.html.

O'Reilly, T. (2007). What is Web 2.0: Design patterns and business models for the next generation of software. *Communications and Strategies, 65,* 17–37.

Ostrom, E. (1990). *Governing the commons: The evolution of institutions for collective action.* Cambridge, UK: Cambridge University Press.

Ostrom, E. (1995). Self-organization and social capital. *Industrial and Corporate Change, 4,* 131–159.

Ostrom, E. (1998). The comparative study of public economies. *American Economist, 42,* 3–17.

Ostrom, V. (1989). *The intellectual crisis in American public administration* (2nd ed.). Tuscaloosa: University of Alabama Press.

Ostrom, V., Tiebout, C. M., & Warren, R. (1961). The organization of government in metropolitan areas: A theoretical inquiry. *American Political Science Review, 55,* 831–1842.

Ott, J. S., & Dicke, L. (Eds.). (2011). *Understanding nonprofit organizations: Governance, leadership, and management.* Boulder, CO: Westview.

Popyack, J. L. (2014). Prohacktivity, or one giant hack for mankind. *ACM Inroads, 5*(2), 40–52.

Rhodes, R. A. W. (1997). *Understanding governance: Policy networks, governance, reflexivity and accountability.* Buckingham, UK: Open University Press.

Sieber, R. E., & Johnson, P. A. (2015). Civic open data at a crossroads: Dominant models and current challenges. *Government Information Quarterly, 32,* 308–315.

Simon, H. A. (1946). The proverbs of administration. *Public Administration Review, 6,* 53–67.

Smith, A. (2008, December 30). From BarackObama.com to Change.gov: Those active in the Obama campaign expect to be involved in promoting the administration. Retrieved from http://www.pewinternet.org/2008/12/30/from-barackobama-com-to-change-gov/

Smith, A., Schlozman, K., Verba, S. & Brady, H. (2009, September 1). The Internet and civic engagement. Retrieved from http://www.pewinternet.org/Reports/2009/15--The-Internet-and-Civic-Engagement.aspx

Smith, D. H. (1997). The rest of the nonprofit sector: Grassroots associations as the dark matter ignored in prevailing "flat earth" maps of the sector. *Nonprofit and Voluntary Sector Quarterly, 26,* 114–131.

Smith, S. R., & Lipsky, M. (1993). *Nonprofits for hire: The welfare state in the age of contracting.* Harvard University Press.

Stepasiuk, T. (2014). Civic hacking: A motivational perspective. *New Visions in Public Affairs, 6,* 21–30.

Suri, M. V. (2013). *From crowdsourcing potholes to community policing: Applying interoperability theory to analyze the expansion of "Open311."* Berkman Center Research Publication No. 2013-18.

Taylor, F. W. (1911). *The principles of scientific management.* New York: Harper & Brothers.

Verba, S., Scholzman, K., & Brody, H. (1995). *Voice and equity: Civil volunteerism in American politics.* Cambridge, MA: Harvard University Press

Warren, R., Rosentraub, M. S., & Harlow, K. S. (1984). Coproduction, equity, and the distribution of safety. *Urban Affairs Quarterly, 19,* 447–464.

Warren, R., Rosentraub, M. S., & Weschler, L. F. (1988). A community services budget: Public, private, and third-sector roles in urban services. *Urban Affairs Quarterly, 23*, 414–431.

West, D. M. (2005*). Digital government: Technology and public sector performance.* Princeton, NJ: Princeton University Press.

Wilson, W. (1887). The study of administration. *Political Science Quarterly, 2*, 197–222.

Wolch, J. R. (1990). *The shadow state: Government and the voluntary sector in transition.* New York: Foundation Center.

Advocacy, Social Change, and Activism

Policy Level

8

Advocacy of, by, and for the Internet

The 2012 Protests against Anti-Piracy Legislation

LORI A. BRAINARD AND JUSTINE AUGERI ■

On January 18, 2012 much of the Internet went dark. Some sites were blacked out; others covered with a banner warning against the then-pending Stop Online Privacy Act/Protect Intellectual Property Act (SOPA/PIPA); others had information about the bills; and some directed visitors to call their member of Congress and/or provided direct mechanisms to do so. This was the hallmark event of the anti-SOPA/PIPA electronic advocacy campaign.

The anti-SOPA/PIPA activists were successful in that they achieved their goal: They killed the bill. Within 48 hours of the blackout, sponsors began backing away from bill, and the bill was shelved. What is significant about this electronic advocacy is not only that it was the first of its kind on the Internet—widespread, dramatic, and successful; it also achieved its goals over the opposition of a group of entrenched interests, including Hollywood, the Chamber of Commerce, and the AFL-CIO.

This chapter provides an exploratory case study of online advocacy and lobbying surrounding the SOPA/PIPA bills in Congress, looking at both sides of the issue. We seek to explain how the two sides differed from each other to isolate possible keys to the unexpected success of the anti-SOPA/PIPA forces. It is exploratory in that it relies almost exclusively on accounts drawn from various newspapers (and also some websites). It is meant to generate an understanding of the details of the case within its context and to develop areas for future research. Finally, by comparing elements of the campaigns to the literature on interest groups and social movements, lobbying, and advocacy, we not only use the literature to shed light on the campaigns; we also use the campaigns to shed light on the literature for those studying electronic advocacy in the future.

We distill from the relevant literature the important elements of advocacy and lobbying efforts. Next, we offer a description of our research process and methods. Then, we look at the case in detail and compare the online pro- and anti-SOPA/PIPA activities to each other and to the literature. While we obviously cannot generalize from a single case, the comparison of the pro- and anti-factions does help us to isolate important factors. This may help us understand the important elements of successful electronic advocacy and shed light on what this teaches us about the literature on the topic. We conclude with areas for future research.

EVOLVING TACTICS AND ACTORS

Advocacy in the US political system has been considered distinct from lobbying. As Libby (2011, quoting Center for Lobbying in the Public Interest, 2008) notes:

> Lobbying is a "specific, legally defined activity that involves stating your position on specific legislation to legislators and/or asking them to support your position. On the other hand, advocacy is a process in which organizations and individuals seek to influence both public opinion and public policy" (p. 14).

This distinction between lobbying and advocacy reflects the distinction between the types of organizations that engage in each activity. An interest group, an "organized body of individuals who share some goals and who try to influence public policy" (Berry, 1989, p. 4), is usually a formal, hierarchically structured organization. Chadwick (2007) notes that interest groups typically have sought their goals without necessarily needing to appeal to the masses or grassroots. Instead, they engage in traditional lobbying by targeting legislators and other government officials.

There are two broad kinds of interest organizations. Private interest groups, such as businesses and their representatives (e.g., the National Association of Manufacturers) have a financial stake in an issue, bill, or law. In contrast, public interest groups, such as environmental organizations like the National Audubon Society, usually do not have a financial stake in the issue, bill, or law. Both groups lobby and advocate.

Social movements, on the other hand, are more amorphous than interest groups. They are nonhierarchical, consensual, and participatory (Chadwick, 2007). They typically include those without formal means of public power and sometimes engage in unconventional political action (Ayers, 1999). The civil rights movement is one such example.

Policymaking in the United States often favors producer interests (Lowi, 1969; Redford, 1969; Wilson, 1982) rather than public interest groups and social movements. Producer groups can make contributions to elected officials and often provide a landing spot for members of an administration after leaving office.

Therefore, elected and appointed officials are often reluctant to make policy that disadvantages producer groups.

Though the system is said to benefit producer interests, there are some factors that contribute to exceptions to that norm. First, in the well-known example of economic deregulation, Derthick and Quirk (1985) show that a political entrepreneur (Kingdon, 2002) can build acceptance for solutions, connect them with problems, and foster political will. Well-known political entrepreneurs include Ralph Nader (auto safety), Steven Bryer (deregulation), and Rachel Carson (environmental issues). Second, Brainard (2004) shows that public interest groups can overcome producer interests when they are able to control the framing of an issue or the definition of a problem (see also Baumgartner & Jones, 1993).

The lines between these categories—interest group, public interest group, social movement, lobbying, and advocacy—are blurring. Some challenge the distinction between social movements and interest groups (see Brainard & Siplon, 2000), arguing that the two are synonymous (Berry, 1999, p. 142; Burstein, 1998, p. 38) because what traditionally has distinguished social movements (advocating for change, representing outsiders, and using nontraditional tactics) can be said about some traditional interest groups. Interest groups, public interest groups, and social movements all can and do engage in both lobbying and advocacy.

While, in general, lobbying targets elected officials and advocacy targets public opinion, campaigns do have some common elements that may be used: (a) identify an issue; (b) research the issue; (c) create educational materials; (d) brand the issue—that is, frame it; (e) identify supporters and opponents; (f) form a coalition; (g) launch a media campaign; and (h) approach elected officials (Libby, 2011). As previously described, Derthick and Quirk (1985) and Kingdon (2002) add to this list by emphasizing the importance of a political entrepreneur.

The Internet adds a new twist by adding the element of electronic advocacy—advocacy that relies on or is heavily dependent on Web technologies and may include a wide array of strategies, tactics, and tools. (McNutt, 2012). By decreasing the effort, time, and energy needed to organize and mobilize, the Internet lowers the costs of action. On the other hand, as Bergan (2009) notes, electronic advocacy campaigns by virtue of their ease and mass quantity may also decrease the perceived value of the action to policymakers. For example, officials may perceive e-mail as less significant than a letter.

In this chapter, we investigate the actions of both the pro- and anti-SOPA/PIPA forces. As these were not formally defined campaigns, we refer to them as "camps." We compare and contrast these two camps to isolate important variables that may have led to the success of the anti-SOPA/PIPA forces. In particular, we consider how Web technologies may have influenced elements of their lobbying/advocacy efforts. We then contribute to theory-building by discussing the implications for the literature.

METHODS

We chose the SOPA/PIPA issue and the activities surrounding it because they are a clear example of success and loss. One side clearly achieved its objective; the other side did not. Such a clear example allows for clearer comparisons. We compare these two camps to each other to discern how the anti-SOPA/PIPA forces were able to overcome the efforts of the pro-SOPA/PIPA forces. We then compare the outcome to the literature to identify how the literature might be adapted to the cyber era.

As an exploratory study, our data sources included three newspapers: *The New York Times* and *The Washington Post* (newspapers of record) and the San Jose's *Mercury News* (based in Silicon Valley and covers technology issues). We coded all relevant articles in the three newspapers for the elements provided in the literature and compared the two camps based on these elements. After coding, we compared our findings to the literature.

There are, of course, limitations to exploratory studies. First, one cannot generalize from a case study. By isolating important elements, however, we can generate areas for future research. Second, our search is limited to the three newspapers previously mentioned. Our search terms (various combinations of the bills' names and campaign names) generated an enormous number of articles that required narrowing by news source. Third, we look only at what happened online as reported by the three newspapers. We do not have interviews with key actors, which could shed light on our findings. Snowball-sampled interviews, for example, may generate a sense of the network—both human and electronic—at play in these events.

"THE ONLY THING MISSING WAS THE THEME FROM JAWS"

As previously discussed, the literature directs our attention to the elements of advocacy campaigns, which we have consolidated as follows: the actors involved (interest groups, public interest groups, the grassroots, and political entrepreneurs, as well as the coalition they may form), the particular actions and tactics they use, and the way they frame the issue and make their arguments.

The Actors

The pro-SOPA/PIPA camp united an interesting mix of industries, from movie studios to pharmaceutical makers, around the single cause of protecting content. Content producers were the most prominent actors and included industries and organizations that have historically wielded a great deal of influence in Congress: Hollywood and major movie studios; the Motion Picture Association of America (MPAA); the Directors Guild of America; labor unions that support

Hollywood production, such as the International Brotherhood of Teamsters (IBT) and the Screen Actors Guild (SAG-AFTRA, a member of AFL-CIO); the American Federation of Musicians; others representing video game makers, publishing houses, musical artists and producers; and the Consumer Electronics Association. The pro-SOPA/PIPA camp also included the US Chamber of Commerce.

The Chamber of Commerce was a flash point for the breakdown into the two sides of the issue. As self-described, the Chamber is the world's largest business organization and represents a spectrum of industries, businesses sizes, and regions (US Chamber of Commerce, n.d.). At the time the SOPA/PIPA legislation was introduced, the Chamber represented both content-producing industries previously described and the Web giants and other Silicon Valley businesses in the anti-SOPA/PIPA camp. Prior to the SOPA/PIPA legislation, disagreements between the Chamber and its members were rarely visible to the public. As an illustration of the power of the entertainment industry, the Chamber came out in support of SOPA/PIPA, and it was the technology firms that left. Implications for the technology industry's exit were at that point unknown, given the well-established strength of the entertainment sector in Congress:

> Spats between the Chamber and its members rarely spill out into public view. And it's unclear how an exodus of technology firms would impact the lobbying group's considerable weight in Washington. The group does not disclose the names of its members, many of whom pay substantial amounts for the Chamber's lobbying prowess. (Kang, 2011)

Several of the organizations in the pro-SOPA/PIPA camp (MPAA, IBT, and the Chamber) have long been among the most powerful interests and, as the previous quote suggests, the lobbying power of a relatively new technology industry was unclear. Certainly, the literature would suggest that if up against a less powerful and less entrenched opposition, MPAA, IBT, and the Chamber would win at least some of their policy wishes. They had teams of lobbyists, both internal and hired firms, and policy shops within their organizations. We are unable to discern whether these organizations formed a formal coalition, but it is certainly safe to say that they were able to fund a large and professionalized initiative, with the Chamber—itself an umbrella organization uniting many organizational members—being one of the more visible actors. Though we lack evidence of a formal coalition, the federated structure of the Chamber, the unions, and other organizations provided organizational direction.

What the pro-SOPA/PIPA camp wanted was a more rigorous copyright law for the Internet. Specifically, they wanted antipiracy legislation that would make it illegal to post copyrighted material. At different stages in the legislative progress the bills' target population varied from individuals, the businesses that own and operate the technology platforms for potentially illegal content (e.g., Facebook, YouTube), and foreign websites that served as conduits for copyrighted material. It was difficult to target the individuals and foreign websites that were perceived to be pirating. As a result, the bill sponsors focus on those they could target best: technology firms that enable pirates to function, including American search engines (e.g., Google and Yahoo), ad servers, and payment processors like PayPal.

As noted, the anti-SOPA/PIPA camp included a range of technology firms, as well as individual actors and the grassroots. This camp included high-tech companies such as Adobe, which were concerned with the overall health of the industry. Social media companies such as Facebook and Twitter, content curators such as Wikipedia and Reddit, and online blog and "zine" sites such as BoingBoing were fearful of being held liable for individuals who independently post copyright material. There were also individual or small-group Web content creators, who constitute the grassroots in cyberspace (or the "netroots") and who were concerned that they might unwittingly post copyrighted material. Consumers and unaffiliated advocates were concerned with a variety of issues ranging from civil liberties to access to free content.

The variety of anti-SOPA/PIPA groups is striking given the range of political perspectives involved: interest groups broadly recognized as liberal (the ACLU and MoveOn) concerned with free speech as well as private interest groups and organizations broadly recognized as conservative. These included traditional media organizations, such as News Corporation, and conservative political organizations, such as the Tea Party. Their concerns included too much government regulation. Interestingly, there seem to have been no political entrepreneurs.

Anti-SOPA/PIPA entities shared a common interest, but we find no evidence that they formed a formal coalition. They acted independently in deciding whether and how to participate in the protest. Wikipedia and 800 of its members, for example, debated and voted on whether to participate in the blackout. Similarly, when Anonymous—the "hacktivist" organization—produced "Operation Hiroshima," a document dump exposing personal information of members of the pro-SOPA/PIPA campaign, other organizations disavowed the method. A striking difference between the pro-SOPA/PIPA camp and the anti-SOPA/PIPA camp was that the pro-SOPA/PIPA camp lacked a grassroots contingent.

Tactics

The two camps used very different tactics, reflecting the kinds of technologies they affiliate with. The pro-SOPA/PIPA camp, comprised largely of corporate content producers, appears to have relied on traditional lobbying—that is, targeting elected officials with crafted messages. While an exact comparison of traditional lobbying across the two camps is not available, it is clearly evident from our research that the actions of the anti-SOPA/PIPA camp relied on new tactics uniquely afforded by the Internet. The pro-SOPA/PIPA camp had congressional campaign funding in its arsenal. According to MacKinnon (2012), during the 2010 election cycle the 32 congressional sponsors of the bills received four times as much in campaign contributions from the entertainment industry as they did from the software industry.

The pro-SOPA/PIPA camp also testified at hearings and engaged in a nationwide ad campaign using TV and radio. During the November 2011 House Judiciary Committee hearings on SOPA, six individuals were given the opportunity to testify. Five of those six individuals represented the pro-SOPA/PIPA camp: Register of Copyrights within the US Library of Congress, the pharmaceutical company Pfizer, the MPAA, MasterCard, and the AFL-CIO. A review of submitted testimony shows that all of these individuals took strong positions of support for SOPA. In contrast, the one representative of the anti-SOPA/PIPA camp, Google (which had hired 15 lobbying firms), did not make a strong statement of opposition, instead describing many "grave concerns" (*Stop Online Piracy Act*, 2011).

The pro-SOPA/PIPA camp did engage in at least one form of online action—tweeting. As Tsukayama and Kang (2011) note, "They tweeted and took to social-media channels. . . . But their efforts hardly made a ripple in the virtual world" (p. A14).

Technology firms did use some traditional tactics. As Wyatt (2011) notes, Google hired at least 15 lobbying firms. Facebook, Google, Yahoo, LinkedIn, eBay, and Mozilla used an open letter to formally request the House and Senate Committees to reconsider the legislation. Companies and, at times, advocates also engaged in traditional advertising in newspapers and magazines:

> Naturally the howls of protest have been loud and lavishly financed, not only from Silicon Valley companies but also from public-interest groups, free-speech advocates and even venture capital investors. They argue—in TV and newspaper ads—that the bills are so broad and heavy-handed that they threaten to close Web sites and broadband service providers and stifle free speech, while setting a bad example of American censorship. (Wyatt, 2011)

Technology firms, however, also used the Internet. Firms such as Tumblr, Reddit, and Mozilla used their sites as billboards to motivate ordinary consumers to oppose the bills. The viral nature of the Internet appears to have furthered the formal methods previously described by enabling ideas and informal efforts to spread as individual sites installed software or posted information enabling consumers to sign petitions, send e-mails to Congress, and call their representative or senator.

Ultimately, three online protests in opposition to SOPA/PIPA took place over three months. American Censorship Day on November 16, 2011 represented a collection of consumers, advocates, and Internet companies such as Tumbler, which posted banners and pop-ups on websites to explain the threat SOPA/PIPS posed. Companies used their online presence to promote traditional tactics:

> In November, Tumblr rigged a tool that "censored" the page its users see when they log into the site, explained the legislation and routed them to contact information for their representatives in Congress. The stunt resulted in 80,000 calls to legislators in a three-day period. (Wortham, 2012)

The second online protest was against the Web hosting company, Go Daddy (rather than Congress), in December 2011. Go Daddy initially supported SOPA/PIPA, but reversed its stance after thousands of websites, one of the most prominent being Wikipedia, threatened to withdraw their domains from Go Daddy.

The culminating protest, the blackout on January 18, 2012, was widespread and dramatic. For example, the nonprofit online-freedom advocacy group, Fight for the Future, created sopastrike.com, which appears to have offered a clear destination for many protestors. By late afternoon on the day of the protest, visitors went through sopastrike.com to send a reported 350,000 emails to Congress. According to Topsy, a tweet-metering site, Twitter users had tweeted "sopa" three million times on the day of the strike (May, 2012). EngineAdvocacy, which helps people call their member of Congress, reported that up to 2,000 calls per second were made. It was reported that many calls did not go through, because demand was so intense. The Wikimedia Foundation, which operates a network of sites including Wikipedia, claimed that four million people used its site to look up contact information on their representative.

It appears many companies used a threatening tone to evoke strong emotion from consumers through direct interaction and illustration of the threat. Sopastrike.com reported one headline that read "Internet Goes on Strike" (May, 2012), and one journalist offered the example of Scribd.com: "Last month Scribd.com introduced a function that made the words on documents gradually fade away. As they did, a pop-up prompted users to contact their representatives. 'Don't let the Internet vanish before your eyes,' it read" (Chozick, 2012).

Overall, the anti-SOPA/PIPA camp appears to have relied more on advocacy than lobbying. Its actions seem viral and nontraditional, even unconventional. Actors used a variety of techniques to spread awareness among the grassroots and consumers. Wikipedia, Reddit, MoveOn, BoingBoing, Cheezburger Network, Fail Blog, and many bloggers blacked out their entire sites/pages for 24 hours—what one observer called a "a political coming of age for a relatively young and disorganized industry that has largely steered clear of lobbying and other political games in Washington" (Wortham, 2012). Some firms did not join the blackout but participated in other ways. Google linked its users to a site that explained its opposition to SOPA/PIPA. Facebook, Twitter, Yahoo, Zynga, and eBay signed an open opposition letter, which went viral. Thousands of other web pages aligned with the anti-SOPA/PIPA camp were filled with warnings about SOPA/PIPA. As one writer put it, "The only thing missing was the theme from Jaws" (May, 2012).

Framing

The camps framed their arguments about SOPA/PIPA using three primary themes: (a) legal principle; (b) the potential impact of the legislation on business, innovation, and the economy; and (c) the potential impact of the legislation in a global context.

The pro-SOPA/PIPA camp's legal argument was that SOPA/PIPA would simply enforce present copyright law on the Internet, thus preventing intellectual property theft. Proponents often appeared dismissive of the opposing camp's claims. As one MPAA proponent stated, "This bill has due process. . . . It covers activities that are, under federal law, illegal, and requires that any order issued is public and transparent" (Tsukayama & Kang, 2011). This enabled pro-SOPA/PIPA activists to analogize intellectual property theft to libel and plagiarism. One constitutional law expert drew a powerful and common sense analogy:

> The judges who have decide, without dissent, that a libel on the Internet is just as subject to punishment as libel in a newspaper were not wrong. The proposition that plagiarism on the Internet must be treated the same as plagiarism by a television program is not controversial. Nor are the rulings—and there are none to the contrary—that make plain that infringements of copyright on the Internet are as criminal there as elsewhere. (Abrams, 2011)

The anti-SOPA/PIPA camp's legal argument was also succinct: SOPA/PIPA constituted censorship. The camp used an altruistic tone, describing SOPA/PIPA as bad for both the nation and the world. As one reported noted, "Wikipedia cofounder Jimmy Wales said SOPA/PIPA would 'endanger free speech both in the United States and abroad, and set a frightening precedent of Internet censorship for the world'" (Owens, 2012). By framing it around a different legal principle, the anti-SOPA/PIPA camp avoided confronting the legal argument made by the pro-SOPA/PIPA camp, arguing that those claims should be dealt with in other ways: "'We oppose these bills because there are smart, targeted ways to shut down foreign rogue websites without asking American companies to censor the Internet,' Samantha Smith, a Google spokeswoman, told Bloomberg News in a Tuesday email" (Owens, 2012).

Interestingly, the anti-SOPA/PIPA camp anthropomorphized the Internet in stressing civil liberties. Talk of "censoring the Internet" was common, and, when opinion started to shift their way, they noted that "the Internet is winning a battle." As described by one teen advocate in an op-ed piece, "Censoring the Internet is not the answer. We need to preserve the Web as a free space for anyone to speak his or her mind" (Mejia-Cuellar, 2012).

The second major argument highlighted the potential effects on business. Both sides claimed that the legislation would harm their respective businesses and the broader economy. Each camp, however, argued this from different angles. One difference was that the pro-SOPA/PIPA camp argued in the present tense about the harmful impact of counterfeiting on business, whereas the anti-SOPA/PIPA camp had to make broad statements about the potential future impact of such a law on their business.

The pro-SOPA/PIPA camp used stark figures to illustrate their point. The Chamber estimated that $135 billion in revenues was lost every year from piracy and counterfeiting and framed the issue broadly, extending it to the technology companies they had previously represented and were now targeting. The Chamber proposed that SOPA/PIPA would improve the quality of media content online, constituting an indirect benefit for technology firms. As stated by the Chamber, "This is a common-sense way forward that is good for the whole industry" (Wyatt, 2011).

Industry actors in anti-SOPA/PIPA camp argued that the legislation would be harmful to their future business and to innovation more broadly. Although lacking hard figures, the camp was still able to invoke fear, noting that the law would stifle innovation and harm a growing sector of the US economy. Michael Petricone of the Consumer Electronics Association described how the tech sector, "perhaps the brightest spot of the economy," would be harmed (Kang, 2011), or as Erick Goldman, director of the High Tech Law Institute at Santa Clara University put it, SOPA/PIPA would "jeopardize the Internets' entire content ecosystem" (Swift, 2011).

The anti-SOPA/PIPA camp appears, at times, to have positioned the issue as generational—a dispute between an older generation that runs Hollywood and the publishing industry and a younger generation that creates and hosts Internet content. Yaney Strickler, a founder of Kickstarter, noted, "The schism between content creators and platforms like Kickstarter, Tumblr and YouTube is generational" (Carr, 2012). Erik Martin of Reddit.com argued, "It's not a battle between Hollywood and tech, it's people who get the Internet and those who don't" (Wortham & Sengupta, 2012).

The third major frame dealt with America's place in the global system. The pro-SOPA/PIPA camp adopted a more old-guard, protectionist tone, using the idea of "piracy." Pirates on the high seas intercept lawfully flowing goods and disrupt the commercial infrastructure. Pirates of intellectual property, who often reside outside the United States, intercept content and disrupt the infrastructure of ideas and entertainment.

There are two facets to the anti-SOPA/PIPA camp's global arguments. In their legal frame, they portrayed themselves as altruistic protectors of civil liberties on a global scale. As previously described, one underlying message was that Internet freedom must prevail to protect individual well-being both nationally and globally. They extended this argument by stressing the potential national security implications. Sandia National Laboratories evaluated the legislation and found that the bill would not prevent intellectual property theft and, further, that it would have a negative impact on American, and even global, security. The process of filtering and blocking made necessary by the law might hinder the US government's efforts at improving security ("Editorial," 2011).

Each camp displayed a unique tendency in its framing. The pro-SOPA/PIPA camp seemed to make technical, impersonal, and protectionist arguments. In stark contrast, the anti-SOPA/PIPA camp appears to have made personal arguments about innovation, individual freedom, nationally, globally, and—by anthropomorphizing it—freedom of the Internet itself.

ADVOCACY AND LOBBYING IN THE INTERNET AGE

Here we place the actors, tactics, and framing of the pro- and anti-SOPA/PIPA camps in the context of prior literature. We seek to understand the extent to which the literature might have predicted certain outcomes.

Actors

The literature draws a distinction between interest groups, public interest groups, and social movements. The activities of the anti-SOPA/PIPA camp support the notion that the conceptual boundaries between groups and movements have blurred. The Internet enabled the actions of private interest groups, public interest groups, "netroots," and consumers to meld together in such a way as to make it difficult to understand what is an interest group and distinguish it from a social movement. These alliances appear to have been informal and characterized by shifting boundaries. For example, bloggers acted in their roles as bloggers and also consumers of the bigger firms, likewise consumers were both creators and users of content.

While the literature points to the importance of a political entrepreneur for overcoming entrenched interests (in this case, Hollywood), the anti-SOPA/PIPA win appears to have happened without one. Newspapers do not mention a single charismatic thought leader at the pinnacle of the movement. It is possible that the Internet—by collapsing producer/consumer boundaries and fostering interorganizational linkages—makes possible not only collective action (Brainard & Siplon, 2002) but also collective action without an entrepreneur, unless we consider the anthropomorphized Internet an entrepreneur of sorts (see chapter 13).

Tactics

While earlier literature notes a distinction between lobbying and advocacy, current literature describes their blurring. The anti-SOPA/PIPA case supports the latter. At times, it is hard to tell where/when one kind of tactic began and another ended. For example, tech firms blurred advocacy and lobbying by using their websites to simultaneously educate the public and urge the public to call their members of Congress. This was enabled by the ease of updating sites and linking actors with tactics.

Framing

Traditional thought would suggest that the pro-SOPA/PIPA camp would have an advantage by making a clear, succinct argument; offering direct evidence of a current problem; and having a powerful industry with abundant lobbying power and campaign finance. Nevertheless, the anti-SOPA/PIPA camp won.

The anti-SOPA/PIPA forces added unique nuances to common themes—legal principle, business and the economy, and America's place in the global community—by adding additional subthemes to each primary theme: "The Internet" to law and civil liberties, innovation to business and the economy, and protector of global freedom and national security to its place in the global community. In this regard, it appears the camp was able to capitalize on the positive characteristics commonly associated with the Internet, such as youth, innovation, global citizenship, and freedom. These advocates thus positioned themselves as fighting for a public good, rather than an industry. The Internet itself allowed users to learn about the issue and act on it almost simultaneously, directly illustrating the power of a free Internet as a venue to directly fight for their freedom.

Further, anthropomorphizing the Internet may have included it as though it were a "thing" in its own right—as distinct from its relationship to law, business, or America's place in the world. This perhaps reinforced the notion of SOPA/PIPA resisters as caretakers of something greater than themselves and their particular interests—the Internet!

CONCLUSION

While the Internet certainly did not preordain a win by the anti-SOPA/PIPA forces, it was a powerful enabler. The success of the anti-SOPA/PIPA campaign offers potential insight into several key topics. First, it demonstrates a continued blurring of the distinction between different kinds of interest organizations and between organizations and movements.

Further, political entrepreneurs may be unnecessary for electronic campaigns, unless the Internet itself can be recognized as one. Second, it also demonstrates a continued blurring of lobbying and advocacy in cyberspace, reflecting the fuzzy boundaries between interest organizations and social movements. Third, the Internet may afford electronic advocates the advantage of framing their issue through both words and action.

REFERENCES

Abrams, F. (2011, December 11). Theft is theft, even online. *Washington Post*, p. A23.

Ayers, J. (1999). From the streets to the Internet: The cyber-diffusion of contention. *Annals of the American Academy of Political and Social Science, 566*, 132–143.

Baumgartner, F., & Jones, B. (1993). *Agendas and instability in American politics.* Chicago: University of Chicago Press.

Bergan, E. E. (2009). Does grassroots lobbying work? A field experiment measuring the effects of an e-mail campaign on legislative behavior. *American Political Research, 37*, 327–352.

Berry, J. (1989). *The interest group society* (2nd ed.). Glenview, IL: Scott, Foresman/ Little Brown.

Berry, J. (1999). *The new liberalism: The rising power of citizen groups.* Washington, DC: Brookings Institution Press.

Brainard, L. (2004). *Television: The limits of deregulation.* Boulder, CO: Lynne Rienner.

Brainard, L., & Siplon. P. (2000). Cyberspace challenges to mainstream nonprofit health organizations. *Administration & Society, 34,* 141–175.

Brainard, L., & Siplon, P. (2002). The Internet and NGO–government relations: Injecting chaos into order. *Public Administration and Development, 22,* 63–72.

Burstein, P. (1998). Interest organizations, political parties, and the study of democratic politics. In A. N. Costain & A. S. McFarland (Eds.), *Social movements and American political institutions* (pp. 39–56). Oxford: Rowman & Littlefield.

Carr, D. (2012, January 2). The danger of an attack on piracy online. *New York Times,* p. B1.

Chadwick, A. (2007). Digital network repertoires and organizational hybridity. *Political Communication, 24,* 283–301.

Chozick, A. (2012, January 14). Fighting antipiracy measure, hackers click on media chiefs. *New York Times,* p. A1.

Derthick, M., & Quirk, P. (1985). *The politics of deregulation.* Washington, DC: Brookings Institution Press.

Editorial. (2011, November 19). Congress should kill online piracy bill. *Mercury News* (San Jose). Retrieved from https://www.mercurynews.com/2011/11/18/ mercury-news-editorial-congress-should-kill-online-piracy-bill/

Kang, C. (2011, November 16). Web giants at odds with Chamber of Commerce over piracy bill. *Washington Post,* p. A17.

Kingdon, J. (2002). *Agendas, alternatives, and public policies* (2nd ed.). London: Longman.

Libby, P. (2012). *The lobbying strategy handbook.* Thousand Oaks, CA: SAGE.

Lowi, T. (1969). *The end of liberalism: Ideology, policy, and the crisis of public authority.* New York: Norton.

MacKinnon, R. (2012, January 22). Why doesn't Washington understand the Internet? *Washington Post,* p. B01.

May, P. (2012, January 18). Wikipedia, Google and other websites protest anti-piracy laws. *Mercury News* (San Jose). Retrieved from https://www.mercurynews.com/2012/ 01/18/wikipedia-google-and-other-websites-protest-anti-piracy-laws/

McNutt, J. (2012). "Electronic advocacy: Why this site?" Retrieved from http://www. policymagic.org/why.htm.

Mejia-Cuellar, K. (2012, January 31). Teens: Internet censorship is wrong. *Mercury News* (San Jose). Retrieved from https://www.mercurynews.com/2012/01/23/ teens-internet-censorship-is-wrong/

Owens, J. C. (2012, January 17). Biz break: Preparing for a dark day on the Web; Yahoo's Yang resigns, and Tesla and Zynga CEOs help stock prices. *San Jose Mercury News* (San Jose). Retrieved from https://www.mercurynews.com/2012/01/17/biz-break-preparing-for-a-dark-day-on-the-web-yahoos-yang-resigns-and-tesla-and-zynga-ceos-help-stock-prices/

Redford, E. (1969). *Democracy in the administrative state.* Oxford: Oxford University Press.

Rheingold, H. (2000). *The virtual community: Homesteading on the electronic frontier* (Rev. ed.). Cambridge, MA: MIT Press.

Stop Online Piracy Act: Hearing before the Committee on the Judiciary House of Representatives, 112th Congress 1 (2011).

Swift, M. (2011, December 8). Silicon Valley fighting proposed law pushed by Hollywood. *Mercury News* (San Jose). Retrieved from https://www.mercurynews.com/2011/12/08/silicon-valley-fighting-proposed-law-pushed-by-hollywood/

Tsukayama, H., & Kang, C. (2011, November 23). A viral war against the piracy act. *Washington Post*, p. A14.

US Chamber of Commerce. (n.d.). About the U.S. Chamber. Retrieved from https://www.uschamber.com/about-us/about-the-us-chamber

Wilson, J. Q. (1982). *The politics of regulation*. New York: Basic Books.

Wortham, J. (2012, January 18). Protest on Web takes on 2 bills aimed at piracy. *New York Times*, p. A1.

Wortham, J., & Sengupta, S. (2012, January 16). Bills to stop Web piracy are inviting a long fight. *New York Times*, p. B1.

Wyatt, E. (2011, December 15). Lines drawn on antipiracy bills. *New York Times*, p. B1.

9

Leave No Org Behind

Exploring the Digital Life of Community Action Agencies

LAURI GOLDKIND AND SUZANNE MARMO ROMAN ■

Social media has become pervasive in the fabric of everyday life as well as a part of many organizational cultures and communications plans. However, in the nonprofit sector where technology uptake has historically been slower than the corporate sector, social media use is less pervasive (Goldkind, 2015; Young, 2013). Social media or Web 2.0 tools are characterized by two-way interactions; one might imagine that nonprofit organizations, especially those with expertise in relationship management at the consumer, donor, and volunteer management levels being especially adept at mastering the use of such tools. Yet little in the literature suggests that nonprofit human services organizations are using social media to leverage the interactive nature and functionality it offers (Phethean, Tiropanis, & Harris, 2013; Waters & Jamal, 2011).

It is possible that an organizational digital divide or even digital chasm exists between human service providers serving the most vulnerable constituents and those organizations serving individuals of means. The idea of an organizational digital divide was first introduced by McNutt in 2008, in the context of an exploration of the ability of grassroots advocacy organizations to compete in the electronic space with or against opponents whose monied connections and access represent significant wealth (McNutt, 2008a). McNutt extrapolates the digital divide recognized for individuals (Van Dijk, 2005) to organizations whose resources are too scarce to participate in the digital discourse in any meaningful way.

This chapter expands on the work of both McNutt (2008a) as well as Edwards and Hoefer (2010) by taking a national cohort of organizations—namely, community action agencies (CAAs)—and performing a content analysis on the 900 organizations' digital presence. CAAs were created by the War on Poverty and Lyndon Johnson's Economic Opportunity Act of 1964. The community action program was meant to serve as a mechanism for civic engagement and poverty alleviation and today remains uniquely positioned to connect stakeholders in their communities to resources in the form of decision makers and power brokers. This study expands on Edwards and Hoefer's (2010) content analysis protocol to investigate three research questions:

1. To what extent social media tools and resources penetrated the human services sphere?
2. To what extent are organizations using Web-based resources to promote policy advocacy engagement?
3. Is there a relationship between engagement in social media use and policy advocacy activities?

LITERATURE REVIEW

Community Action Agencies

Now roughly 50 years old, CAAs are locally based human services providers founded to alleviate poverty and engage and empower citizens in the United States. Johnson declared the War on Poverty in his State of the Union address on January 8, 1964. At that time 35 million Americans were living in poverty, nearly 30% of the total population, and about 25% of Black youths could expect to live life without regular employment. He also signed the Economic Opportunity Act (PL 88-452)—the signature legislation creating the Office of Economic Opportunity and providing the teeth for the War on Poverty (Wolman, 1972). The passage of the Economic Opportunity Act not only created the Office of Economic Opportunity, it also engendered a mechanism for fostering federal to local relationships. This approach developed a channel of bypassing state and local involvement in federal funding of local programmatic initiatives. This office would go on to create many of the core human services programs that are considered important to human services today such as VISTA, Job Corps, Neighborhood Youth Corps, Head Start, adult basic education, community health centers, congregate meal preparation, economic development, foster grandparents, legal services, neighborhood centers, and summer youth programs. The Office of Economic Opportunity was dismantled under the Nixon administration. Many of the programs created have continued to survive at both the federal and local level.

The CAAs and community action programs that were created by Office of Economic Opportunity have, in many cases, survived into the information age. This evolution has created a situation where technology tools have become important.

Web 2.0 and Social Media Tools

Social media and interactive Web-based communication tools have changed the fabric of organization to constituent communications. It is no longer sufficient for organizations to use a website as a megaphone or channel of information out into the universe with an expectation that interested parties will accept at face value the static media offerings being put forth. Instead constituents and stakeholders expect a two-way transmission of information offering a more personalized relationship with the organization via channels such as Facebook, Twitter, LinkedIn, and the like (Briones, Kuch, Lui, & Jin, 2011). Social media is a group of Internet-based applications that build on the technological foundations of Web 2.0 and allow users to share content that they have generated (Smith, 2015). Web 2.0 is focused on interactivity, feedback loops, and the world of social media as well as user-generated content such as blogs and wikis. The most pervasive examples of social media are social networking sites (e.g., Facebook, LinkedIn). These sites allow the users to both generate and exchange content within open or semi-open platforms (Goldkind, 2015; Kaplan & Haenlein, 2010).

While the spread of social media has significantly increased the opportunities for nonprofits to communicate with constituents of all stripes, including clients, donors, volunteers, the media, and the general public (2012; Nah & Saxton, 2012), it is generally agreed that nonprofits have not used social media to its fullest potential with regard to meeting organizational goals. One criticism has been about the nature of nonprofit communications over social media, with some authors highlighting that the paradigm changes of interactive two-way constituent communication, which is a hallmark of social media, have not been embraced by the sector (Lovejoy & Saxton, 2012).

Under the Web 2.0 rhetoric of information exchange and interactivity, social media networks and platforms such as LinkedIn, Facebook, Myspace, hi5, Friendster, and Ning allow users to create profiles; connect to family, friends, and acquaintances; and share information and data. Specialized social network channels allow for the distribution of specific types of information such as video files (e.g., YouTube, Vimeo, Vine, Periscope, Ocho, Metacafe) and photography files (e.g., Pinterst, Flickr, Instagram, Photobucket, GifBoom). Blogs are online journals that involve a series of entries or posts and allow blog readers to comment on the posting; some popular blog hosting websites include Blogger, Medium, Squarespace, and Tumblr (Goldkind & McNutt, 2014). The "blogosphere" is a public opinion arena with more than 100 million blogs, and their interconnections cannot be ignored (Kietzmann, Hermkens, McCarthy, & Silvestre, 2011). Lastly, microblogging, or Twitter, a social network made up of very short predominately text-based messages, has made communicating daily activities and updates accessible to everyone from celebrities to academics to teenagers. Founded in 2006, Twitter has more than 145 million users, sending on average 90 million "tweets" per day, each consisting of 280 characters or less (Kwak, Lee, Park, & Moon, 2010; Madway, 2010). These tweets are mostly short status updates of what users are doing, where they are, how they are feeling, or links to other sites.

This broad range of new electronic tools present a range of options and choices for nonprofits interested in pursuing connecting to constituents and stakeholders. As previously mentioned, the literature suggests two distinct organizational goals that may be supported with social media communications tools: fundraising and policy advocacy.

Fundraising Online

Often seen as less expensive and more efficient than traditional fundraising activities, electronic fundraising is certainly one tool in the fundraiser's arsenal that cannot be denied. E-mail, social media, Web 2.0, and social networking technologies have become important strategies for nonprofits engaged in building new relationships and cultivating new donors. However, the value of social media in particular, as a fundraising and volunteer procurement strategy is controversial. In terms of securing donations and attracting volunteers, the evidence is mixed, suggesting that social media can support the garnering not only of new contributors but also of smaller-scale donations. Although perceptions of social media use are high, the challenge—particularly for smaller and medium-sized nonprofits, defined as having budgets of $1 million to $5 million per year by—is that there is a persistent mismatch between perceptions, motivations, results, and the investment required to participate relative to the rate of return can be suspect.

Goecks, Voida, Voida, and Mynatt (2008) studied 150 instances of technology for nonprofit fundraising, including Facebook Causes and Network for Good. They assert that e-mail is amplifying an immediate need and framing a contribution as helping individuals rather than groups. They found that online fundraising can be significantly more cost-effective than offline fundraising. In their study, they suggested that for every $1 raised offline it cost a nonprofit up to $1.25 to generate; while online, it costs as little as $0.05 to raise $1. Additionally, they found there is a significant difference between the average age of donors who give online (39 years old) versus those who give offline (usually estimated to be 60 years or older), suggesting an affinity for online giving among the next generation of donors. This last finding has been supported by others including Flannery, Harris, and Rhine (2009) who study 24 national nonprofit agencies and find that online giving has become a major source of new donor acquisition, that online donors tended to be younger, and that these new donors gave larger gifts than traditional donors.

Policy Advocacy and Social Media

Advocacy and social change practice have rapidly become linked with technology tools and Internet-based outreach (Goldkind, 2014; McNutt, 2008b; McNutt & Menon, 2008; McNutt & Boland, 1999; Saxton, Niyirora, Guo, & Waters, 2015). In addition, electronic advocacy, defined as "the use of technologically intensive media as a means to influence stakeholders to effect policy change" (Fitzgerald & McNutt, 1997, p. 3), which is driven by social media tools, is revolutionizing policy advocacy practices in the United States and around the world. Electronic,

Internet-based interactive tools (e.g., social media) are facilitating the increased ease through which individuals and organizations can engage in advocacy campaigns (Guo & Saxton, 2012; Saxton et al., 2015).

The Internet can serve as a gathering place for those interested in activating change as well as a hub for connecting advocates. For organizations interested in creating and fomenting social change, the ability to quickly and efficiently identify groups and allied organizations with common interests and agendas as well as empathic individuals is greatly enhanced by the use of social networking sites (Goldkind & McNutt, 2014; Rohlinger, Bunnage, & Klein, 2012). Social networking sites allow organizations and users to rapidly connect and assemble like-minded communities that can be leveraged for social change (Rohlinger, Bunnage, & Klein, 2012). The interaction between social media and different political and economic aspects of life can also create a multiplying effect that can stimulate the creation and formation of social movements (Leenders & Heydemann, 2012).

According to Shirky (2011) and McNutt (2008a, 2008b), political use of social media such as Facebook, Twitter, YouTube, blogs, and cell phones has permanently changed the traditional way of organizing social movements by providing more channels for knowledge transfer and far more accelerated transfer of knowledge and information without a media bias and by dramatically accelerating individual's ability to coordinate efforts. One of the most revolutionary aspects of the use of social media in mobilizing and movement building is that it trivializes the need for elite support (Lopes, 2012; Shirky, 2011). First, "social media introduces speed and interactivity that were lacking in the traditional mobilization techniques, which generally include the use of leaflets, posters, and faxes" (Eltantawy & Wiest, 2011, p. 1213). Facebook and Twitter are able to reach millions of people from all over the world as events are happening. The diffusion of information between different countries through traditional media outlets generally takes longer than information going through social media. The fast spread of information—especially internationally—helps with validation, mobilization, and scope enlargement. Perhaps one of the most exciting functions of these new communication tools is the ability to bypass the mass media and give a voice to ordinary citizens in transforming the political landscape of their country.

METHOD AND PROCEDURE

This study adopts a methodology first put forward by Edwards and Hoefer (2010), which through a simple, yet highly effective content analysis presents a summary of interactive electronic advocacy activities of social work advocacy groups. Edwards and Hoefer analyzed a cohort of 63 advocacy-focused social work organizations to assess their use of Web 2.0 and Web sites for advocacy activities. The present study expands on their original design in several ways as detailed in the following discussion.

Sample

All free-standing CAAs with a functioning website were eligible to be including in the sample. A total of 902 CAAs exist nationally, with 732 of those being independent, private nongovernmental organizations or private nonprofits, not county health departments or county human services departments run by the state.

Data Collection

Content analysis was used to collect the data for this study. The principle investigator created a data collection instrument based on Edwards and Hoefer (2010) as well as the literature on Web 2.0 advocacy practices and the emergent literature on social media use for the sector, including the authors' own work. Lastly, the organizational characteristic data such as number of employees, volunteers, board members, and revenue information were collected from Internal Revenue Service Form 990. These forms were obtained from Guidestar.

Data Gathering

Data gathering was conducted by the author and three research assistants over a period of two months in the spring of 2014. With the exception of 50 (six percent) community action organizations, used for training purposes, each organization's website was reviewed by one team member. The data collected from the training sites were compared to ensure intercoder reliability. By dividing the number of times that the researchers agreed by the number of coding possibilities, researchers determined an agreement rate of 0.86. This rate exceeds the acceptable rate of 0.81 (Brank, Fox, Youstin, & Boeppler, 2009; Schutt, 2006).

FINDINGS

A total of 732 CAAs' websites, representing all 50 states, were analyzed. Table 9.1 displays characteristics of the CAAs analyzed in this sample. Organizations ranged in age from 5 to 122 years old with an average age of 45 years old. Over 50% of the sample of CAAs had budgets of $5 million or more and had a mean total budget of $12,061,413 (SD = $12,959,456). The mean number of employees was 234.3 (SD = 205.6). The mean total expenses were $11,195,608 (SD = $12,577,489); mean program expenses were $11,195,608 (SD = $12,577,489); and mean management expenses were $775,435 (SD = $772,043). Large standard deviations in expenses, particularly the dependent variable in this study, total expenses, did reveal some skewness to these distributions, but visual inspection of the distribution showed limited outliers within the data with a majority of values on the lower side of the distribution.

Table 9.1. ORGANIZATIONAL CHARACTERISTICS

Characteristic	N	M (SD) or %
Board members	700	16.9 (6.3)
Number of employees	701	234.3 (205.6)
Pre	701	69,607.0 (13,6408.3)
Volunteers	647	880.2 (1998.8)
Total expenses	701	12,061,413 (12,959,456)
Program expenses	700	11,195,608 (12,577,489)
Management expenses	698	775,435 (772,043)
Fund expenses	679	23,088 (98,667)
Organization lobbies	58	8.3
United Way member	182	26.8
Other coalition member	332	47.2
Agency has organizational blog(s)	52	7.7
Agency has links to twitter	164	24.2
Agency has links to Facebook	328	48.3
Agency has links to LinkedIn	38	5.6
Agency has links to photosharing	21	3.1
Agency has links to other social media	21	3.1
Org links video	149	22.0
Org uses text message	4	.6
Org uses podcast	3	.4
Org uses RSS	63	9.3
Org has advocacy materials online	47	6.9
Org has clear statement of policy perspective	65	9.2
Website has internal search engine	266	39.2
Org accepts online donations	328	48.4
Org hosts online petitions	2	.3
Mission posted on website	623	91.9
Advocacy mention in mission	161	23.7
Empowerment mention in mission	136	20.1
Org facilitates identification of decision makers	48	7.1
Org asks people to contact decision makers	11	1.6
Org provides tools for writing decision makers	5	.7

Only 8.3% of CAAs reported to using lobbying. United Way membership was reported by 26.8% of the sample, and 47.2% were members of other coalitions. Social media use was reported among CAAs, but the majority did not report using any of the most popular social media outlets. The most popular social media outlet was Facebook with 48.3% of sample utilizing, followed by Twitter (24.2%), LinkedIn (5.6%), and photosharing such as Instagram or Flickr (3.1%).

Examination of CAAs' websites revealed the following information. Twenty-two percent had a video link of the organization. Less than 10% used RSS, had advocacy materials posted online, or had a clear statement of policy perspective.

Websites were also used less than 10% of the time for identifying or facilitating communication with policy decision makers. Less than one percent used text messaging, podcasts, hosted online petitions, or provided tools for writing decision makers.

Almost half (48.4%) of CAAs used their website for accepting donations, and 39.2% had an internal search engine for assistance with negotiating the website. Websites were most often used to promote the agency mission with 91.9% of CAAs posting their mission on their website. Examination of these missions revealed that 23.7% mentioned advocacy, and 20.1% mentioned empowerment in their mission statements.

Bivariate Analyses

Table 9.2 displays the bivariate analyses of all study variables with total expenses of the program. Independent samples t tests were conducted to determine significant differences in CAAs that utilized and did not utilize various social media sources. In bivariate analyses, total budget was significantly different between CAAs that used the more popular social media outlets such as Twitter and Facebook, with both Twitter and Facebook users having approximately $4.3 million higher mean budgets compared to non-Twitter and non-Facebook users ($p < 0.001$). Differences in budget size were noted with advanced website characteristics such as the presence of a video link, with a $5.8 million higher budget when compared to those that did utilize a video link ($p < 0.001$). Those that posted their agency mission had a $3.6 million higher budget compared to those who did not ($p < 0.05$). Additional differences in budget size were noted for those CAAs that had an internal search engine ($3.6 million higher; $p < 0.001$) or that accepted online donations ($4.6 million higher; $p < 0.001$). No significant differences in total budget were noted for organizations that were part of United Way or other coalitions or that mentioned advocacy or empowerment in their mission.

Table 9.3 displays the correlation between the social media scale score, social advocacy scale score, and the budget variables. A social media scale score was created by counting each use of different social media items (blogs, Twitter, Facebook, LinkedIn, Photosharing, other social media, and organizational video sharing). A similar policy advocacy scale score was created by counting each use of different policy advocacy (provides information to raise awareness, statement of organization's policy perspective, and website hosts online petitions; facilitates identification of decision makers; asks people to contact decision makers; and provides template to write decision makers). Budget variables were total expenses, management expenses, and fundraising expenses. Social media scale score had a small positive correlation with all variables, including the policy advocacy scale score and all budget variables. This indicates that the greater the rate of social media use in the agency is, the higher the engagement with policy advocacy activity in the agency and the larger the budgets are. The policy advocacy scale

Table 9.2. T-Test Analysis

Use of social media and budget size of organization

	Does not utilize or participate in			Utilizes or participates in			
	N	M	SD	N	M	SD	*p*
Org Blogs	626	11,611,225	10,614,600	52	19,221,080	29,021,244	0.07
Links to Twitter	515	11,162,570	12,402,629	164	15,499,688	14,622,842	0.001
Links to Facebook	351	10,130,166	8,523,757	328	14,435,927	16,375,499	<0.001
Links to LinkedIn	640	12,114,166	13,285,959	38	12,114,166	9,421,461	0.51
Links to Photo sharing	657	12,095,770	13,121,967	21	15,295,345	12,227,949	0.27
Links to other social media	563	11,725,557	13,383,274	115	14,492,474	11,378,944	0.04
United Way member	496	11,792,026	13,676501	182	13,292,736	11,337,330	0.19
Other Coalition Membership	346	11,952,546	15174276	332	12,447,417	10525768	0.62
Org links, video, you tube, vimeo	529	10,909,490	10,112,642	149	16,758,409	19,826,875	0.001
Org uses RSS	616	12,055,351	13,297,902	63	13,723,435	10.886,361	0.34
Org has advocacy materials online	631	11,923,166	13,138,390	47	15,842,673	12,097,390	0.05
Organization has a clear statement of policy perspective	613	12,110,317	13,355,401	65	12,992,289	10,418,326	0.60
Website has internal search engine	412	10,743,534	12,473,935	266	14,442,809	13,734,630	<0.001
Organization accepts online donations	328	9,957,815	8,452,528	350	14,291,313	16,023,845	<0.001
Mission is posted on website	55	8,800,137	7,772,634	623	12,494,568	13,430,820	0.05
Advocacy is mentioned in mission	517	12,124,671	13919400	161	12,420,298	10,052,126	0.80
Empowerment mentioned in mission	542	11,893,858	11,062,810	136	13,394,502	19,186,662	0.23

(continued)

Table 9.2. CONTINUED

	Use of social media and budget size of organization						
	Does not utilize or participate in			Utilizes or participates in			
	N	M	SD	N	M	SD	p
Org facilitates identification of decision makers and contact info	630	12,336,800	13,340,386	48	10,332,059	9,263,299	0.31
Org asks people to contact decision makers	667	12,168,152	13,162,720	11	13,815,042	8,568,312	0.68

score was only correlated with social media scale score and had no significant correlations with any of the budgetary variables.

DISCUSSION

CAAs in many respects mirror human service providers and can provide an interesting window into nonprofit online behavior and priority setting. These organizations, which rely strongly on government contracts for support, are not heavily engaged in social media and electronic communications. However, there is some evidence that there is a relationship between budget size and social media activity. Similarly, it does seem that there is a relationship between organization's budget size and its policy advocacy activities, and we find a cautious link between social media engagement and policy advocacy activities. It is somewhat disheartening that for a cohort of organizations founded to energize civic participation and empower citizens for the purposes of poverty alleviation greater rates of policy advocacy activities are not observed. It is difficult to posit or conjecture why these activities are not more prominent in the fabric of the organizations without gaining access to senior leadership and engaging in qualitative investigation with boards and executive

Table 9.3. CORRELATION BETWEEN SOCIAL MEDIA SCALE SCORE, POLICY ADVOCACY SCALE SCORE, AND BUDGET VARIABLES

Scales	M (SD)	2	3	4	5
1. Social Media Scale score	1.28 (1.51)	0.18*	0.20*	0.21*	0.18*
2. Policy Advocacy Scale score	0.26 (.69)		0.03	−0.02	0.01
3. Total budget	12,061,413 (12,959,456)			0.57*	0.18*
4. Management expenses	49.2 (5.3)				0.56*
5. Fundraising expenses	18.9 (5.1)				

*$p < 0.01$.

directors. However, we can maintain at the public media level, as a group, CAAs are not widely engaged in policy advocacy activities as a core business activity.

LIMITATIONS

This study was designed to understand the social media behavior and level of electronic civic engagement activities among a specific type of nonprofit organizations, specifically, CAAs. While some literature exists describing specific social media channels such as Twitter use among environment advocacy groups or Facebook use for fundraising purposes, the purpose of this investigation is to gain a broader understanding of how multipurpose human service organizations are using social media tools to engage a range of stakeholders to meet their goals for conducting policy advocacy activities. The two main limitations of this study are the limited generalizability of the findings and the quantification of qualitative data during the content analysis. The presence of inter-rater reliability results in this study lessens the likelihood that bias considerably influenced results.

FUTURE DIRECTIONS

The nonprofit sector is constantly evolving. This investigation attempted to link the use of social media tools to a specific type of nonprofit human services provider, the CAA. In the spirit of Edwards and Hoefer (2010), it used a content analysis-like model to scan organization's websites to understand the range of social media tools and range of policy advocacy activities the organizations were engaged in. Next iterations of such work might include an examination of the depth of social media use by nonprofit organizations where a team or researcher could consider investigating an organization's commitment to one particular tool such as Twitter, Facebook, YouTube, or LinkedIn and examine the depth and level of interactivity between the agency and its stakeholders to begin to understand the dimensions of purpose for which the organization is using the tool. For example, because several authors have commented on organizations' inability to capitalize on the two-way nature of social media communication (Goldkind, 2015; Saxton et al., 2015), it would be useful to understand how agencies are cultivating two-way communications with constituents; for instance, are they broadcasting information out for fundraising purposes only or for policy advocacy purposes only, or are there missed opportunities where organizations can collaborate together to form communication webs and engage stakeholders with shared visions for a shared purpose? Another area of inquiry is around agencies that are not participating in social media marketing at all. Given the dominate narrative of pervasive social media use in the nonprofit sector (Goldkind, 2015), one would believe that most nonprofit organizations are engaging heavily in social media use. However, this research appears to point to other outcomes. Little research has directly asked nonprofit leaders to prioritize and evaluate their choices for resource investment with regard to social media use versus other possible communications tools. Further research on this is certainly required to help scholars as well as educators understand how to shape choices.

CONCLUSION

Fifty years after their initial founding CAAs are still a big part of providing essential services to communities across the United States. Perhaps because of their reliance on government contracts for funding or perhaps because their primary constituents are less-affluent individuals, this specific group of nonprofit organizations is not heavily invested in social media and Web 2.0 activities. This finding is consistent with the author of other nonprofit agency's experiences and use of social media tools. While the popular narrative suggests that social media is a must-use tool for nonprofit communications, many nonprofit leaders seem to adopt these strategies haphazardly or without a thoughtful plan at best (Goldkind, 2015). The lackluster policy advocacy activities, while not surprising, are more noteworthy for this group of organizations. One of the signature functions of the community action initiative is civic engagement and citizen empowerment with a goal of poverty alleviation. Founded with a goal of reducing inequality, CAAs continue to provide valuable community services but certainly struggle in a climate of growing inequality and community disengagement.

REFERENCES

Brank, E. M., Fox, K. A., Youstin, T. J., & Boeppler, L. C. (2009). Changing the latitudes and attitudes about content analysis research. *International Journal of Teaching and Learning in Higher Education, 20,* 476–480.

Briones, R. L., Kuch, B., Lui, B. F., & Jin, Y. (2011). Keeping up with the digital age: How the American Red Cross uses social media to build relationships. *Public Relations Review, 37,* 37–43.

Edwards, H. R., & Hoefer, R. (2010). Are social work advocacy groups using Web 2.0 effectively? *Journal of Policy Practice, 9,* 220–239.

Eltantawy, N., & Wiest, J. B. (2011). The Arab spring| Social media in the Egyptian revolution: reconsidering resource mobilization theory. *International Journal of Communication, 5,* 18.

Flannery, H., Harris, R., & Rhine, C. (2009). *2008 DonorCentrics Internet giving benchmarking analysis.* Charleston, SC: Target Analytics.

Goecks, J., Voida, A., Voida, S., & Mynatt, E. D. (2008, November). Charitable technologies: Opportunities for collaborative computing in nonprofit fundraising. In *Proceedings of the 2008 ACM conference on Computer supported cooperative work* (pp. 689–698). ACM.

Goldkind, L. (2014). E-advocacy in human services: The impact of organizational conditions and characteristics on electronic advocacy activities among nonprofits. *Journal of Policy Practice, 13,* 300–315.

Goldkind, L. (2015). Social media and social service: are nonprofits plugged in to the digital age? *Human Service Organizations: Management, Leadership & Governance, 39,* 380–396.

Goldkind, L., & McNutt, J. G. (2014). Social media and social change: Nonprofits and using social media. In J. A. Ariza-Montes & A. M. Lucia-Casademunt (Eds.), *ICT management in non-profit organizations* (pp. 56–72). Hershey, PA: Business Science Reference.

Kaplan, A. M., & Haenlein, M. (2010). Users of the world, unite! The challenges and opportunities of social media. *Business Horizons, 53,* 59–68.

Kietzmann, J. H., Hermkens, K., McCarthy, I. P., & Silvestre, B. S. (2011). Social media? Get serious! Understanding the functional building blocks of social media. *Business Horizons, 54,* 241–251.

Kwak, H., Lee, C., Park, H., & Moon, S. (2010). What is Twitter, a social network or a news media? In M. Rappa & P. Jones (Eds.), *Proceedings of the 19th International Conference on World Wide Web* (pp. 591–600). New York: ACM.

Leenders, R., & Heydemann, S. 2012. Popular mobilization in Syria: Opportunity and threat, and the social networks of the early risers. *Mediterranean Politics, 17,* 139–159.

Lopes, A. R. (2014). The impact of social media on social movements: The new opportunity and mobilizing structure. *Journal of Political Science Research, 2014.* Retrieved from https://www.creighton.edu/fileadmin/user/CCAS/departments/PoliticalScience/Journal_of_Political_Research__JPR_/2014_JSP_papers/Lopes_JPR.pdf

Madway, G. (2010). Twitter remakes website, adds new features. Retrieved from https://www.reuters.com/article/us-twitter-website/twitter-remakes-website-adds-new-features-idUSTRE68E02620100915

McNutt, J. (2008a). Advocacy organizations and the organizational digital divide. *Currents, 7*(2), 1–16.

McNutt, J. G. (2008b). Web 2.0 tools for policy research and advocacy. *Journal of Policy Practice, 7,* 81–85.

McNutt, J. G., & Boland, K. M. (1999). Electronic advocacy by nonprofit organizations in social welfare policy. *Nonprofit and Voluntary Sector Quarterly, 28*(4), 432–451.

McNutt, J., & Menon, G. (2008). The rise of cyber activism: Implications for the future of advocacy in the human services. *Families in Society, 89,* 33–38.

Nah, S., & Saxton, G. D. (2012). Modeling the adoption and use of social media by nonprofit organizations. *New Media & Society, 15*(2), 294–313.

Phethean, C., Tiropanis, T., & Harris, L. (2013). Rethinking measurements of social media use by charities: A mixed methods approach. In Association for Computing Machinery (Ed.), *Proceedings of the 5th Annual ACM Web Science Conference* (pp. 296–305). New York: ACM.

Saxton, G. D., Niyirora, J. N., Guo, C., & Waters, R. D. (2015). #AdvocatingForChange: The strategic use of hashtags in social media advocacy. *Advances in Social Work, 16,* 154–169.

Schutt, R. K. (2006). *Investigating the social world: The process and practice of research* (5th ed.). Thousand Oaks, CA: Pine Forge.

Shirky, C. (2011). The political power of social media: Technology, the public sphere, and political change. *Foreign Affairs,* 28–41.

Smith, J. (2015). *The social network? The use and efficacy of Facebook and Twitter to expand nonprofit reach and user engagement* (Unpublished doctoral dissertation). University of Oklahoma, Norman.

Van Dijk, J. A. (2005). *The deepening divide: Inequality in the information society.* Thousand Oaks, CA: SAGE.

Waters, R. D., & Jamal, J. Y. (2011). Tweet, tweet, tweet: A content analysis of nonprofit organizations' Twitter updates. *Public Relations Review, 37,* 321–324.

Wolman, H. (1972). Organization theory and community action agencies. *Public Administration Review,* 33–42.

Young, J. (2013). A conceptual understanding of organizational identity in the social media environment. *Advances in Social Work, 14,* 518–530.

10

A Long Strange Trip

*Social Media Adoption in a Group of Technologically
Sophisticated Child Advocacy Organizations*

JOHN G. McNUTT, JANICE BARLOW,
AND DAVID B. CARTER ■

One of the most critical things that the nonprofit sector does is to advocate for those who cannot speak for themselves (Jenkins, 2006; Salamon, 1994). An obvious example is children and nonprofit efforts to ensure their welfare, which date from the middle ages. In more recent times, nonprofit organizations helped to create the juvenile court, child welfare, family income support and child health programs, and a host of related policy innovations. Child advocacy is, therefore, a key function of the nonprofit sector, as is services to combat child welfare problems.

While nonprofit organizations provide services for children and their families, the work of influencing policies at the national and state levels often falls to specialized organizations. These organizations exist at national level and state level. In the last three decades, owing to devolution and other changes in the nature of the child and family policy enterprise, much of the effort has been conducted at the state level.

Most advocacy organizations, regardless of level, use a common set of intervention techniques that are well known and well understood by advocates. These have always included lobbying, community organizing, policy research, political fundraising, get-out-the-vote efforts, advertising, and so forth. The last two decades have seen a move toward technology-based interventions. This appears to have progressed in three steps: pre-Web technologies (e-mail, discussion lists, newsgroups, etc.), Web 1.0 or early Web-based technologies (web pages, online petitions, etc.), and Web 2.0 or social media (social networking sites, blogging, microblogging, etc.). Most of the base technologies of the latter group are well over 10 years old, and the movement to the next phase is well underway. While it is not completely clear how this phase will develop, it is clear that social media/

Web 2.0 is now a mature technology with a stable user base and a well-developed set of political techniques associated with it. This means that it is appropriate to examine the progress of a group of advocates in adopting these technologies.

The research questions are:

1. What types of social media/Web 2.0 tools are state-level child advocacy organizations using in their policy work?
2. What presocial media tools are they continuing to utilize?
3. What technologies have been discarded?

This study builds on earlier work with this population. Three previous studies were conducted in 2000, 2004, and 2008.

This research is important because it examines the experience that organizations that have used technology for advocacy in the past have with social media. This should provide a more nuanced understanding of the adoption of these new technologies in nonprofit organizations.

REVIEW OF THE LITERATURE

Changing public policy is a central function of the nonprofit sector (Jenkens, 2006; Salamon, 1994). While individual nonprofits might eschew policy involvement and advocacy (Bass, Arons, Guinane, & Carter, 2007; Berry & Arons, 2002), the sector as a whole has a robust involvement in the political world. Political parties, political action committees, and a host of other policy-related organizations are nonprofits. This is especially important in the wake of the Citizens United (*Citizens United v. Federal Election Commission,* 2010) and McCutcheon (*McCutcheon v. Federal Election Commission,* 2014) decisions of the US Supreme Court.

Within this universe of politically active nonprofits, interest groups and advocacy organizations lead most of the traditional efforts to advance the sector's policy change function. Occasionally, service delivery organizations also advocate, but this is less common (Bass et al., 2007; Berry & Arons, 2002).

Child advocacy organizations represent an important aspect of the nonprofit advocacy enterprise (Bremner, 1989; DeVita & Mosher-Williams, 2001; Imig, 1996). They exist at multiple levels but largely at the state and national levels. Much of the heavy lifting for major national legislation falls to the national organizations. On balance, much of the legislation that affects children is at the state and occasionally local levels. The bulk of policymaking for child welfare, education, and family law are largely at the state and local levels. The state level advocates were represented by an organization called Voices for America's Children, formally the National Association of Child Advocates and the National Association of State-Based Child Advocacy Organization. Voices ceased operations in 2013 (see McNutt & Barlow, 2012).

Nonprofit advocates have a standard range of techniques that they use to effect policy change. These include policy research, community organizing, political fundraising, electoral strategies, and so forth. In the past few decades, these tradi-tional approaches have been joined by a series of new technology-based techniques, which have supplemented or replaced the traditional techniques. Collectively known as electronic advocacy techniques, the technologies offered much to the ad-vocate and his or her organization (Hick & McNutt, 2002; McNutt & Boland, 1999).

In general, the development of these advocacy techniques paralleled the de-velopment of technology and reflected the skill and ingenuity of the advocates who use them (see McNutt & Appenzeller, 2004). Many of the technologies that have proved so useful in a host of social change situations were created for quite different uses. It takes skill and imagination to adapt and repurpose a technology from one solution to another.

Early advocacy technology made use of the limited capacity of early per-sonal computers combined with other types of computing and networking (Downing et al., 1991; Wittig & Schmitz, 1996; Yerxa & Moll, 1994). PeaceNet, for example, was an early form of advocacy-based networking (Downing, 1989). Bulletin boards, newsgroups, and other technologies were used for advocacy by nonprofits, as was e-mail and discussion groups (often called listservs after the popular software). This type of electronic advocacy was bolstered by the commu-nity networking movement (Schuler, 1996) throughout the 1980s and early 1990s. Many of these technologies continue to prove useful today.

As the World Wide Web developed, more possibilities emerged. Web pages allowed organizations to create visually positive images in cyberspace. The crea-tion of web pages also facilitated the development of online petitions, fundraising, volunteer recruiting, and so forth. This stage combined evolving technology with a larger group of technology-savvy advocates to create a more substantial base. Eventually, political parties and large advocacy groups began to engage the Internet as a partner in their work.

The movement toward Web 2.0 or social media developed gradually over a number of years (Germany, 2006). Both social media and Web 2.0 are more popularized and less precise terms. O'Reilly (2005) offers the following definition:

> Web 2.0 is the network as platform, spanning all connected devices; Web 2.0 applications are those that make the most of the intrinsic advantages of that platform: delivering software as a continually-updated service that gets better the more people use it, consuming and remixing data from mul-tiple sources, including individual users, while providing their own data and services in a form that allows remixing by others, creating network effects through an "architecture of participation," and going beyond the page meta-phor of Web 1.0 to deliver rich user experiences.

In sum, these are technologies that are based on the Internet—"Web as platform" to use O'Reilly's (2007) term—harnessing collective knowledge or collective in-telligence, facilitating the creation of user generated content, software as a serv-ice, and so forth (O'Reilly, 2005, 2007). Figure 10.1 has a list of popular Web 2.0 technologies:

Blogs	Image Sharing (Flickr)
Wikis	Videosharing Sites (YouTube)
Microblogging (Twitter)	Artificial Worlds (Second Life)
Social Networking Sites (MySpace,	Storify
Facebook; Pinterest)	Vine
Meetup	
Podcasting	

Figure 10.1 Web 2.0/Social Media Technologies

These are also technologies that can be combined with each other or additional types of applications to build new systems via a process known as mash-up.
Theoretically, the mash-up process could yield an almost unlimited supply of Web
2.0 applications.

The growth of Web 2.0 as a political technology probably begins with Howard
Dean's run for the democratic nomination for President in 2004. Dean's campaign
staff (Cornfield, 2004; Trippi, 2004) incorporated many of these new tools in their
innovative campaign.

These are mature technologies. The most popular applications were developed
almost a decade ago and are well understood. Their use in political work is also
well documented (Guo & Saxton, 2013; McNutt, 2011). There is a substantial research literature about social media. While some organizations are later adopters
than others, it is difficult to argue that the use of social media is somehow novel
or new. The parallel growth of wireless technologies has made these applications
far more powerful.

What is likely to happen next in advocacy technology is the merging of big data
with advocacy techniques (McNutt & Goldkind, 2018). Systems like microtargeting
will take advantage of substantial available data to narrowcast messages to specific stakeholders. This will change the nature of advocacy campaigns (a process
that has already begun) and will tie advocacy more to policy and constituency
research. Most of the earlier technologies will support the evolving advocacy
technology model.

This approach will make the collecting and processing of data ever more important. It will further fuel the movement toward open government and transparency and will dovetail nicely with evidence-based policymaking. The growth of
civic technology is an exciting parallel.

This progression will eventually leave some technologies unused while others
will remain important for a long time. New technologies will continually be developed. The likely path is presented in the Figure 10.2.

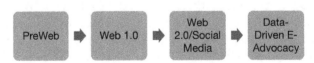

Figure 10.2 The Evolution of Electronic Advocacy

THEORETICAL FRAMEWORK

Rogers' (2003) diffusion of innovation theory provides the theoretical underpinnings for the study. This is a well-respected theory that explains the phenomena of interest well. An innovation is something that is new to the system of interest. Rogers (2003; also see Dillon & Morris, 1996; Robinson, Swan, & Newell, 1996; Strang & Soule, 1998) argues that an innovation is communicated via networks to successive population groups who decide whether or not to adopt it. Different innovations are adopted at a faster or slower rate depending on innovation characteristics, and users go through a series of steps in deciding to adopt an innovation.

Innovations are introduced by a change agent who exists outside of the system. The change agent presents the innovation to a motivated group called the innovators. Innovators are those who are willing to experiment with new ideas. This group communicates the innovation to the early adopters. The early adopters are important in communicating the innovation to the early majority. The early majority brings in the rest of the majority and later (if possible) the laggards. The process proceeds slowly until a critical mass of the population adopts and the process accelerates. Each of these conversions depends on communication networks and the functioning of opinion leaders within those networks.

What determines how quickly (if at all) an innovation is adopted? Rogers (2003) observes that five factors are important: trialability (the ability to try before committing), compatibility (with existing practices), relative advantage, complexity, and observability. This would mean that easier-to-use technology would be adopted at a faster rate. It would also probably mean that organizations with more proficiency and experience with technology would be more likely to adopt. Larger organizations with more slack resources tend to be more innovative, but there are a host of additional factors such as structure and environment to consider.

We would expect, from diffusion of innovation theory, that in a population of child advocacy organizations different organizations would be at different points in the adoption population. This means that adoption rates would vary. It would also be likely that different technologies would be adopted at different rates. Those technologies that were more complex, less triable, and less compatible and with lower relative advantage and observability would not be adopted as readily and, in some cases, would be discontinued.

RESEARCH OBJECTIVES

Considering our research questions and available literature and theoretical approaches, we offer the following research objectives:

1. To identify what types of high technology state-level child advocacy organizations are using in their policy work.

2. To identify what types of social media/Web 2.0 applications state-level child advocacy organizations are using in their policy work.
3. To determine what technologies have been adopted and then discarded.

RESEARCH METHODOLOGY

This study examines social media adoption in a national group of state-level organizations (n = 70) engaged in advocacy for policy issues involving children. These organizations are former members of Voice for America's children and previous organizations. All of these organizations are independent members of the network. While some are part of a larger entity (often a university), they are separate from the former corporate organization.

The questionnaire was developed from the three previous rounds. It was updated to include new technologies, particularly those in social media/Web 2.0. An electronic survey was used for data collection. Data collection used a modified tailored design method (Dillman, 2011).

Previous studies (McNutt, 2007; McNutt & Barlow, 2012; McNutt, Keaney, Crawford, Schubert, & Sullivan, 2001) used a mailed questionnaire. So there may be some minor issues of comparability. Results are compared with data from the 2008 study. This study had a lower response rate.

RESULTS

The study was administered in the late spring to early fall of 2014. Two organizations had ceased operations in the past five years. They were removed from the sampling frame for a total of 68. We received 47 usable questionnaires for a response rate of 69%. There was some missing data. Data were coded and cleaned. There were some initial issues with the Web-based survey instrument, but they appear to have been resolved.

Organizational Size

These are largely small organizations. The smallest had 2 employees while the largest had 33 employees. The mean (9.7713) and median (8.0000) are similar with standard deviation of 6.86928, suggesting a significant amount of variability.

Time Spent on Policy

Table 10.1 contains the reported amount of staff time spent on policy-related work. Most of the organizations reported spending at least half their time on

Table 10.1. REPORTED TIME SPENT ON POLICY WORK

	N	%
25% or less	4	8.7
26–50%	7	15.2
51–75%	14	30.4
76–100%	21	45.7
Total	46	100.0

policy related work. The biggest segment spent at least three quarters of their time on policy-related work.

Effectiveness and Usage

Respondents were asked to rate the effectiveness of electronic advocacy techniques. The mean ranking on a seven-point scale was 5.2308 with a standard deviation of 1.28681 (higher is better). This suggests a high degree of confidence in the techniques. Respondents were also asked to rate (again, on a seven-point scale with higher being better) the extent to which electronic advocacy techniques were used by other groups. The mean ranking was 5.5476 with a standard deviation of 1.17291. This suggests that advocates feel their counterparts in other organizations were using the technology.

Electronic Communications Techniques

Some of the earliest advocacy technologies use electronic mail and telephone-based systems. Table 10.2 contains the reported data about this set of tools. The largest declines appear to be in the area of fax and related techniques. There are a mixed pattern of declines and increases. At least some of these variations may be due to differences in the two samples.

The next type of technology to develop was websites. Since most organizations in the sample had a website, we concentrated on information and other materials available on the website. The results are presented in Table 10.3. Fewer organizations offered statistics, copies of legislation, and links, but far more used streaming video and banner ads.

Most of the respondents (61.7%) reported using a content management system for the website. Social media usage is reported in Table 10.4. Both Twitter and social networking sites (such as Facebook) demonstrated substantial utilization, while other types of social media are less favored. Podcasting and wikis are actually less well supported.

Table 10.5 examines which social networking sites organizations tend to favor. While nearly 77% of the organizations reported that they had adopted a social networking site, the nature of that site was unclear. Facebook is the most often

Table 10.2. OLDER ELECTRONIC ADVOCACY TECHNIQUES REPORTED

Technique	2008		2014		% change 2008–2014
	N	%	*N*	%	
Electronic mail (e-mail) to coordinate policy influence efforts within your organization	39	92.9	41	87.2	−5.6
E-mail to coordinate policy influence efforts outside of your organization	37	88.1	41	87.2	−0.9
E-mail to decision makers	34	81.0	41	87.2	6.2
E-mail mail discussion list about policy issues (listserv)	21	50.0	27	57.4	7.4
Newsgroups	8	19.0	15	31.9	12.9
Chat rooms	2	4.8	3	6.4	1.6
Standard fax	33	78.6	15	31.9	−46.7
Broadcast fax	14	33.3	3	6.4	−26.9
Fax on demand	7	16.7	2	4.3	−12.4
Distribution lists (mass e-mail distribution)	41	97.6	43	91.5	−6.1
Conference calls	39	92.9	40	85.1	−7.8

identified followed by LinkedIn. Pinterest is next. Only one organization reported having a MySpace site.

Table 10.6 looks at a range of advocacy technologies that are not social media but emerged in the past two decades. Online fundraising continues to be a popular set of techniques. More than three quarters of the respondents' reported engage in it. The secure donation site remains the most popular method, but a host of other possibilities are presented by the data. Fundraising is a critical nonprofit function.

Table 10.3. REPORTED WEBSITE CHARACTERISTICS

Technique	2008		2014		% change 2008–2014
	N	%	*N*	%	
Copies of legislation	31	73.8	34	72.3	−1.5
Case studies	16	38.1	21	44.7	6.6
Statistics	40	95.2	41	87.2	−8.0
Links to important policy sites	37	88.1	36	76.6	−11.5
Advocacy technique how to's	28	66.7	29	61.7	5.0
Banner ads on other websites	6	14.1	7	41.2	27.1
Streaming video	12	28.6	28	61.7	33.1

Table 10.4. REPORTED SOCIAL MEDIA ADOPTION

Technique	2008		2014		% change 2008–2014
	N	%	N	%	
Meet ups	1	2.4	6	12.8	10.4
Blog/weblogs	6	14.3	22	46.9	32.6
Wiki	4	9.8	3	6.4	−3.4
Podcasting	2	4.8	1	2.1	−2.7
Video sharing	5	11.9	8	17.0	5.1
Image sharing	4	9.8	9	19.1	9.3
Social networking site	6	14.3	36	76.6	62.3
Virtual reality simulation	1	2.4	2	4.3	1.9
Twitter			41	87.2	
Storify			8	17.0	
Vine			1	2.1	
Foresquare			1	2.1	

There was a substantial increase in database use and wireless applications and important reductions in online volunteer recruitment, online surveys, and comprehensive advocacy software.

Technology for issue research tools are reported in Table 10.7. In general, most of these more traditional techniques are in slight decline. Infographics has emerged as an important new technique. Social bookmarking is also a social media technology, but its reported use is less frequent.

Electronic communication techniques include a huge range of technology and represents a considerable investment in time, talent, and money.

DISCUSSION AND CONCLUSIONS

This research has presented a changing portrait of advocacy technology in a group of state-level child advocates. These descriptive findings are part of a larger effort to predict and explain the nature of technology adoption in state-level child advocacy organizations. This group reports making substantial use of technology in their work, and they have adopted both social media technology and other types of technology.

Table 10.5. SOCIAL NETWORKING SITES
REPORTED

Application	N	%
Facebook	41	87.2
MySpace	1	2.1
Linked In	23	48.9
Pinterest	9	19.1

Table 10.6. GENERAL ELECTRONIC ADVOCACY TECHNIQUES REPORTED

Technique	2008		2014		% change 2008–2014
	N	%	N	%	
Online fund raising	28	66.7	37	78.7	12.0
Secure donation Site	29	69.0	38	80.9	11.9
Shop for a cause site	3	7.1	6	12.8	5.7
Text to donate			3	6.4	
Crowdfunding			4	8.5	
Auction			7	14.9	
Video teleconferencing	2	4.8	6	12.8	8.0
Databases	9	21.4	34	72.3	50.9
Online survey research	34	81.0	29	61.7	−20.7
Online volunteer recruiting	18	42.9	3	6.4	−36.5
Geographic information systems	10	23.8	12	25.5	1.7
Online mapping	10	23.8	12	25.5	1.7
Secure intranet	9	21.4	8	17.0	−3.4
Wireless applications and tools	11	26.2	29	61.7	35.5
Instant messaging and short message	11	26.2	11	23.4	2.8
Online petitions	10	23.8	17	36.2	12.4
Comprehensive advocacy software	18	42.9	9	19.1	−23.8
Web-based conferencing	5	11.9	14	29.8	17.9
QR codes			11	23.4	

What Types of Social Media/Web 2.0 Tools Are State-Level Child Advocacy Organizations Using in Their Policy Work?

The organizations reported using social networking sites, blogging, and Twitter most often. Facebook appears to be the most common application in the social networking sites area. Other types of tools are used less often. Some social media tools have actually declined in use, although that maybe due to sample differences.

Table 10.7. ISSUE RESEARCH TECHNIQUES

Technique	2008		2014		% change 2008–2014
	N	%	N	%	
Policy-related listservs	26	61.9	25	53.2	−8.7
Policy-related websites	29	69.0	30	63.8	−5.2
Social bookmarking sites	3	7.1	1	2.1	−5.0
RSS feeds/tagging/sharing	9	21.4	11	23.4	2.0
Infographics			33	70.3	

On balance, Pinterest (founded in 2010) managed a very respectable showing. It is possible that some social media tools will never be popular among advocates or even the general public. Facebook's huge user base in the United States makes it a likely choice for an advocacy organization in the United States. Since many of their employees probably already use Facebook, little training is needed.

In terms of Rogers's (2003) diffusion of innovation theory, social media has likely reached critical mass in the population of interest. Most of the organizations are using a social network system and Twitter. Not all of these technologies are of equal interest. Wikis and social bookmarking seem to have declined in use (although the decline is small), and both of these applications might be seen as more complex and less compatible. This all seems to support Rogers's (2003) approach.

What Presocial Media Tools Are They Continuing to Utilize?

Older technologies, with some exceptions, continue to soldier on after new technologies are developed. There are some minor instances that can easily be explained by differences in samples or other issues. E-mail, a very old application, continues to be a vital part of electronic advocacy as well as many other types of online activity. E-mail still enjoys comparative advantage over a host of applications and is easy to use, compatible, and easily experimented with.

What Technologies Have Been Discarded?

It is clear from the data that fax and related applications are losing adherents. These are systems that are rapidly being replaced by other more capable arrangements. It is useful to consider that fax, at one time, was almost the gold standard for advocacy messages.

The reduction of interest in comprehensive advocacy suites might have to do with their cost and complexity. They might also be more prescriptive than advocates might prefer. The reduction of interest in surveys and volunteer recruiting is more difficult to explain. Third-party applications might be used in place of resident systems.

In general, these findings seem to support diffusion of innovation theory. The components of the theory that involve the progression of innovations through population groups and the characteristics that support adoption appear to be consistent with the data at this point in time.

LIMITATIONS

This study needs to be considered in terms of its limitations. As a survey, it is subject to all of the issues that affect that data-collection strategy. They include question misinterpretation, social desirability effect, nonresponders, and so forth (Babbie, 1994). While the response rate is excellent, there are still those that did not contribute. Converting the survey from a mailed survey to an electronic survey has a number of possible consequences, and there were issues with the conversion.

FUTURE RESEARCH

This is part of a larger research effort. A regression-based model for predicting adoption decisions is being created based on these data. Additional work will focus on relating technology adoption to other organizational variables.

REFERENCES

Babbie, E B. (1994). *Survey research methods.* Belmont, CA: Wadsworth.

Bass, G., Arons, D., Guinane, K., & Carter, M. (2007). *Seen but not heard: Strengthening nonprofit advocacy.* Washington, DC: Aspen Institute.

Berry, J. M. & Arons, D. (2002). *A voice for nonprofits.* Washington, DC: Brookings Institution Press.

Bremner, R. H. (1989). Encouraging advocacy for the underserved: The case of children. In V. Hodgkinson (Ed.). *The future of the nonprofit sector* (pp. 203–218). San Francisco: Jossey-Bass.

Citizens United v. FEC, 130 S. Ct. 876, 898 (2010).

Cornfield, M. (2004). *Politics moves online.* Washington, DC: Brookings Institution Press.

DeVita, C. J., & Mosher-Williams, R. (Eds.). (2001). *Who speaks for America's children?* Washington, DC: Urban Institute.

Dillman, D. A. (2011). *Mail and Internet surveys: The tailored design method—2007 update with new Internet, visual, and mixed-mode guide.* New York: Wiley.

Dillon, A., & Morris, M. G. (1996). User acceptance of information technology: Theories and models. *Annual Review of Information Science and Technology, 31,* 3–32.

Downing, J., Fasano, R., Friedland, P., McCollough, M., Mizrahi, T., & Shapiro, J. (Eds.). (1991). *Computers for social change and community organization.* New York: Haworth.

Downing, J. D. (1989). Computers for political change: PeaceNet and public data access. *Journal of Communication, 39,* 154–162.

Germany, J. B. (Ed.). (2006). *Person to person to person: Harnessing the political power of on-line social networks and user generated content.* Washington, DC: Institute for Politics, Democracy and the Internet, George Washington University.

Guo, C., & Saxton, G. (2013). Tweeting social change: How social media are changing nonprofit advocacy. *Nonprofit and Voluntary Sector Quarterly, 43,* 57–79.

Hick, S., & McNutt, J. (Eds.). (2002). *Advocacy and activism on the Internet: Perspectives from community organization and social policy.* Chicago: Lyceum.

Imig, D. (1996). Advocacy by proxy: The children's lobby in American politics. *Journal on Children and Poverty, 2,* 31–53.

Jenkins, C. (2006). Nonprofit organizations and political advocacy. In W. P. Powell & R. S. Steinberg (Eds.), *The nonprofit sector: A research handbook* (pp. 307–332). New Haven, CT: Yale University Press.

McCutcheon v. Federal Election Commission. 134 S. Ct. 1434 (2014).

McNutt, J. G. (2007). Adoption of new wave electronic advocacy techniques by non-profit child advocacy organizations. In M. Cortes & K. Rafter (Eds.), *Information technology adoption in the nonprofit sector* (pp. 33–48). Chicago: Lyceum.

McNutt, J. G. (2011). Fighting for justice in cyberspace: The role of technology in advocacy. In P. Libby (Ed.), *The lobbying strategy handbook* (pp. 251–268). Thousand Oak, CA: SAGE.

McNutt, J. G., & Appenzeller, G. (2004, August). *The three ages of cyberadvocacy: Prospects for the future of advocacy in cyberspace.* Paper Presented at Communication & Democracy: Technology & Citizen Engagement Colloquium, Fredericton, NB.

McNutt, J. G., & Barlow, J. (2012). A longitudinal study of political technology use by nonprofit child advocacy organizations. In A. Manoharan & M. Holzer (Eds.), *E-governance and civic engagement: Factors and determinants of e-democracy* (pp. 405–422). Harrisburg, PA: IGI Books.

McNutt, J. G., & Boland, K. M. (1999). Electronic advocacy by non-profit organizations in social welfare policy. *Non-Profit and Voluntary Sector Quarterly, 28,* 432–451.

McNutt, J. G., & Goldkind, L. (2018). E-Activism Development and Growth. In M. Khosrow-Pour, D.B.A. (Ed.), *Encyclopedia of Information Science and Technology, Fourth Edition* (pp. 3569–3578). Hershey, PA: IGI Global. doi:10.4018/978-1-5225-2255-3.ch310

McNutt, J. G., Keaney, W. F., Crawford, P., Schubert, L., & Sullivan, C. (2001). Going on-line for children: A national study of electronic advocacy by non-profit child advocacy agencies In A. Chib, J. May, & R. Barrantes (Eds.), *The impact of information technology on civil society: Working papers from the Independent Sector's 2001 Spring Research Forum* (pp. 213–228). Washington, DC: Independent Sector.

O'Reilly, T. (2005). Web 2.0: Compact definition. [Web log post]. Retrieved from http://radar.oreilly.com/2005/10/web-20-compact-definition.html

O'Reilly, T. (2007). What is Web 2.0: Design patterns and business models for the next generation of software. *Communications and Strategies, 65,* 17–37.

Robinson, M., Swan, J., & Newell, S. (1996). The role of networks in the diffusion of technological innovation. *Journal of Management Studies, 33,* 333–359.

Rogers, E. (2003). *Diffusion of innovations* (5th ed.). New York: Free Press.

Salamon, L. (1994). The nonprofit sector and the evolution of the American welfare state. In R. Herman (Ed.), *The Jossey-Bass handbook of nonprofit leadership and management* (pp. 83–99). San Francisco, CA: Jossey-Bass.

Schuler, D. (1996). *New community networks: Wired for change.* ACM Press/Addison-Wesley Publishing Co.

Strang, D., & Soule, S. A. (1998). Diffusion in organizations and social movements: From hybrid corn to poison pills. *Annual Review of Sociology, 22,* 265–291.

Trippi, J. (2004). *The revolution will not be televised: Democracy, the Internet and the overthrow of everything.* New York: Reagan Book/Harper Collins.

Wittig, M. A., & Schmitz, J. (1996). Electronic grassroots organizing. *Journal of Social Issues, 52,* 53–69.

Yerxa, S. W., & Moll, M. (1994). Notes from the grassroots: On-line lobbying in Canada. *Internet Research, 4*(4), 9–19.

Global and International Social Change

11

Social Media and Governance in China

Evolving Dimensions of Transparency, Participation, and Accountability

ROBERT WARREN AND YINGYING ZENG ■

INTRODUCTION

A good deal of attention is being paid to the record of the use of social media to challenge dictatorial governments, especially related to the Arab Spring cases. China is another particular focus of attention in this discourse. It has a large and growing rate of Internet penetration. By December 2013, the total of Chinese netizens rose to 618 million with 281 million (45.5%) using Weibo, which has become the most popular Internet communication trend in China (China Internet Network Information Center, 2014). Yet, China, generally viewed as an authoritarian regime, has not been subverted or threated by social media-facilitated efforts to challenge it.

In looking at the many recent failures in regime-change efforts in which social media played a part, Shirky (2011) concluded that social media's potential is not revolution but mainly in supporting the building of "civil society and the public sphere—change measured in years and decades rather than weeks or months."

This view also is reflected in research concerning governance in China. Some find that, although there have been successful protests against Chinese government officials and policies using social media, they have not been linked to an explicit and continuing movement to bring about regime change and are possible only because the central government chooses to allow them to happen. Huang and Yip (2012) argue that "the influence of the Internet has been exaggerated" in initially mobilizing protests (p. 201). Sullivan (2014) concludes that microblogging dissent in China is "bounded" because of the government's "control of the information revolution continues . . . to keep the lid on mobilization of either large-scale, cross-cutting protests or a viable opposition movement." He goes on to say that, despite ostensible victories of netizen protests, their actual effect can be to strengthen authoritarian rule because in these cases people vent their anger, guilty officials are removed, and the Party is "able to propagate its image as benevolent protector of the nation let down by the wrongdoings of its representatives" (Sullivan, 2014, p. 7).

Meng (2010), however, takes a different perspective, arguing that there has been a "fixation" in social media research in China that focuses "on whether the Internet could democratize" the governmental system (p. 501). MacKinnon (2008, p. 45) and Wu (2012, p. 2238) make similar comments, and Esarey and Qiang (2011, p.298) call for "new approaches to consider how popularization of the Internet is changing Chinese politics." Meng also points out that the revolutionary origin of the authoritarian Chinese government gives it "historically grounded legitimacy" and "no one should assume an antithetical relationship between the regime and the Chinese people" (p. 502). He concludes that a "pre-formed lens of democratization" in China Internet research can lead to "oversimplification of the very diverse activities taking place in Chinese cyberspace, many of which contribute to a more inclusive communication environment without pursuing overt political agendas" (p. 501).

This is not a new critique. Yang (2003) wrote that "technological diffusion is not shaped only by political and economic factors, nor is the impact of technology confined to the political sphere and state behavior" (p.408) and that "it is crucial to examine how Chinese civil society shapes the development of the Internet, and vice versa" (p. 410).

Meng's (2010) and Yang's (2003) comments suggest there is need for analysis of the actual impact of social media on governance in China, a nation effectively dominated by a single party that utilizes advanced information technology for control but also that has the greatest number of "netizens" in the world. As a step in this direction, the intent here is to examine the use and evolving impact of social media within Chinese governance, broadly defined, and from a bottom–up citizens' perspective. To do this, the chapter identifies and examines (a) a variety of social media-related elements and infrastructure and their dynamics as used by citizens in the generation, reception, and redistribution of information; (b) ways in which this enhances their ability to act spontaneously and collectively from the bottom up in cyber and terrestrial space; (c) how netizens exercise influence within the socio-cultural and economic sectors as well as the formal institutions of government; and (d) how single social media incidents that are not part of an organized long-term movement can have cumulative governance effects. Ways in which the national and local governments seek to interact with and influence citizens through social media are also of relevance.

Two dimensions of this bottom–up and multisectoral governance construct are used to frame the analysis. First, to include, but go beyond, the state–citizen focus, the study looks at the use of social media by citizens that relate to other citizens, private sector actors, government agencies and officials, and government actions directed toward citizens. The second dimension involves what can be called infrastructure elements of social media. They are produced by individuals using information and communication technology (ICT) as well as by the space/time effects of the technology itself. These include human flesh search engines (HFSE), surrounding gaze, code language, cyber and terrestrial space action linkages, and reduction of time/space barriers to communication and action.

These interrelated and evolving multisectoral and infrastructure dimensions of social media have increased citizen influence from below in both individual cases and in the aggregate. As Shirky (2011, p. 5) points out, institutionalized groups, whether government or business, normally have an advantage over citizens because they "have an easier time . . . of directing the action of their members." However, he goes on to say that social media can compensate for this by reducing the cost of both creating a common body of information and understanding and of spontaneously coordinating action for large numbers of spatially dispersed netizens.

Social Media Infrastructure Elements

Human Flesh Search Engine
HFSE is a method that Chinese netizens can employ to generate both information and action online and offline. The term, first applied in 2001, is a literal translation of 人肉搜索 (renrou sousuo). There is no record of the exact number of cases of HFSE although one study, focusing primarily on China, identified 404 major cases between 2001 and 2010 (Wang et al., 2010).

The use of HFSE to identify individuals and dig up facts about them is seen by some as vigilante-like. Sterling (2010) describes it as Internet users hunting down and "punishing people who have attracted their wrath." Tong and Lei (2010) assert it is one of the worst features of massive social media actions. Others, however, view it in more neutral terms, and the meaning adopted here is drawn from Wang et al. (2010). They define it as "people-powered" online information seeking and sharing that usually relies on voluntary crowdsourcing and involves strong offline elements in a variety of ways.

Surrounding Gaze
In 2011, a Xinhua News Agency article claimed that 2010 was the year that China's Internet culture entered "the era of the national surrounding gaze" (全民围观时代; quanmin weiguan shidai; "2010 China Internet Public Opinion," 2010). The origins of the term come from a novel by Lu Xun (1928). He used the phrase "culture of the gaze" to characterize the coldness and indifference of crowds when people gather and just look at a public spectacle. In its adaptation to the social media world, it refers to an "online surrounding gaze" (网络围观; wangluo weiguan), or "surrounding gaze politics," which can influence things and result in changes by gathering massive digital public opinion around certain issues and events (Hu, 2011).

While Hu (2011) considers participation in an online surrounding gaze a kind of minimal form of public participation, he believes it is still a significant platform for netizens. They act individually without central direction to express their views and make demands that are recognized by other citizens and those in power as a formidable massing of public opinion. As Hu puts it, the surrounding gaze is organized strength without organization and an important form of "wei dongli" (微动力), a Chinese Internet phrase meaning micro force or the power of social media.

CODE LANGUAGE

A major government online censorship tactic is blocking messages that contain words critical of the state or deal with controversial issues. In turn, Chinese netizens have used "coded language, neologisms, and satire to evade censorship and repression" (Esarey & Qiang, 2011, p. 312). What has evolved amounts to a reverse form of Orwellian doublethink that is from the bottom up—originating with the people not the state. Further, this coding of language "has given rise to a surprising number of new terms for exposing, criticizing, and ridiculing" those in power (Qiang & Link, 2013). They can also be incorporated into general offline language.

Constructing a harmonious society has been a government-favored term used to characterize national policy that was initiated under Hu Jintao's leadership in 2004. Consequently, saying anything negative about the word *harmonious* (和谐; hexie) is subject to censorship. To escape this, netizens have substituted the similarly sounding word *river crab* (河蟹; hexie) and, for example, will say online that their blog was "river-crabbed" instead of censored or harmonized. A few other examples of the many code words that have been used by bloggers are Celestial Empire, poison jackal, calamity TV, and frog for China, dictatorship, China Central TV, and former president Jiang Zemin, respectively.

When code terms are censored, netizens can change the code or use other avoidance techniques. An example of the latter was generated during several days of protest rioting in Guizhou province that involved 30,000 people but received no coverage by the government-controlled mass media. In response, netizens provided real-time online reports that made news of the protest available throughout China. To avoid government blockage, one strategy adopted by bloggers was writing backwards. Software was used that "flips sentences to read right to left instead of left to right, and vertically instead of horizontally" to make it difficult for government software to automatically censor terms (Ye & Fowler, 2008). According to Ye and Fowler (2008), an editor at the Tianya.cn forum, who had responsibilities for deleting posts about the riots, said that, despite the government's sophisticated censorship regime, "the country also has the most experienced and talented group of netizens who always know ways around it."

Words and phrases that gain coded meaning can originate from the offline statements of government officials and citizens as well as be invented by bloggers. In 2008, Lin Jiaxiang, a government administrative official, appeared to be molesting an 11-year-old-girl in a restaurant. When others there came to stop it, Lin said to them, "Do you people known who I am? . . . You people are worth less than a fart to me!" This exchange was recorded by a surveillance camera in the restaurant and subsequently a video clip that included Lin's statement was put online. In turn, Lin was fired from his government position and "fart people" has come to be used as a term of pride in reference to ordinary people both on and offline ("A Man Attacks 11-Year-Old Girl," 2008).

Another quote that gained a coded political meaning grew out of the 2011 Wenzhou train crash in which many people were killed and injured. While the accident site was still being cleared away, a reporter asked a Railway Ministry spokesperson why the government had so quickly given orders to bury the derailed train cars rather than continue rescue efforts to find possible survivors. When his answer was met with skepticism, he said "Whether you believe it or not, it's up to you, but I do anyway." The quote is now widely used online and offline to indicate that the explanations and answers given by a person, especially by officials, are questionable ("Word of the Week," 2012).

A number of events involving local police actions and statements have also generated code language that has built-in governmental criticism. In one well-known 2009 example, police in Yunnan Province initially said the death of a 24-year-old man who died while in jail was caused by an injury he received while playing "duo maonao" (躲猫猫), the Chinese name for hide-and-seek, (literally, "eluding the cat") with other prisoners. This explanation quickly produced extensive negative online comments and *duo maonao* has become a term widely used to mean a lack of credibility, fairness, and transparency in law enforcement and other public agency statements (Schott, 2009; Tong & Lei, 2010). In 2008, a teenage girl drowned in a river in Guizhou Province. According to the police report, after she had a quarrel with a boy there, the boy began doing push-ups, and the girl jumped in the river and drown. In turn, "doing push-ups" has become another widely used code phrase for questionable official explanations (Ye & Canaves, 2008).

CYBER AND TERRESTRIAL SPACE LINKAGES

The role of social media in governance can only be understood and assessed in relation to its linkage to offline phenomena and the two-way causal flows that are involved. On the one hand, social media information, messages, and interactions can foster and then provide video images and reports of resulting terrestrial actions that stimulate further offline citizen actions. On the other hand, citizen actions and demonstrations can occur first offline and subsequent social media messages related to them can produce further offline action. The following discussion provides some examples.

Reduction of Time/Space Barriers to Citizen Communication and Action

Because of its vast space and ethnic differences many parts of China, prior to social media, citizens were provided with news of distant happenings only by officially sanctioned media, if at all. This made it very difficult for activists to create linkages with others elsewhere, who may have had similar concerns or been willing to support a popular movement (Esarey & Qiang, 2011). Now, social media allows almost instantaneous communication among millions of widely dispersed people. Further, news distributed by bloggers about events of public importance may be the only reports available or be faster and more accurate than information provided by state and the mass media it basically controls.

A classic example of this change can be seen in a comparison of the current "Digital Democracy Wall" with the terrestrial Democracy Wall. The latter was a small portion of wall space on a street in Beijing where citizens were able to attach uncensored written comments. It existed for a brief period during the winter of 1978–1979.

Today, the central government's extensive ICT technical resources and ability to censor social media and block access to particular sites has been labeled the "Great Firewall." Even so, in contrast to its past ability to quickly eliminate the Democracy Wall, it cannot close down or fully control constantly evolving and accessible social media. As Erasey and Qiang (2011) put it, now "via blogs, online video clips, email, and text messages, activists can utilize interactive relationships to garner broad support for their causes" (p. 312). Thus, today the Digital Democracy Wall makes it possible for millions anywhere in China to post or receive messages—not just in word form but also video—that the state cannot fully censor. As Yang and Cao (2012) observe, with Weibo "information can be posted online anytime, anywhere and by anyone" (p. i).

An example of this and of cyber/terrestrial linkages can be seen in a recent dispute over the censorship by the Guangdong provincial government of an editorial in the *Southern Weekly,* one of China's more freewheeling papers. Many throughout China first learned about the censorship conflict online. According to Mozur (2013), one person who was involved for several days in street demonstrations outside the paper's offices in Guagzhou indicated that this loosely organized group was "reaching out to others, contacting thousands on China's instant-messaging service QQ and Sina Weibo microblogging service." In reporting on this conflict, Mozur goes on to say,

> In an earlier era of protests, their voices would have been lost in the vastness of China. The Internet has provided the platform to turn local protests national, with instant mobs able to form and activists able to bring their protest experience to bear at the latest political hot spot.

THE MULTISECTORIAL SOCIO-CULTURAL, ECONOMIC, AND POLITICAL DIMENSIONS OF NETIZEN ACTION

Citizens-to-Other Citizens

Citizen-to-citizen social media interaction, as discussed here, can range from efforts to enforce cultural and moral values to providing needed information and services that government or other organizations are not.

Public reaction to cruelty to a kitten provides an illustration of the first type. Photos posted online in 2006 showed a young woman using her high-heel shoes to torture a kitten to death. Angered netizens quickly located where the incident took place and the woman's identity. As a result, there was wide online disapproval of her, and she lost her job ("High-Heeled Kitten Killer Apologizes," 2006).

In another case, a woman killed herself in 2007 because her husband was engaged in an extramarital love affair. Subsequently, a sister of the dead woman put the wife's final blog post online. In it she talked about her husband's affair and her impending suicide. This video produced widespread condemnation of the husband and the "other woman," and HFSE detective work was used to identify and post their names and details about them. This generated a great number of negative and harassing comments received by the pair. In turn, he also lost his job (Downey, 2010).

A quite different example relates to the estimated 20,000 children who are abducted annually in China. Some are sold to families and others are forced to beg (SMG Research Team, 2011). After he was contacted by a mother who saw a photo of her abducted son online, Professor Yu Jianrong started a Sina Weibo account in January 2011 labeled "Taking Pictures to Rescue Begging Children." He put the picture of the woman's missing boy on it. Within a month the blog had over a quarter of a million followers who uploaded more than 2,500 images of children begging in all parts of China along with what information they could include about the child (SMG Research Team, 2011).

Going back to the issue of animal cruelty, in April 2011, some netizens noticed a truck on a highway loaded with caged dogs and concluded that they were going to be killed and used for human food. They put photos of the truck on Weibo that were seen by "hundreds of thousands of people across China" and "at least 100 animal lovers quickly answered an appeal to jump in their cars and block the truck's path" (Hewitt, 2012). After stopping the truck, the matter was resolved when the netizens blocking it paid over a thousand dollars to the trucker to have the dogs taken to an animal protection shelter (Hewitt, 2012). Since then, this process has become quasi-institutionalized, and there have been a number of similar dog rescues carried out via linked Weibo and terrestrial action.

In the absence of government-provided information about food safety problems in China, a graduate student at a Shanghai university and 34 volunteers started a website (http://www.zccw.info) in 2011 to make timely data available to citizens. The site had over 190,000 hits in its first few months. By May 2012 it had posted more than 3,000 relevant news items and a map of China pinpointing where food problems existed ("Student's Food Safety Website," 2012). Similarly, when the government failed to provide adequate information concerning deaths in Beijing's July 2012 extensive flooding, residents in the city's "worst-affected district took matters into their own hands and published their own death toll numbers using public and private chat rooms" (Chong & Liu, 2013).

A final example relates to a major and unpredictable problem in China—earthquakes. In April 2013 a 7.0-magnitude earthquake hit Lushan County in Sichuan province, and both governments and citizens used social media to gather and communicate real-time information about the earthquake that the formal media could not.

According to Levin (2013), Sina Weibo enhanced efforts by civil society and volunteers to directly aid quake victims, to coordinate with each other, and "in some instances outsmart a government intent on keeping them away." Another report described Weibo and WeChat as playing a significant role as "technological tools for relief" through which microbloggers "quickly launched their earthquake relief channels" to provide the latest disaster reports, information about missing persons, and options to make donations ("Is Ya'an Different?" 2013). The nongovernmental organization Disaster Relief Information Sharing Platform, enabled over 50 nongovernmental organizations to post information through Weibo and other online channels (Brown-Inz, 2013).

Citizens-to-Private Sector Actors

Weibo events involving the relationship between citizens and the private sector that involve product quality are seldom looked at in detail, although social media can enhance the capacity of consumers to come together and fight for their interests.

Drawing upon a 2011 survey of Chinese Internet users, Chiu, Lin, and Silverman (2012) concluded that there was "a remarkably vocal group of consumer advocates who don't hesitate to condemn products they consider shoddy or substandard." In one example cited, a popular blogger raised an issue with a firm about a defective product. The company responded using Weibo but denied their product had a quality problem. In turn, other "consumers soon joined in and uploaded videos of and posts about their own problematic appliances, severely damaging the brand's equity" (Chiu et al., 2012).

In 2008, two students in Zhengzhou, Henan province, were required to pay an extraordinary high price, 200 times the advertised cost, for haircuts at a local salon. In their efforts to force this payment, salon staffers threatened to use their personal connections with local officials. After social media reporting of the story, citizens started both online and offline HFSE to identify the salon staff and what connections they had with officials. Street protests were also staged in front of the salon. Ultimately, a government investigation resulted in the salon being closed and the owner fined for illegal pricing and tax dodging ("The Top 10 Human Flesh Search Incidents," 2010).

Three other quite different cases reflect the broad range of private-sector matters that netizens have become involved in. In one, bloggers reported that an advertising claim that a luxury brand of furniture, DaVinci, was imported from Italy was a false and that it was produced in China. Many angry buyers launched social media discussions about how to gain compensation from the company. In turn, there were Internet posts about other brands that claim to be from Europe, which helped foster a national scandal (Barboza, 2011). In 2013, the Guizhentang Pharmaceutical Company planned to triple the number of captive bears whose abdomens would be used to extract bile for company products. However, it withdrew the plan after protests by animal rights advocates in which social media played an important part (Jacobs, 2013a).

The third example relates to a long-standing pattern of corruption between construction firms and government agencies. In the aftermath of the deadly 2008 Great Sichuan earthquake, protests spontaneously developed among parents who had lost children in the collapse of schools that had been poorly built as "the result of collusion between construction firms and the local government" (Shirky, 2011). Prior to this, the corruption in the country's construction industry was an open but unchallenged fact. "But when the schools collapsed, citizens began sharing documentation of the damage and of their protests through social media tools" (Shirky, 2011).

In assessing the overall importance of netizens in generating critical information about businesses, Esarey and Qiang (2011) compared the content of blogs and articles in newspapers in China. They concluded, "Bloggers, more than journalists, appear to be acting as watchdogs in a country plagued by faulty products, hazardous business practices, and corporations engaging in illegal pollution" (p. 309).

Citizens-to-Government

Tong and Lei (2010), using data from 2003 to 2009, identified 24 of what they refer to as "large-scale Internet mass events" that were critical of government behavior and had over one million clicks (p. 4). They suggest that these events have generally involved "exposing corruption cases, supervising officials' behavior, interfering with judicial process, and pressing for policy adjustments" (p. 5).

Looking only at cases related to the behavior of officials, Esarey and Qiang (2011) found that more than 80 local government officials had become the target of questions by bloggers and one third had "lost their positions due to exposure of the misconduct online" (p. 300). They also note that there has been a steady increase in what they call "'mass Internet incidents' that involve one million visits by users" and go on to say that

> These mass incidents have contributed to the abolition of the custody and repatriation system for migrant workers, the halting of state-sponsored urban development projects, the overhauling of the criminal justice system to reduce the abuse of inmates in prisons, the reconsideration of a murder case involving the slaying of a local official, and the investigation and dismissal of numerous local party officials. (p. 300)

Many of the cases that arouse bloggers involve how government agencies and officials treat ordinary people as well as relate to major policy issues. In the fall of 2012, staff members of a local Civil Affairs Bureau refused to accept the small donations that elementary school students had collected to aid people recovering from the Yi Liang earthquake. The Weibo posting of this refusal produced a great number of online messages critical of the Civil Affairs Bureau's action, forcing it to apologize, punish and retrain the staff involved, and promise to provide better service ("Small Change Earthquake Donation," 2012).

A woman in Hunan province, hurriedly driving her son to a hospital, was stopped by a police officer. He took her driver's license but did not return it. Subsequently, when she went to a number of local police stations trying to get her license back, she was told that no officer there had taken the license. She spent 10 days trying to get it back. She then put a report of her experience online. It generated over a million responses in which a number of people described similar experiences with the police. This mass criticism from all over China resulted in the local police apologizing to the woman and more generally promising the community they would do a better job of providing services ("A Lady from Hunan Province," 2012).

The 2012 outrage of netizens over a forced abortion has contributed to the growing demands for change in the government's one-child policy. In that year, a woman, in the seventh month of pregnancy with a second child, was required to have an abortion by a local government in Shaaxi province. Virtually immediately, her family posted a photo online of the mother lying on a hospital bed next to the body of her seven-month-old fetus. This produced a vast number of social media responses expressing strong opposition to the forced abortion along with many comments that the one-child policy should be ended or relaxed (Johnson, 2012).

Government-to-Citizens

Apart from control and censorship, one of the first government responses to the development of the Internet was to expand the use of "50-centers" to generate social media messages. These are persons who initially had been paid by the national and local governments to plant propaganda items in the print media and television (Sullivan, 2013, p. 9).

A more important factor, however, has been the rapid growth, under pressure from central authorities, of all governmental levels in utilizing social media for communicating with citizens. Premier Li Keqiang, for example, highlighted the importance of transparency in the era of Weibo, during a speech in the State Council's meeting on clean governance in March 2013. He warned that delay in disclosure would lead to rumor, speculation, dissatisfaction, and even panic among some sections of the public and leave the government in a passive position (Guo, 2013).

By the end of 2012, there were 176,700 verified government Weibo accounts compared with 126,100 in 2011. Among them, approximately two thirds are operated by government agencies and one third by individual officials (E-Government Research Center, 2013).

The fact that social media is influencing the style of language people use in ways that make the "official talk" of state agencies increasingly ineffective also is being recognized. A 2011 article in the *People's Daily* underscored the importance of the "language environment of the grassroots" and went on to advise Communist Party and state officials that "only by abandoning bureaucratic or empty talk can one's microblog message resonate with the public" (Bristow, 2011). Further, the speed of Internet-sent messages and the virtual guarantee that citizen protesters will be reached by this means has resulted in a growing government strategy of using social media during conflicts (Young, 2013).

In Kunming, Yunnan province, in 2009, for example, thousands of shop owners in a wholesale market area went to the streets to protest what they viewed as unsatisfactory government compensation for them when it demolished the market for redevelopment. They blocked traffic and had battles with the police. Initially, the government and official media provided no credible information about the protests. As the conflict grew, however, the Yunan government started its own Weibo account and began to provide accurate reports of events. The results were looked upon as a positive step for the government in dealing with crisis management through social media (Liu, 2012).

Announcing government concessions online to citizens engaged in protests has also come into use. After demonstrations in the streets and online protests over a decision by the city of Shifang to allow a copper alloy plant to be built, the government used Sina Weibo to make an official announcement that it was canceling plans for the plant to be constructed (Goldman, 2012). Similarly, in response to demonstrations (that included breaking into a government building and smashing furniture and computers) against the location of a waste discharge plant in the city of Qidong, local officials used their website to tell citizens that it had abandoned plans for the facility (Perlez, 2012).

These and other environmentally related mass protests led national environmental minister, Zhou Shengxian, to comment that the growing local protests and their extensive discussion on Sina Weibo tend to happen because of government "mistakes that involve projects that start without official approval, without proper environmental impact assessments and without an assessment of community sentiment." (Bradsher, 2012). Relatedly, in 2012, the central government's State Council ordered relevant government agencies "to make public all environmental impact assessments by posting them on the Internet, with a description of what the government planned to do about the assessments" (Bradsher, 2012). Such directives, however, have far from eliminated environmentally related protests.

In 2013 Jiangmen City, Guangdong province, announced approval of building a uranium processing plant in there. Citizens had been given no prior information about the project, and they were to have only 10 days to submit comments. In response to ensuing local opposition, the city provided a question-and-answer section on its website. However, many of the answers it gave "were decidedly lacking in substance" (Jacobs, 2013b). Citizens then staged a protest (coded as "take a walk") against the plant that was made known on social media "despite government efforts to censor the discussion on Sina Weibo" (Mullany, 2013). One day after hundreds of people marched in protest and planned a second such "walk," the Jiangmen City website carried news that the project had been canceled (Mullany, 2013).

A quite different dimension of social media in governance is its growing use by political leaders involved in national policymaking. During the 2013 National People's Congress (NPC), 2,987 delegates from across the country gathered together in Beijing to make decisions about public policy and central leadership. A number of the delegates were active on the Internet. Most made use of Weibo to communicate policy proposals they favored, interact with the netizens, and solicit public opinion ("Renmin Weibo," 2013).

Beyond the delegates' individual online presence, a number of Weibo platforms were set up to provide the public with multiple channels to ask questions and contribute their suggestions. Examples are NPC and CPPCC (Chinese People's Political Consultative Conference) Micro Scene, on Xinhua Weibo; NPC & CPPCC Press Conference, on Tencent Weibo; and Focusing on NPC and CPPCC, Micro-NPC and CPPCC, and Weibo Questioning, on Sina Weibo. In turn, in March 2013, after the NPC and CPPCC 2013 Annual Sessions, a Weibo account, State Council Bulletin, was created on Tencent Weibo for the highest-level national government agency, the State Council. This was considered a milestone in China's governmental microblogging ("The State Council Bulletin Launched Tencent Weibo," 2013).

Finally, there is another dimension of importance in the central government's selected tolerance of citizen use of the Internet to be critical of the state, especially in cases involving lower levels of government. As Young (2013) notes, Chinese leaders have discovered that "social media, can be an effective tool in gauging public opinion on everything from broader national topics . . . down to very local issues." Young continues, "Such feedback was difficult to get in the past due to interference by local officials, who tried to filter out or downplay anything with negative overtones and play things up to their own advantage." Hassid (2012) makes a similar point, explaining that the Internet is "one of the few tools Beijing can rely upon" to obtain the information and commentary from the periphery needed to monitor and try to control "otherwise unaccountable local officials" (p. 226).

CUMULATIVE POLICY AND GOVERNANCE EFFECTS

The occurrence over time of a number of individual cases involving netizens that are in the same policy area but seldom directly related to one another can have important cumulative policy and governance effects. The large number of corrupt official exposed online has both been facilitated by the central government's tolerance of such citizen initiatives and, in turn, influenced the central government's increasingly strong, at least rhetorically, anticorruption campaign that was initiated during the latter part of Xi Jinagping's leadership and is being continued. A report in the *Xinhua Press* in December 2012 concluded that online anticorruption campaigns have "forced China's disciplinary authorities to combat corruption in a more proactive way." ("China's Craze for Online Anti-Corruption," 2012)

There have also been cumulative effects of issues raised by bloggers relating to railway services and the roles of charitable organizations. In 2011, the head of the

Railway Ministry was removed due to accusations he received extensive bribes to influence the awarding of contracts. In the same year, as previously noted, two high-speed trains collided in the suburbs of Wenzhou with a number of passengers killed and injured. News of the accident and photos were put on Weibo by citizens more than two hours before reports were carried by mass media. In the immediate aftermath of the collision, dominant public opinion was reflected in questions and criticism raised online about serious inefficiencies in the rescue operation, lack of transparency in reporting about passenger deaths and injuries, and the adequacy of the initial investigation into the causes of the accident.

This social media discourse played an important role in the government's undertaking a more extensive investigation into the causes of the crash. The resulting report found mismanagement and flaws in equipment design in relation to the collision and contributed to the government's taking a more general look at corruption throughout the management and operation of the railways (Watt, 2013).

Another and long-standing critique of rail service on social media concerned the degree to which people using train travel, particularly during high demand times, found the ticket booking system inefficient and food, drink, and other services on trains very poor (Watt, 2013).

The extensive critical online comments about the operation of rail transportation was an important factor in the central government's 2013 announcement of its major reorganization (Watt, 2013). The Railways Ministry, which had been in control of the most-used rail system in the world, is to be dismantled. The management of the railway services is to go to a newly created China Railway Corporation and authority to set and enforce technical standards moved to the Transport Ministry. The aggregate significance of extensive negative social media comments on rail management and services, according to Watt (2013), is suggested by the fact that the Railways Ministry had been able to resist government efforts to reform its operations for a decade and a half.

Another cumulative impact of social media relates to the status of the Red Cross Society of China (RCSC) and the number and role of nongovernmental charity agencies involved in natural disaster responses. A Red Cross agency has existed in China since the early twentieth century. In 1949, with the creation of the People's Republic of China, the RCSC became "a pseudo-governmental aid organization" and has been the primary agency recognized by the state and dominant in charity and disaster relief (Sauer, 2013). However, after the RCSC raised several hundred million dollars in donations in 2008, primarily in response to the Great Sichuan earthquake, "rumors began to spread about graft within the organization" that were fueled by the lack of financial records open to public (Sauer, 2013).

Adding to this, in April 2011, a photo was put online that showed a restaurant bill of $1,500 paid for by a small group of people working for the Red Cross in Shanghai ("Businessman Quits," 2011). The pivotal social media event, however, was in June 2011 when an Internet mass incident caused trust in the RCSC to further drop and its ability to raise funds to be seriously affected.

Guo Meimei, an attractive young woman, put several little-noticed posts on Weibo showing her enjoying a lavish life with ultra-expensive sport cars and top-of-the-line clothes. She identified herself as the "commercial general manager at the Red Cross" (Wong, 2011). When an Internet user reposted Guo's blogs, there was immediate and massive public outrage, and she and the Red Cross became "the most talked-about subjects on the Chinese Internet" (Wong, 2011).

Initial online responses included calls for digging up information about Guo, and within hours "netizens began a massive human flesh search" (Fauna, 2011). An array of personal information was soon put online that showed she had, in less than two years, moved from ordinary housing and no evidence of wealth to a large villa and now had luxurious belongings. Both Guo and the Red Cross issued statements denying any connection, but that did little to reduce public suspicion and negativity toward the latter.

As Kazar noted in 2013, the RCSC still has not been able to fully regain public confidence. When its Weibo site called for donations to aid people affected by the 2013 Lushan earthquake, many who made donations chose online charity platforms other than RCSC (Low, 2013). Further, online responses to the RCSC contained "thousands of caustic replies" ("Red Cross Reopens Guo Meimei Scandal," 2013), a flood of "thumbs-down icons" (Kazar, 2013), and a "resounding chorus of . . . get lost" (Brown-Inz, 2013). Further, pedestrians generally ignored RCSC's traditional sidewalk collection boxes (Levin, 2013). Although, based on incomplete data, the China Charity and Donation Center reported several months after the quake that the Red Cross received only about 40% of all money raised by charities to aid Lushan victims ("RCSC raises $194m," 2013).

The RCSC's reputation had so deteriorated that, according to Sauer (2013), any rumor about it was being taken as the truth. Then, yet another Guo-related incident negatively affected the RCSC. Early in 2013, Guo, as part of an "online spat" with a boyfriend, posted a photo of herself with hundreds of thousands of dollars worth of chips in a Macau casino. The spat became "a top trending topic on Weibo" for several weeks immediately prior to the Lushan earthquake in April, and this timing of Guo's return to public attention was detrimental to the RCSC (Sauer, 2013).

Immediately after the Lushan quake and the poor response to calls for donations, officials from the Red Cross supervision committee, a third-party watchdog group created in 2012, announced there would be a reopening of the probe into the 2011 Guo case ("Red Cross Reopens Guo Meimei Scandal," 2013). Many netizens saw this as an effort to rebuild public trust, but three days later the RCSC's general secretary stated online that news reports were inaccurate and there would be no new investigation.

On the day prior to this denial two things happened online that further undermined the Red Cross. A netizen's post quoted Guo as saying that if the Red Cross dared to harm her, she would "immediately expose insider stories of its corruption." On the same day "rumors of a sex tape featuring Guo and a few high-ranking China Red Cross officials started to go viral" online ("A Mysterious 17.2g Sex Tape," 2013). Although there was no verification of either Guo's statement or the existence of the sex tape, one report concluded that most netizens believed the Red Cross reversed its decision in fear that online revelations by Guo would make things worse ("A Mysterious 17.2g Sex Tape," 2013).

Given this history, it is clear that blogging from the bottom up and the use of HFSE have influenced the structure and governance of the charity sector in China. The Red Cross no longer has a near-monopoly position, and the government has become more willing to allow the creation and operation of more charity organizations. The One Foundation is the first privately founded foundation to obtain a "public foundation" status from the government that allows public fundraising. It received a large amount of donations in response to the Lushan quake and has implemented transparency in its operations "intended to offer a professionalized alternative to organizations such as the Chinese Red Cross" (Brown-Inz, 2013).

Some observers have suggested that the significant increase in funds collected by privately created charities may have received some help from the government. In the past, it had only encouraged direct citizen contributions to the Red Cross and several other organizations it controlled. This was the first time it recommended that the public donate to social organizations with a background in disaster relief (Brown-Inz, 2013).

CONCLUSIONS

The analysis and findings of this chapter support Yang's (2003) warning that it is misleading to examine social media in China only in terms of the government's efforts at political control and citizen actions to use it for regime change. The same is true for Meng's (2010) caution that doing so reflects a Western hegemonic view that will fail to identify and understand the range of activities and effects that are being generated by social media in relation to governance broadly defined.

By adopting these assumptions, this study has sought to build a framework to examine dimensions of social media processes in China from the bottom up that (a) involve citizens in the creation, distribution, and reception of information and (b) generate actions that can enhance their ability to interact spontaneously and collectively in both cyber and terrestrial space in ways that enhance their influence within the socio-cultural and economic as well as formal governance sectors.

Two steps were basic to doing this. One was to identify and examine a set of social media infrastructure dimensions that are produced by citizen actions and by effects of the technology itself. These included HFSE, surrounding gaze, code language, cyber and terrestrial space linkages, and reduction of time/space barriers to communication and action. The other step was to distinguish social media messages initiated by citizens that primarily involve linkages with other citizens, private sector actors, and with government agencies and officials as well as those generated by the state, directed toward citizens.

It is also important to note that, in the formal governance sphere, the state can contribute to the expansion of citizen power as well as seek to suppress it. For example, there is evidence that the central government has reduced or refrained from blocking citizen use of social media directed at local government related to corruption, opposition to projects on environmental grounds, and demands to change in oppressive policies. This behavior arises in some cases from the central government's inability to control local officials and their networks of power.

Many analysts also point out that a critical factor in the increasing influence of netizens is the extensive growth in the size and Internet activity of the middle class. There are spatial aspects as well. Significant growth is taking place in Internet users outside Tier 1 cities (Beijing, Shanghai, Guangzhou, and Shenzhen), and according to a report in July 2012, over 50% of new Internet users are from rural areas who primarily connect with smartphones (Chong & Liu, 2013).

In the aggregate then, without any netizen-led mass movement seeking regime change, significant expansions have occurred and are growing in the ability of citizens over the vast space of China to act collectively and quickly using social media to exercise influence in the private sector, all levels of government, and in relation individual behavior. This can be expected to expand along with continued rapid innovation and technological advances in ICT so long as they are widely available to increasingly numbers of citizens of all classes and all areas of the nation.

Perhaps, even more important, the reconceptualized analytic framework developed for this study that deals with the infrastructure elements and the evolution of social media produced by citizens themselves and by the technology and governmental responses can be applied to other nations. This would be the basis of comparative research and more extensive and detailed understanding of citizen use of social media to increase their influence from the bottom up in multiple sectors, not just in relation to the formal government sector.

REFERENCES

2010 China Internet public opinion analysis report: We-media challenges the Internet regulation (2010中国互联网舆情分析报告: "自媒体" 挑战网络规范). (2010, December 17). *Xinhua News.* Retrieved from http://news.xinhuanet.com/politics/2010-12/17/c_12890073.htm

Barboza, D. (2011, July 18). Chinese upset over counterfeit furniture. *New York Times.* Retrieved from http://www.nytimes.com/2011/07/19/business/global/chinese-upset-over-counterfeit-furniture.html?_r=0

Bradsher, K. (2012). "Social risk" test ordered by China for big projects. *New York Times*, p. A8.

Bristow, M. (2011). Can microblogs change China's rulers? Retrieved from http://www.bbc.co.uk/news/world-asia-pacific-14422581

Brown-Inz, A. (2013, May 13). A view from the media: Response to the quake. Retrieved from http://www.chinadevelopmentbrief.cn/?p=2087

Businessman quits amid China Red Cross scandal. (2011, July 5). Retrieved from http://www.bbc.co.uk/news/world-asia-pacific-14026592?print=true

China Internet Network Information Center. (2014). 第三十三次中国互联网络发展状况调查统计报告 [The 33th statistical report on Internet development in China]. Retrieved from http://www.cnnic.cn/hlwfzyj/hlwxzbg/hlwtjbg/201301/P020130122600399530412.pdf

China's craze for online anti-corruption. (2012, December 7). *Xinhua News.* Retrieved from http://news.xinhuanet.com/english/china/2012-12/07/c_124059507.htm

Chiu, C., Lin, D., & Silverman. A. (2012). China's social-media boom. Retrieved from https://www.mckinsey.com/business-functions/marketing-and-sales/our-insights/chinas-social-media-boom

Chong, E., & Liu, R. (2013). The power of connectedness: How social media usage among China's digital natives is evolving. Retrieved from http://allthingsd.com/20130308/the-power-of-connectedness-how-social-media-usage-among-chinas-digital-natives-is-evolving/

Downey, T. (2010, March 7). China's cyberposse. *New York Times.* Retrieved from http://www.nytimes.com/2010/03/07/magazine/07Human-t.html?pagewanted=all&_r=0

E-Government Research Center. (2013). The 2012 Chinese Government Affairs Weibo assessment report [2012 年中国政务微博客评估报告]. Retrieved from http://www.govweibo.org/art/2014/4/5/art_550_1064.html

Esarey, A., & Qiang, X. (2011). Digital communication and political change in China. *International Journal of Communication, 5,* 298–319.

Fauna. (2011, June 29). Guo Meimei Red Cross controversy pissing off Chinese netizens. *China SMACK.* Retrieved from http://www.chinasmack.com/2011/stories/guo-meimei-red-cross-controversy-pissing-off-chinese-netizensw.html

Goldman, L. (2012, July 18). Chinese microbloggers fill vacuum left by state media in coverage of popular protests. Retrieved from http://techpresident.com/news/22586/chinese-microbloggers-fill-vacuum-left-state-media-coverage-popular-protests

Guo, J. (2013). Li Keqiang talks open government: Must "tell the truth, be completely honest" with the masses [李克强谈政务公开：要向群众"说真话、交实底"]. *China News.* Retrieved from http://www.chinanews.com/gn/2013/03-26/4678154.shtml

Hassid, J. (2012). Safety valve or pressure cooker? Blogs in Chinese political life. *Journal of Communication, 62,* 212–230.

Hewitt, D. (2012, July 16). Weibo brings change to China. *BBC News Magazine.* Retrieved from http://www.bbc.co.uk/news/magazine-18773111

High-heeled kitten killer apologizes. (2006, March 16). *China Daily.* Retrieved from http://www.chinadaily.com.cn/english/doc/2006-03/16/content_540375.htm

Hu, Y. (2011). Interview: Can online surrounding gaze change China [Web log post]. Retrieved from http://yyyyiiii.blogspot.com/2011/01/no2.html; partial English translation retrieved from http://cmp.hku.hk/2011/01/04/9399/

Huang, R., & Yip, N. M. (2012). Internet and activism in urban China: A case study of protests in Xiamen and Panyu. *Journal of Comparative Asian Development, 11,* 201–223.

Is Ya'an different? Lessons from Lushan and Wenchuan quakes. (2013). Retrieved from http://www.sino-us.com/141/Is-Yaan-different-Lessons-from-Lushan-and-Wenchuan-quakes.html

Jacobs, A. (2013a, May 22). Folk remedy extracted from captive bears stirs furor in China. *New York Times,* p. A8.

Jacobs, A. (2013b, July 13). Rally in China protests plant for making nuclear fuel. *New York Times,* p. A6.

Johnson, I. (2012, July 12). China to pay family in a case of forced abortion. *New York Times*, p. A9.

Kazar, W. (2013, April 30). China's Red Cross tries to rebuild after self-inflicted disaster. *Wall Street Journal*. Retrieved from http://blogs.wsj.com/chinarealtime/2013/04/30/chinas-red-crosstab/print-tries-to-rebuild-after-self-inflicted-disaster/

A lady from Hunan province gave the local traffic police brigade a pennant saying "Advanced Unit of Roundaround" [湖南女子赠交警大队"踢皮球先进单位"锦旗]. (2012). *China News*. Retrieved from http://www.chinanews.com/fz/2012/05-25/3914545.shtml

Levin, D. (2013, May 12). Social media in China fuel citizen response to quake. *New York Times*. Retrieved from http://www.nytimes.com/2013/05/12/world/asia/quake-response.html?_r=0

Liu, Y. (2012). Microblog: A new hand of government public relations in crisis (微博: 政府危机公关新手段). *Journal of Ningbo University* (Liberal arts edition), *25*, 125–128.

Low, S. (2013). Raising earthquake relief funds through Weibo. CNET Asia. Retrieved April 5, 2014 from http://asia.cnet.com/raising-earthquake-relief-funds- through-weibo-62221263.htm

Lu, X. (1928). A prose "Mr. Fujino" [TengyeXiansheng]. In *Morning Flowers Plucked at Dusk* [Zhaohua xi shi]. Beijing, Weimingshe.

MacKinnon, R. (2008). Flatter world and thicker walls? Blogs, censorship and civic discourse in China. *Public Choice, 134*, 31–46.

A man attacks 11-year-old girl, claimed from Beijing and with the same ranking as the major [男子猥亵11岁女童 自称"京官"与市长平级]. (2008, October 31). *Fenghuang News*. Retrieved from http://news.ifeng.com/society/1/200810/1031_343_855737.shtml

Meng, B. (2010). Moving beyond democratization: A thought piece on the China Internet research agenda. *International Journal of Communication, 4*, 501–508.

Mozur, P. (2013, January 10). A protest unites far-flung activists, *Wall Street Journal*, p. A9.

Mullany, G. (2013, July 14). After protest, China cancels plans for uranium plant. *New York Times*, p. Y4.

A mysterious 17.2g sex tape of Guo Meimei and another PR nightmare for China Red Cross. (2013). Retrieved December 12, 2014 from http://offbeatchina.com /a-mysterious-17-2g-sex-tape-of-guo-meimei-and-another-pr-nightmare-for-china-red-cross

RCSC raises $194m for Lushan quake. (2013, September 16). *China Daily*. Retrieved from http://www.chinadaily.com.cn/china/2013-09/16/content_16972860.htm

Red Cross reopens Guo Meimei scandal. (2013). *People's Daily Online*. Retrieved from http://english-people.com.cn/90882/8221644.html#

Renmin Weibo: The Report of 2013 NPC & CPPCC representatives' Weibo influence [人民微博: 2013 两会代表委员微博影响力报告]. (2013). *People's Daily Online*. Retrieved from http://www.people.com.cn/NMediaFile/2013/0326/MAIN201303260825000353929512169.pdf

Perlez, J. (2012, June 26). Waste project is abandoned following protests in China. *New York Times*, p. 12.

Qiang, X., & Link, P. (2013, January 4). In China's cyberspace, dissent speaks code. *Wall Street Journal*. Retrieved from http://online.wsj.com/article/SB10001424127887323874204578219832868014140.html

Sauer, A. (2013). China's Red Cross Comes under fire again when country needs it most. Retrieved from http://www.brandchannel.com/home/post/2013/04/24/China-Red-Cross-Under-Fire-042413.aspx

Schott, B. (2009, March 2). Duo Maomao [Web log post]. *New York Times*. Retrieved from http://schott.blogs.nytimes.com/2009/03/02/duo-maomao/

Shirky, C. (2011). The political power of social media. *Foreign Affairs, 90,* 28–41.

Small change earthquake donation from elementary school was refused by local Civil Affairs Bureau [教师为地震捐款被民政局拒收嫌弃零钱多捐的少]. (2012). *Sina News.* Retrieved from http://news.sina.com.cn/s/2012-09-28/045925270788.shtml

SMG Research Team. (2011, February 28). How Weibo reunites kidnapped children with their families. Retrieved from http://www.starcomchinablog.com/2011/02/28/how-weibo-reunites-kidnapped-children-with-their-families

The state council bulletin launched Tencent Weibo: The communique matrix will be born [国务院公报开通腾讯微博"公报矩阵"将诞生]. (2013). *Xinhua News.* Retrieved from http://news.xinhuanet.com/info/2013-03/29/c_132271254.htm

Sterling, B. (2010). Human flesh search engines—renrousousuoyinqing. Retrieved from https://www.thechinastory.org/yearbooks/yearbook-2013/chapter-6-chinas-internet-a-civilising-process/human-flesh-search-engine-renrou-sousuo-yinqing-%E4%BA%BA%E8%82%89%E6%90%9C%E7%B4%A2%E5%BC%95%E6%93%8E/

Students food safety website fuels his fame. (2012, May 8). *China Daily* .Retrieved from http://www.chinadaily.com.cn/china/2012-05/08/content_15230564.htm

Sullivan, J. (2014). China's Weibo: Is faster different? *New Media & Society, 16,* 24–37.

Tong, Y., & Lei, S. (2010). *Creating public opinion pressure in China: Large-scale Internet protest* (East Asian Institute Background Brief No. 534). Retrieved from http://www.eai.nus.edu.sg/publications/files/BB534.pdf

The top 10 human flesh search incidents on Internet from 2001 to 2008 [互联网十大著名"人肉搜索"事件]. (2010). *CNW News.* Retrieved from http://www.cnwnews.com/html/soceity/cn_shlw/20100304/196929.html

Wang, F. Y., Zeng, D., Zhang, Q., Feng, Z., Gao, Y., Lai, G., . . . Wang, H. (2010). A study of the human flesh search engine: Crowd-powered expansion of online knowledge. *Computer, 43*(8), 45–53.

Watt, L. (2013, March 10). China's leaders take aim at railways ministry. Retrieved from https://www.cnsnews.com/news/article/chinas-leaders-take-aim-railways-ministry

Wong, E. (2011, July 4). An online scandal underscores Chinese distrust of state charities. *New York Times*. Retrieved from http://nytimes.com/2011/07/04/world/asia/04china.html?pagewanted=all&_r=0

Word of the week: Believe it or not, I do. (2012, July 25). *China Digital Times*. Retrieved from http://chinadigitaltimes.net/2012/07/word-week-believe-it-not-i-do/

Wu, A. X. (2012). Jail the independent thinker: The emergence of public debate culture on the Chinese Internet. *International Journal of Communication, 6,* 2220–2244.

Yang, G. (2003). The co-evolution of the Internet and civil society in China. *Asian Survey, 43,* 405–422.

Yang, L., & Cao, S. (2012, August). *Weibo and its political and social impacts on China* (EAI Background Brief No. 750). Retrieved from http://www.eai.nus.edu.sg/publications/files/BB750.pdf

Ye, J. & Canaves, S. (2008, July 3). Here for soy sauce or push-ups? *Wall Street Journal.* Retrieved from http://blogs.wsj.com/chinarealtime/2008/07/03/here-for-soy-sauce-or-push-ups/

Ye, J., & Fowler, G. A. (2008, July 2). Chinese bloggers scale the "great firewall" in riot's aftermath. *Wall Street Journal*. Retrieved from http://online.wsj.com/article/SB121493163092919829.html

Young, D. (2013, January 13). Censorship row reveals tolerant side of China's new leadership. Retrieved from http://www.cnn.com/2013/01/13.opinion/china-censorship-young/index.html

12

Policing Digital Sanctuaries

Exploring Environmental Advocacy through Technology-Enabled Monitoring and Enforcement Network Organizations

STEPHEN KLEINSCHMIT ■

The last fallen mahogany would lie perceptibly on the landscape, and the last black rhino would be obvious in its loneliness, but a marine species may disappear beneath the waves unobserved and the sea would seem to roll on the same as always.

—G. Carleton Ray

Advocacy takes many forms, from consumer education campaigns to traditional lobbying, even direct action. The world's pressing environmental problems have resulted in an increased urgency by advocates to find new strategies that can produce results. While international nongovernmental organizations (INGOs) are "primarily seen as the passive subjects of external oversight and punishment" (Ebrahim 2007, p. 193) and primarily pursue information and socialization politics, there is evidence to suggest that direct interventions enhance the potential for obtaining compliance with global norms (Eilstrup-Sangiovanni, & Bondaroff, 2014). Within the international community, a substantial collective action problem exists with regards to the enforcement of international law: Many countries lack the capacity (or political will) to police the world's oceans. Barring an unlikely collective response, the existing nature of global common pool resource management (CPR) institutions will not prove adequate to solve this problem. This chapter explores an emerging form of hybrid organization that may be used as a model by INGOs to engage in new forms of technologically enhanced advocacy and complement the capacity of the existing resource management regimes.

No more complicated resource management challenge exists than in the world's oceans, whose lonely expanses remain largely unmonitored, enabling industrial-scale exploitation of marine fisheries. The United Nation's (UN) Convention on the Law of the Sea (1982) treaty formally established territorial waters and exclusive economic zones as a means to apportion property rights, with even most nonsignatory states also acknowledging the provisions of the convention (Nandan, 2012). The treaty ceded primary responsibility to nations to enact and enforce their fisheries management programs, which have often used marine sanctuaries as a tool to expand fishing grounds into natural habitats. This tool is primarily intended to regulate commercial activity, with resource closures used as means to protect the economic and environmental interests of the state.

Despite enforcement, large-scale illegal fishing occurs in these reserves, including UNESCO World Heritage sites (Carr et al., 2013), many nations have not ratified or implemented other multilateral fishery treaties, such as the UN Fish Stocks Agreement (1995). A small sliver of the globe has enhanced protected status; only 1.2% of the world's oceans are protected by Marine Protected Areas, and 90% of those areas do allow forms of fishing (World Wildlife Fund, 2014). The UN Food and Agriculture Organization estimates that 70% of the world's fish species are fully exploited or depleted, and most may be unviable in a few short decades (UN Fisheries and Aquaculture Department, 2014). Additionally, the substantial threats of ocean acidification and pollution are conspiring to make the world's oceans inhospitable for marine life (Zheng, Chen & Zhuang, 2015). Whether the question of protecting fisheries is tied to sustainability goals, the economic utility of commercial industry, or the public welfare, the impetus for action grows stronger as the resource deteriorates.

The reason for the continued abuse of the world's oceans is clear: Resource managers lack strong monitoring and enforcement mechanisms needed to police its expanses. Global policies have proved insufficient to reduce demands on marine environments, which is in no small part a result of the massive scale of the problem. Most notably, nations within Asia and the European Union have large distant-water fishing fleets, with thousands of vessels implicated in illegal fishing around the globe (Kende-Robb, 2014). The scale of this resource exploitation hastens the transfer of wealth from the poor to the wealthy, worsening global poverty, and is a violation of human rights. The size and remoteness of large maritime sanctuaries often lead regulators and industry alike to consider them unenforceable. The realities of perpetual resource scarcity adding fire to a conflict-riddled world present a pessimistic outlook toward humankind's ability to address such problems without resorting to conflict.

As declining resource estimates attest, traditional forms of INGO advocacy have proved ineffectual. To prevent irreversible damage to marine fisheries, alternative governance arrangements must arise to address these failures. The institutions that emerge are likely to benefit from the development the integration of information and communications technology (ICT) technologies, which have demonstrated potential within the realm of e-governance. Marginalized groups may find the current structure unconducive to addressing their issues and might find their preferred alternative to be somewhat disruptive in nature. Such a strategy may include combining ICT with an alternative organizational infrastructure—one designed to wield influence in ways previously thought impossible.

The growth of multisectoral (hybrid) network organizations present new possibilities for institutional development. In doing so, they take clues from existing forms of institutions, as INGO are comprised of a combination of informal cultures, formal systems, and technologies (Brown, Ebrahim, & Batliwala, 2012). Their development enables new forms interest representation, but their "architectures may enable or constrain choices of advocacy strategies or targets" (Brown et al., 2002, p. 1107). The organizations seek to accomplish a number of standard functions of governance-based institutions (a) to decrease information the symmetries about market conditions goods and participants, (b) define and enforce property rights and contracts and, (c) restrict the actions of politicians and interest groups (World Trade Organization, 2004, p. 176). To purpose the organization optimally toward its missions, it must be structured to address these challenges.

INGO ADVOCACY THROUGH TECHNOLOGY

INGOs are involved in policy advocacy as a means to scale up their impact, "gaining leverage through communicating their ideas to policymakers and becoming sources of knowledge" (Salazar, 2010, p. 366). Their impact has grown as ICT platforms have allowed for improved coordination between similarly purposed organizations. Initiatives like the UN World Summit on the Information Society have formally incorporated INGOs as partners in its consultations and decisions (Franklin, 2007). Its most recent iteration, WSIS+10, reaffirmed the UN's commitment to inclusivity in December 2015, welcoming "the remarkable evolution and diffusion of information and communications technologies, underpinned by the contributions of both public and private sectors" (UNGA 2016, 4/8). By explicitly recognizing the role of ICT in promoting collaborative governance, it highlighted the value of its use for engaging in multisectoral deliberative processes.

While ICT is used as a means to promote collaborative processes, it need not be its sole purpose. The monitoring capacity of environmental nonprofits has grown considerably due to their employment of networked data collection and remote-sensing technologies (Hoekstra, 2014). The ability to conduct timely (real or delayed) intelligence has enabled a much more expansive functionality than previously thought possible. Commercial satellites are a technology that has scaled organizational capacity up, allowing nonstate actors to monitor entire domains of global society. Such enormous leaps in capacity are reshaping the dynamics of governance, as the emergence of a new institutional architecture to promote new forms of regulatory monitoring by multisectoral hybrid organizations. By integrating traditional advocacy approaches with spatial technologies, new CPR management institutions may prove transformative. This chapter details the possibilities and pitfalls of integrating ICT into hybrid network organizations.

TECHNOLOGY-ENABLED MONITORING
AND ENFORCEMENT NETWORKS

Elinor Ostrom's institutional analysis and design framework proved an important theoretical advancement in understanding the mechanisms for effective CPR management regimes (Ostrom, 1990). She hypothesized "a tremendous institutional diversity would flourish as a result of socio-ecological demands" (Munger 2010, 264). These institutions were important for controlling the self-interested behavior of individuals, who in the absence of regulation would abuse public resources until they faced ruin (Hardin, 1968). Answers to the problem of "tragedy of the commons" include regulatory policy, privatization, and social pressure. The introduction of ICT in this context extends the traditional social pressure axiom of intergroup dynamics hierarchically, expanding the scale of conflict both downward and upward as groups disseminate information across multiple outlets.

New hybrid governance arrangements, which I term *technology-enabled monitoring and enforcement networks*, provide the capacity that will change the mechanisms of global fisheries governance. Real-time remote sensing and tracking, combined with new ICT forms, provide institutional capacity for monitoring and enforcement—essential elements needed for successful CPR management institutions at all levels (Ostrom et al., 2012). Incorporating this into a soft power strategy, based on influencing governance institutions and resource users, can afford INGOs increased influence and legitimacy.

Global Fishing Watch

An initiative known has *Global Fishing Watch* evidences the disruptive potential of technologically enhanced CPR management institutions. It is a collaborative partnership between private-sector Google, nonprofit advocacy organizations SkyTruth and Oceana. This partnership enables fisheries monitoring and reporting beyond the scope of sovereign jurisdictions, such as territorial seas and exclusive economic zones, into the open ocean. Satellites collect ship-based automatic position indicator (API) beacon information, reporting vessel location and movement patterns. Under testing in 2016, a planned public Web-based information portal is to be made available to citizens and organizations to report illegal entry of vessels in territorial waters and sanctuaries. Countries that are signatories to international fisheries treaties will now possess the data needed to identify and prosecute those who violate protected areas and resource closures. Data logging enables behavioral analyses to identify more complex avoidance behaviors, exposing unregistered commercial vessels that operate as fishing vessels, discovered through movement patterns consistent with long-line fishing or trawling. Though ships may try to disable their API system to avoid detection, doing so may flag them for further scrutiny.

With regards to terminology, I seek to make a meaningful distinction between technologically-*enhanced* and technologically-*enabled* networks. The infrastructure supporting each does not augment existing capacities; it creates new networks of organizations and individuals that provide government-scale monitoring capacity to help overcome the failures of governance. Their use reflects an evolutionary development and fundamentally changes the way that environmental problems may be addressed. Fisheries exemplify "wicked" environmental problems are technically complex and politically contentious (Hoppe & Petersen, 1993) and demand adaptable institutional mechanisms that recognize this complexity. Technologically enabled network institutions are such a step in the evolution of complex resource governance network arrangements.

Enabling Advocacy through Networked Organizations

Technology has become "integral to global agenda-setting in the intertwined areas of ICT, media, and social-cultural policy" (Franklin 2007, 309). A strategy combining ICT accomplishes many of the same functions of traditional media, providing transparency and accountability functions, and serves as a catalyst for reform (Misuraca & Viscusi, 2014). It is worthwhile to note that the transparency function is not simply designed toward ensuring accountability for political actors but also the officials who are obliged to enforce the laws and to influence the actions of the regulated entities themselves.

New mechanisms for participatory and democratic governance emerge through the availability of open data (Misuraca & Viscusi, 2014). This undermines the ability of governments to act as the "information gatekeeper" and may be useful in areas where regulatory processes are captured or rife with corruption, providing monitors with a much more comprehensive assessment of activity than would otherwise be reported. Real-time data provision and behavioral analytics mean that enforcement orientation can be proactive, as preventing an environmental catastrophe is preferable to enforcement after the damage has occurred.

The monitoring capacity of the networks is in itself useful, though its information will not accomplish its intended mission unless communicated effectively. Social media is recognized as an effective tool for achieving advocacy goals, proving its effectiveness in numerous social movements, including the Arab Spring protests and Occupy Wall Street (Chalmers & Shotton, 2015). An ICT-based strategy can quickly disseminate information to numerous institutions and potential users. It allows free-flowing, interactive discourse with governments, companies, news organizations, nonprofit organizations, and other stakeholder groups in resource management activities. Through a public relations campaign, it also retains the ability to help frame the nature of the debate, helping to shape public opinion and its preferred policy alternatives.

An Emerging Global Network CPR Institution

Resource demands evidence a substantial disconnect between consumers and their base, a troubling reality that has defined the realm of fisheries and causes difficulty in mobilizing public opinion (Oosterveer & Spaargaren, 2011). Long-distance trawlers from Asia and Europe regularly find themselves in the waters of the Southern Ocean; industrial-scale fishing occurs within the lightly policed territorial seas of the African coasts, which have led to the degradation of local fisheries. The resultant collapse of the resource base has been cited as the primary factor of the rise in piracy within the Indian Ocean (Beri, 2011). With linkages to so many visible policy realms, shortcomings of existing resource institutions evidence the need to collaborate across organizations with similar policy goals.

Global Fishing Watch is first example of this hybrid global institutional form. While other entities have used position-locating technologies for management purposes, they have not been integrated with ICT on a global scale. Though the propagation of this organizational form is somewhat limited, initial reports find its monitoring and enforcement strategy has been successful. Oceana paints the picture of a resounding success; their estimates indicate a drastic (99.7%) reduction in detected fishing activities after a commercial fishing ban was instituted in Kiribati's Phoenix Islands Protected Area (Witkin, 2016). It cites three important factors in explaining the success of the protected area through a multifaceted strategy. First, the nation established a commercial "no-take" designation for the area in 2015, though the marine-protected area had been formally established in 2006. Second, its technology was used to complement the 17-nation Pacific Islands Forum Fisheries Agency, supplementing the efforts by other small island nations to monitor their large ocean expanses. Finally, the monitoring technology provided a performance measurement capacity to assess the success of the policies, enabling feedback and a means by which to modify its operations. The integrated approach will be tested as the technology's use is expanded to larger operational environments, such as their proposed collaboration with Indonesia ("Indonesia," 2015).

Global Fishing Watch provides a new means to base enforcement action against those who violate international sanctions, as spatial location data evidence interactions between parties and states. Entities that violate marine reserves and then interact with others (such as the offloading of illegally taken fish to other vessels) reveal cooperative networks in ways that traditional enforcement activities never could. Additionally, the technology may prove useful for addressing a host of environmental and social problems, including illegal dumping, illicit arms sales, and human trafficking—all linked to illegal fishing (Hattendorf, 2013). As a result, they can expand their network of support to organizations within other realms of policy that might not share their implicit goals.

An INGO opens itself for criticism if it is unable to sustain adequately its value within its policy domain. The elements the organization's technical legitimacy are primary components of its overall legitimacy, primarily its standards of effectiveness, expertise, efficiency, audit (certification), and legality (Pallas, Gethings, & Harris, 2015). INGOs that are able to perform highly within these realms may be afforded more legitimacy than those of individual states—particularly those with an extensive history of graft or corruption. A high degree of institutional buy-in from trusted organizations can elevate the trustworthiness of these networks, improving their stature and allowing them to wield power in multiple policy domains. Thus, forming a transparent and trusted global governance institution is of utmost importance.

The following sections will detail some of the possibilities of these networks, detailing their strengths within the realm of regulatory activity and policy, as well as the technical attributes of their systems. Later, I will discuss the possible drawbacks to the strategy, including unforeseen consequences that can arrive from its use.

Regulatory and Policy Considerations

Aside from its utility for advocacy, these networks are constructed to be a complementary regulatory enforcement mechanism. As such, consideration should be placed on how such an institution can indirectly influence the realms of policy and enforcement. ICT-based networks can address regulatory fragmentation and can actively monitor behavior in the open oceans where little or no effective enforcement mechanism exists. There is a substantial disparity in the degree of capacity of the naval and fisheries fleets of the world: Very few are funded to an extent at which they can prove responsive and effective. By "flattening" regulatory disparities between the developed and developing world, it may undercut collective action problems that lead to disengagement from governance processes. Alternatively, the global community may seek to impose a common regulatory standard through alternative mechanisms such as voluntary, consensus-based partnerships like the International Standards Organization.

Supply chain restrictions have been used previously to address such social and environmental problems with regards to illegal mining, logging, and poaching. Whether imposed by trade bodies or manufacturers, supply chain standards assist in overcoming asymmetries of information, removing portions of "the black box" of global supply chains through a soft policy approach (Friedrich, 2013). Influencing large retail operations may prove substantial; an entity with sizable market share implementing such policies influences a larger market and regulatory environment. Engaging these actors in policy subsystems may help mitigate forms of conflict through an integration of scientific research and social values (Weible & Sabatier, 2009). Additionally, this allows for expanded interaction between similarly tasked organizations that help form larger advocacy coalitions. By contributing to these policy networks; interest groups enjoy increased capacity and legitimacy through their collective responses to environmental challenges. They can create network governance organizations that pursue multimodal public relations strategies toward national governments, international governing bodies, trade associations, and other strategic partners.

Technological Considerations

These organizations are unusual not only because of the composition of their constituent organizations and mission; they assemble a level of capital investment, network infrastructure, and technological capacity that mirrors those traditionally held by national governments. It is uncommon for a private enterprise to possess such substantial monitoring capability and even less common that it would be employed in a manner that promotes the public interest. The degree to which this distinctive institution is driven by its technological core is noteworthy, as is its unique approach to wielding influence.

With regards to the ICT network applications of the technology, their advantages mirror those of cloud computing, including the ability to implement measures faster and more efficiently than democratic institutions and scalable technology that does not require a large capital investment for governments (Kamensky, 2014). When combined with internal and locally adapted rules, it assists in overcoming collective action problems by implementing a common technological framework across the globe but contextualizing the application to the requirements of each member state.

Real-time analytics can quickly discover anomalies in operational contexts, resulting in substantially increased response times by regulatory agencies. Within moments of a vessel entering a protected marine sanctuary on the other side of the world, regulatory agencies receive notification of the violation. As a result, networks can expand the de facto range of national sovereignty. This "over-the-horizon capacity" for fisheries enforcement is a paradigmatic shift in how regulatory authority can be implemented. Upon analyzing patterns of vessel data, resource closures and management areas may be able to shift from those defined by arbitrary political boundaries to those delineated by habitats. Thus, a new framework for habitat preservation, digital sanctuaries, enables both governments and industries to independently create and enforce resource protection closures and can be applied and withdrawn as needed. Such boundaries are conditions of the socio-ecological systems for CPR management institutions to exclude parties who operate in irresponsible manners (Ostrom, 1990).

QUESTIONS AND CONSIDERATIONS

This new form of technologically based advocacy is not without its downside. Though a substantial degree of optimism that should result from its propagation, there are concerns that should be addressed before such systems become institutionalized. The potential "revenge effect of technology" should be noted—the ability of advancements to create new unforeseen problems, often worse than the ones they set out to solve (Segal, 1996). One potential problem: the use of API data logging creates an incentive for vessels to turn off their transponders to avoid tracking. As the system is intended to prevent collisions, those who disable the system increase risk for catastrophic accidents.

The network seeks to give citizens "a simple, online platform to visualize, track and share information about fishing activity worldwide" (Skytruth, 2016). The initiative is intended to benefit from decentralized information sharing, its users disseminating its data to help accomplish its public relations goals. But the potential for misreporting (or other malicious uses) under such systems cannot be ignored. Some forms could be considered rent-seeking behavior, where economic actors seek to gain a competitive market advantage over their competitors through the misuse of regulatory policy and enforcement, seeking to hamper competitors to secure a larger market segment.

Disparities in governing law could provide a significant challenge to the authority of data derived from these systems. Regarding legality, will data collected from a nonstate source, located in a foreign country be considered valid for the basis of considering enforcement actions? Many legal systems would not consider this valid admissible evidence in a court, undercutting the efficacy of the reported information, irrespective of its accuracy. It is also possible that the organization's "software code, architecture design, and technological standards— can have significant consequences for human rights" and are worthy of further consideration before becoming institutionalized in international law (Land 2013, p. 393).

While the development of these technologies will increase the capacity of government, unforeseen problems could emerge as a result of their dependency on these tools. Political actors may use this as a rationale for alternative action, cutting the budgets of fisheries enforcement under the guise that these tools provide an adequate basis for enforcement, ultimately undermining part of the multifaceted approach needed to enforce fisheries laws. Supplanting a publicly held and accountable monitoring entity for a private one begs the consideration of many elements of its operations. With regards to accountability, due process, organizational ethics, management processes, and other organizational considerations, whose are the most valid?

Will the adoption of technology from a major distributor undercut innovation? The emergence of new solutions could be hampered by their lack of ability to be integrated into the existing system, creating a version of "vendor lock-in." In such instances, both the dependence on technology and the development of proprietary technologies undermine the adoption of innovative alternatives by competing organizations. Certainly the scale and model of Google's operations might hand it a natural monopoly. Is it their responsibility to ensure the continuation of the tool and the investment needed to maintain its infrastructure indefinitely? An enterprise begun under the auspices of corporate citizenship are certainly noteworthy, but the continuing cost of operations and the potential fallout to their activity in this and other policy realms could create a strong incentive for canceling the project. For example, Google may find its efforts toward expanding its core business missions hampered by governments that feel their economy is being harmed by the use of Global Fishing Watch. As a means to broaden their market share, shareholders and governing boards may be compelled to return their company's operations to that of their core mission. Aside from corporate citizenship and the ability to test a system that might have further commercial applications, it is worth questioning what shareholder value is to be derived by the company in its continued partnership.

CONCLUSION

Technological innovation will play an important part of innovations in environmental advocacy and governance in the future. As the use of ICT becomes more institutionalized at all levels of governance, INGOs can derive improved capacity for influencing policy processes through adopting new technologically driven organizational innovations. Much like smartphone technology has enabled a paradigm shift within the realm of mobile government, the integration of spatial information into public information portals can change the way we govern the world's oceans.

Technology-enabled monitoring and enforcement networks are not a panacea. They alone will not solve issues of abuse of CPRs, but they offer a glimmer of hope toward addressing a global environmental problem in a domain where no effective solution exists. There are obvious shortcomings that are exposed by such an approach including the potential for avoidance, a regulatory emphasis on large industrial fishing over fleets of smaller vessels, displacing market demand to threatened species or habitats—perhaps even the enabling of vigilantism and piracy. Still, it constitutes a new institutional governing form—one that may prove instrumental in solving a host of environmental problems in the global commons. This emerging solution may change the landscape of fisheries management, and its approach invites both serious consideration and further study from those interested in environmental management.

REFERENCES

Beri, R. (2011). Piracy in Somalia: Addressing the root causes. *Strategic Analysis, 35,* 452–464.

Brown, L., Ebrahim, A., & Batliwala, S. (2012). Governing international advocacy NGOs. *World Development, 40,* 1098–1108.

Carr, L. A., Stier, A. C., Fietz, K., Montero, I., Gallagher, A. J., & Bruno, J. F. (2013). Illegal shark fishing in the Galápagos Marine Reserve. *Marine Policy, 39,* 317–321.

Chalmers, A., & Shotton, P. (2015). Changing the face of advocacy? Explaining interest organizations' use of social media strategies. *Political Communication, 33*(3), 374–391.

Ebrahim, A. (2007). *Towards a reflective accountability in NGOs. Global accountabiliti es: Participation, pluralism, and public ethics.* Cambridge University Press, 193–224.

Eilstrup-Sangiovanni, M., & Bondaroff, T. (2014). From advocacy to confrontation: Direct enforcement by environmental NGO s. *International Studies Quarterly, 58,* 348–361.

Friedrich, J. (2013). *International environmental soft law: The functions and limits of nonbinding instruments in international environmental governance and law.* New York: Springer.

Franklin, M. (2007). NGOs and the "information society": Grassroots advocacy at the UN—A cautionary tale. *Review of Policy Research, 24,* 309–330.

Hardin, G. (1968). The tragedy of the commons. *Nature, 162*(3859), 1243–1248.

Hattendorf, J. B. (Ed.). (2013). *The International Seapower Symposium: Report of the proceedings, 18–21 October 2011.* Newport, RI: Naval War College Press.

Hoekstra, J. (2014). Networking nature: How technology is transforming conservation. *Foreign Affairs, 93,* 80–89.

Hoppe, R., & Peterse, A. (1993). *Handling frozen fire: Political culture and risk management.* Boulder, CO: Westview.

Indonesia: Govt to launch Global Fishing Watch. (2015, November 3). *Asia News Monitor.*

Kamensky, J. (2014, January 2). Government in the cloud: Minimizing the risks [Web log post]. Retrieved from http://www.governing.com/blogs/bfc/col-government-cloud-computing-contract-12-issues-ibm-center-report.html

Kende-Robb, C. (2014, June 19). Why illegal fishing off Africa's coast must be stopped. *The Guardian.*

Land, M. (2013). Toward an international law of the Internet. *Harvard International Law Journal, 54,* 393–458.

Misuraca, G., & Viscusi, G. (2014). Is open data enough? E-governance challenges for open government. *International Journal of Electronic Government Research, 10,* 18–34.

Munger, M. C. (2010). Endless forms most beautiful and most wonderful: Elinor Ostrom and the diversity of institutions. *Public Choice, 143,* 263–268.

Nandan, S. (2012). Remarks by Satya N. Nandan, UNCLOS Anniversary: What are the challenges?). *Proceedings of the Annual Meeting-American Society of International Law, 106,* 400–402.

Oosterveer, P., & Spaargaren, G. (2011). Organising consumer involvement in the greening of global food flows: The role of environmental NGOs in the case of marine fish. *Environmental Politics, 20,* 97–114.

Ostrom, E. (1990). Governing the commons: The evolution of institutions for collective action. Cambridge [England]. New York: Cambridge University Press.

Ostrom, E. (2005). *Understanding institutional diversity.* Princeton, NJ: Princeton University Press.

Ostrom, E., Chang, C., Pennington, M., & Tarko, V. (2012). *The future of the commons—Beyond market failure and government regulation.* London: Institute of Economic Affairs.

Pallas, C., Gethings, L., & Harris, D. (2015). Do the right thing: The impact of INGO legitimacy standards on stakeholder input. *Voluntas: International Journal of Voluntary and Nonprofit Organizations, 26,* 1261–1287.

Salazar, L. (2010). Enablers and constraints to knowledge creation, sharing and use: The case of policy advocacy networks. *VINE: Journal of Information and Knowledge Management Systems, 40,* 362–375.

Segal, H. (1996). Why things bite back: New technology and the revenge effect. *Nature, 382*(6591), 504.

Skytruth. (2016). Global fishing watch. Retrieved from http://skytruth.org/mapping-global-fishing/

United Nations Convention on the Law of the Sea. 1833 UNTS 3; 21 ILM 1261 (1982).

United Nations Fish Stocks Agreement. 34 ILM 1542 (1995); 2167 UNTS 88.

United Nations Fisheries and Aquaculture Department. (2014). *The state of world fisheries and aquaculture*. Rome.

United Nations General Assembly (2016). Resolution adopted by the General Assembly on 21 December 2016 [on the report of the Second Committee (A/71/460)] 71/212. Information and communications technologies for development.

Weible, C. M., & Sabatier, P. A. (2009). Coalitions, science, and belief change: Comparing adversarial and collaborative policy subsystems. *Policy Studies Journal, 37*, 195–212.

Witkin, T. (2016). Global Fishing Watch put to the test: Monitoring the Phoenix Islands Protected Area. Oceana. Retrieved from: http://usa.oceana.org/blog/global-fishing-watch-put-test-monitoring-phoenix-islands-protected-area

World Wildlife Fund. (2014). Fishing problems: Poor fisheries management. Retrieved from http://wwf.panda.org/about_our_earth/blue_piblelanet/problems/problems_fishing/fisheries_management

World Trade Organization. (2004). *World trade report 2004: Exploring the linkage between the domestic policy environment and international trade*. Geneva: Author.

Zeng, X., Chen, X., & Zhuang. J. (2015). The positive relationship between ocean acidification and pollution. *Marine Pollution Bulletin, 91*, 14–21.

13

Social Media and Leaderless Social Movement Organizations

Implications for Transnational Advocacy

LORI A. BRAINARD, KATHERINE M. BOLAND,
AND JOHN G. McNUTT ■

Transnational advocacy organizations exist in a turbulent, politically charged, and even physically violent organizational environment (Batliwala, 2002; Warkentin, 2001; Young, Koenig, Najam, & Fisher, 1999). Addressing issues of war and refugees, world hunger, poor or nonexistent healthcare, trafficking, and violence means negotiating a bewildering array of organizational arrangements.

In the past few years we have seen the emergence of a variety of new forms of organizations that make extensive use of technology for many of their operations. These include everything from flash mobs to online organizing efforts. The emergence of essentially leaderless organizations, still largely face to face, that depend on technology (and particularly social media) can make that world more chaotic. On balance, they can provide a set of additional capacities that advocates can use in their vital work.

The emergence of these efforts also has implications for all types of nonprofit social change organizations and, perhaps, the nonprofit sector in general. This chapter will discuss how these new efforts are structured, what they mean for transnational advocacy efforts, and what the implications are for voluntary action theory.

The chapter will look at several examples of this type of organizing effort. We will examine the Tea Party, Occupy Wall Street, and the movements in the Middle East collectively described as Arab Spring. We will briefly look at a few other examples as well. We will contrast these with traditional nonprofit advocacy and social movement organizations. We will discuss some of the theoretical base that informs the examination of such organizations. Finally, we will look at implications of this discussion for theory and practice.

THREE RECENT CASES

In the past few years, several movements have caught the attention of the public. Many of these are traditional social movements but others are configured in a different fashion. These new movements lack many of the structural characteristics of earlier organizations. Equally important is the extensive use of technology. This is an interaction between structure and technology. One of these organizations is domestic, one is international, and the other is a combination of both.

The Tea Party

The Tea Party movement appeared on the domestic US national stage in early 2009. Many point to a rant given by commentator Rick Santelli in 2009 as the beginning of the Tea Party movement (Cohen, 2010a, 2010b, 2010c; Zernike, 2010). Some see the movement as a response to the recession, the bailouts of the financial and auto industries, and the concerns and fears of conservative Americans (Klimp, 2010; Lepore, 2010; Zernike, 2010). The election of Barak Obama is also an important factor in the creation of the Tea Party movement.

The Tea Party movement calls itself a leaderless movement. There are several national organizations but no central leadership. Local groups are free to explore their own agendas and create their own action plans. It frequently appears that coordination and control is nonexistent. Some of the local organizations are probably not affiliated with any of the major national groups. A hierarchical or vertical control would run counter to the ideology of the movement (Zernike, 2010).

A leaderless organization, in this context, does not mean that there are no leaders. It means that leadership is distributed throughout the membership rather than being tightly controlled by a small group or an individual.

What do Tea Party members stand for? There are things that are consistent with Republican values including a healthy free-market economy, lower taxes, smaller government, state's rights, and a limit to federal government powers. Most opposed the bailouts of the financial services industry and the auto industry, and most are also opposed to national health care reform (Obamacare) (Cohen, 2010a, 2010b, 2010c; Rasmussen & Schoen, 2010; Zernike, 2010). While they argue that the US government has departed from the constitution and the vision of the founding fathers, there is some strain within the movement about the so-called social agenda (e.g., abortion, gay marriage, etc.) as some feel that this would be an intrusion by government into an unacceptable area. This is often an issue between traditional conservatives and evangelical conservatives within the mainstream Republican Party and can make internal policymaking difficult. The struggle between the Tea Party-backed candidates and the mainstream GOP candidates was visible in several contests in the 2010 midterm elections and the primary elections for 2012. While movement members often identify with former Governor Sarah Palin, Senators Marco Rubio and Jim DeMint, commentator Glenn Beck, and former congressman and House Minority Leader Dick Armey, there is not an agreement that they speak for the Tea Party movement.

Most of the activity appears at the local level, despite the fact that a few national events (such as the Tea Party Convention and several marches on Washington) garnered more media attention. This highlights circumstances where national groups and local groups can sharply differ.

There are a number of national organizations that are influential in the Tea Party movement (Cohen, 2010a, 2010b, 2010c; Klimp, 2010; Zernike, 2010). The Tea Party Nation (http://www.teapartynation.com) (2012) bills itself as "Tea Party Nation is a user-driven group of like-minded people who desire our God-given individual freedoms written out by the Founding Fathers. We believe in Limited Government, Free Speech, the 2nd Amendment, our Military, Secure Borders and our Country." The Tea Party Nation sponsored the 2009 National Tea Party Convention in Nashville. Tea Party Patriots (http://www.teapartypatriots.org/), founded in Houston, aims at creating a clearinghouse for the Tea Party movement. It has a large online data base of Tea Party groups. Tea Party Express (http://www.teapartyexpress.org/) sponsors a fundraising bus tour across the country to raise money for a group of recommended candidates. The Tea Party Express has been a successful fundraiser. 9-12 Patriots was related to former Fox contributor Glenn Beck. It operated on observance to a set of 12 principles and 9 values. This group sponsored the March to Restore Honor. The Project's mission statement states, "This is a non-political movement. The 9-12 Project is designed to bring us all back to the place we were on September 12, 2001" (9-12 Project, 2009). The group's website listed substantial number of local affiliates.

FreedomWorks chaired by former Speaker Dick Armey, predated the Tea Party movement (Zernike, 2010). Essentially a think tank, it provides resources to Tea Party groups. FreedomWorks has a political action committee. None of these organizations claim to speak for the Tea Party. Some local Tea Party groups are not associated with any one (or any) organization. On balance, because of their money and visibility, it would be difficult to conclude that these national level organizations lack clout in the movement (Cohen, 2010b).

The Tea Party was originally vulnerable to the charge that the Tea Party organizations are a form of AstroTurf. There was no national organization, and Tea Party efforts had been supported by conservative donors (see Rich, 2010) and conservative media (particularly Fox News). Also, as McNutt and Boland (2007) have argued, AstroTurf is better thought of as a matter of degree rather than a dichotomy. In any event, it is difficult to make that claim numerous years later.

The Tea Party has been self-described as a leaderless organization or a leaderless movement. *The Starfish and the Spider* (Brafman & Beckstrom, 2006), a popular business book about decentralized organizations, typifies the Tea Party's approach (Rauch, 2010; see also Cohen, 2010a, 2010b, 2010c). In this approach, an organization composed of semiautonomous cells. The cells organize together but have considerable autonomy. Destroying one cell will not materially damage the whole; it will just be replaced. Traditional social movement organizations are hierarchical. Arresting or incapacitating the leadership of the organization can have considerable undesirable consequences. This type of organization has assets and liabilities. While it makes attacking the organization difficult, it is not always clear if these organizations can manage a substantial action that requires a sustained effort (Rauch, 2010).

It is evident that technology is a major driver of the Tea Party movement (McNutt, Curtis, O'Boyle, & Fox, 2010; Sarno, 2009; Zernike, 2010). Technology makes many of the things that they do possible and creates the opportunity to build a national movement without a central hub. McNutt et al. (2010) found that Tea Party groups employed a wide variety of technologies.

Occupy Wall Street

On the other end of the ideological spectrum is Occupy Wall Street (Lang & Levitsky, 2012). Occupy Wall Street started as a demonstration on September 17, 2011, that evolved into a movement with many similar efforts throughout the United States and eventually throughout the world. The effort has had far more substantial legs than many pundits had predicted. While it has been called the Tea Party of the left, the actual similarities are really not due to ideology.

The initial demonstration was promoted by a Canadian group Adbusters (http://www.adbusters.org/) and led to an occupation of Zuccotti Park in New York City. This demonstration centered on the issues of corporate control, inequality, and the role of money in politics. Other issues, such as conflict, political inclusion, and even student loans, quickly became part of the agenda. Some of the original discussion compared Occupy Wall Street with the Arab Spring movement in Egypt. Occupy Wall Street took control of Zuccotti Park from September to November in 2011, when they were removed by the City of New York. The original demonstration was a face-to-face movement operated on collectivist lines.

Occupy Wall Street became an international movement with demonstrations and occupations throughout the world. It clearly has a message that resonates with a diverse set of populations. There is no central governing body or clearinghouse. Since there is no central organization nor is there a central voice.

In that way, it has some common ground with the Tea Party. This tends to create consternation in the traditional media, because an anointed spokesperson is not available. In many ways, this can be seen as one of the reasons that some have charged the movement as being unfocused.

Technology is clearly used to recruit participants, inform the public, and engage decision makers (Gaby & Caren, 2012; Orcutt, 2011). Gaby and Caren (2012) observe:

Based on data acquired from Facebook, we find that Occupy groups have recruited over 170,000 active Facebook users and more than 1.4 million "likes" in support of Occupations. By October 22, Facebook pages related to the Wall Street Occupation had accumulated more than 390,000 "likes," while almost twice that number, more than 770,000, have been expressed for the 324 local sites.

Orcutt (2011) notes that Twitter was helpful in organizing and building awareness about the movement.

While dissimilar in ideology, the Occupy Wall Street movement has some things in common with the Tea Party movement. First, there is the leaderless and devolved form of organizing the movement. As Earl and Kimport (2011) note, this makes both efforts dissimilar from traditional social movements. They also differ substantially from the way that nonprofit advocacy groups are organized and managed. Both movement make substantial use of technology although neither is a purely virtual effort. While other, earlier technologies such as websites and discussion lists are important, the real stars of the technological universe are the social media/Web 2.0 technologies—particularly Facebook and Twitter.

The Arab Spring

On December 17, 2010, Tarek al-Tayeb Mohamed Bouazizi set himself on fire. Bouazizi was a street vendor of fruit and claimed that two municipal police officers of the city of Sidi Bouzid attempted to take his goods. Though eventually allowed to keep his fruit, Bouazizi's uncle appealed to the city's police chief for help. The chief instructed the police officer in question to allow Bouazizi to continue to sell his fruit. Furious, she confiscated the fruit and allegedly pushed and hit him. Other officers joined in on the slapping of Bouazizi's face in front of a crowd. Bouazizi demanded to see a city official, but nobody would see him. He later set himself on fire in front of city hall. Three weeks later, Bouazizi died of his burn injuries. Bouazizi's cousin had captured on his phone images of a protest that vendors had waged in front of city hall. Posted on Facebook, the images spread, as did the protests they triggered, via Facebook, other social media, and traditional media that broadcast the images. Protests spread throughout the Arab world including Egypt, Libya, Yemen, Bahrain, Syria, Algeria, Iraq, Jordan, Kuwait, Morocco, Sudan, Lebanon, Mauritania, Oman, Saudi Arabia, and Djibouti. Governments fell in Tunisia, Egypt, Libya, and Yemen. This phenomenon became known as the Arab Spring (Fisher, 2011).

Though Bouazizi's self-immolation was the trigger for these uprisings, the protests had larger, more systemic causes. Among these were the fact that citizens in these countries had been living under various forms of dictatorships, complete with corruption, human rights infractions, economic malaise, high unemployment (particularly among highly educated youth and young adults), and poverty (Fisher, 2011).

The Arab Spring is a movement composed of individuals and informal groups across the Arab world. Thus, for example, Wael Ghonim, a Google employee, became an electronic activist; Wael Abbas blogged on the issue; Kefaya (Egyptian movement for change), the April 6th movement, We Are ALL Khaled Said (a Facebook group), and soccer supporters in Cairo (Lim, 2012) were all important to the Arab Spring movement in Egypt, though as a movement, no centralized leadership existed.

The Arab Spring movement made extensive use of social media, sometimes with an assist from traditional media. As previously noted, the original story of Mohamed Bouazizi was passed around via social media and images of the protest were posted on Facebook, which were picked up by Al-Jazeera and spread through the Arab world. In Egypt, which has received the most scholarly attention thus far, activists used the Twitter hashtag #Egypt to note and spread ideas about the various protests and stand-offs as they occurred on the ground. In this example, as the news about the movement and its activities was spread via ordinary people who had become activists over Twitter—a platform supporting at the time 140-character, often spontaneous posts—the spread of ideas was organic (rather than strategic) and was often emotional and human interest, rather than technical news about the regime or policies (Papacharissi & Oliveira, 2012). In fact, social media, which activists used to frame the protests as a movement for freedom and justice, was an important complement to the state-owned newspapers that gave voice to regime interests. Social media was also an important complement to the news spread by independent news organizations (which were not state-owned but nevertheless needed state approval to operate), which was ambivalent and torn about the significance of the protests (Hamdy & Gomaa, 2012). Similarly, social media enhanced the network of Egyptians active in the movement and helped to facilitate relationships between activists. Social media globalized the issue in an immediate way, bringing the eyes of the world on Egypt, making it more difficult for the regime to crack down on activists (Lim, 2012). In addition, those who got their news from social media were more likely to participate in the movement (Tufekci & Wilson, 2012).

There are certainly other cases where technology-assisted leaderless organizations jumped onto the world stage. There is the Green movement in Iran, the Twitter revolution in Moldavia, and the London riots, as well as others.

The technology that drives these organizations is different from the websites, e-mail, and discussion lists that drove earlier organizations. This is social media, Web 2.0, or social software (Germany, 2006; Madden & Fox, 2006). It is blogs, wikis, social networking sites, and so forth. They are interactive, pool-collective intelligence and allow for user-generated content.

What these recent cases suggest is that social movements are changing, and transnational advocacy organizations will be faced with new efforts that can be friends or foes or both. The recent conflict between US nongovernmental organizations and the post–Arab Spring Egyptian government might be one example of this (Londoño & Wan, 2012). These organizations operate by different rule and operate in a different manner. Understanding the emerging global civil society will require understanding what these efforts bring to the table. In the next section, we will look at the applicable theoretical tools that we can use to understand this phenomenon.

TRADITIONAL TRANSNATIONAL ADVOCACY ORGANIZATIONS

Like most other nonprofit organizations, transnational advocacy organizations are formal organizations with a set structure and formal procedures. Some are more bureaucratic that others. Most of the larger ones make use of technology and, as McNutt and Flanagan (2007) found, many make use of social media.

In the 1960s, many advocacy organizations moved away from a membership model toward a model based on professional advocates (Berry, 1977, 1999). This paralleled the developments in electoral campaigning that emphasized professional consultants.

What this means for transnational advocacy organizations is that the membership, if any, participates in a general way while decisions are made by professional staff. This approach tended to put more emphasis on the crafting and control of advocacy messages. Early technology supported this approach. While technology was more interactive than traditional broadcast media, it still lacked some of the capacities that future technology would allow. Newer approaches from the social media/Web 2.0 school change this dynamic, and they are also an ingredient of newer forms of social movement efforts.

EMERGING THEORY AND EXISTING MODELS

To fully understand these new phenomena, it is essential to look at what applicable theory base is available. Much of the literature in organizational theory and most of the social movement literature have a strong orientation toward traditional hierarchical formal organizations. There is often some departure from the major tenants, but theoretical change comes slowly. The organizational literature on innovation, organizational learning, and knowledge management is the most similar to what we envision.

In actuality, many of the ideas that become salient start now in the physical and biological sciences. Certainly developments like chaos and catastrophe theory are important here, as well as ideas from organizational learning and knowledge management. The role of technology, particularly new and emerging technology, sweetens the discussion.

Distributed perspective/distributed leadership theory is a promising possibility to understanding the management of these organizations within the more traditional management disciplines. The distributed perspective is a recent addition to the scholarship on leadership and leadership practice. Proponents of this view consider leadership to be both a process of social influence and an activity orientated toward social change (Conger & Pearce, 2003; Foster, 1989;

Spillane, Halverson, & Diamond, 2004). They argue that the demands of leadership are so varied that a group is best served by spreading the responsibilities among the members of the group (Conger & Pearce, 2003; Foster, 1989; Hooker & Csikzentmihalyi, 2003; Seers, Keller, & Wilkerson, 2003). The focal point is on the influence dynamics between and among the members of an interdependent system, rather than one individual leader (Harris, Leithwood, Day, Sammons, & Hopkins, 2007; Seers et al., 2003).

The distributed perspective encompasses the literatures on distributed leadership and shared leadership. Although scholars have not yet settled on a common definition for either term or definitions of these concepts, Spillane et al. (2004) and Conger and Pearce (2003) provide useful conceptions. That is, distributed leadership can be defined as a "'person-plus' perspective on human activity," one that "shifts the unit of analysis from the individual actor or group of actors to the web of leaders, followers, and situation that give activity its form" (Spillane et al., 2004, p. 10). And shared leadership can be defined as "a dynamic, interactive influence process among individuals in work groups in which the objective is to lead one another to the achievement of group goals. This influence process often involves peer, or lateral, influence and at other times involves upward or downward hierarchal influence" (Conger & Pearce, 2003, p. 286). Both definitions reference notions like mutual influence, interdependence, and the whole is greater than the sum of its parts. This approach is characterized by four foundational beliefs. The first is a shift in the unit of analysis, from the leader to the leadership practice (Spillane, 2006; Spillane & Sherer, 2004). Proponents explain that leadership is a group-level phenomenon that is practiced among all the members of the group (Fletcher & Kaufer, 2003; Gronn, 2002). To make sense of the leadership activity, one must look beyond individual actions and appreciate the reciprocal influence and the interdependencies within the interactive web of relationships connecting actors, artifacts, and their shared situation (Spillane, 2006; Spillane & Sherer, 2004).

The second foundational belief is that leadership practice results from the interactions between and among elements in the interactive Web (Spillane, 2006). Every element in the Web is connected to another, so each person's practice affects and is affected by the other (Harris et al., 2007; Spillane, 2006; Spillane et al., 2004). This reciprocity creates a multiplicative dynamic. The impact of each person's leadership is more substantial than the sum of his or her activities, so formal role and positional power become less important (Fletcher & Kaufer, 2003; Gronn, 2002; Harris, 2005; Harris et al., 2007; Kets De Vries, 1999; Spillane et al., 2004).

The third foundational belief in the distributed perspective is that leadership and context are tied. That is, the shared situation both defines and is defined through leadership practice of the members of the group (Spillane, 2006). There is a reciprocal relationship; the "material, cultural, and social [elements in an environment] enable, inform, and constrain the human activity [in that environment]" (Spillane et al., 2004, p. 10), and the group affects the structure, norms, and language in the environment (Gronn, 2002). This means that one's leadership practice is situated in a specific context and is subject to change in response to changes in the context.

The fourth foundational belief relates to the distributed perspective on the role of a leader. In this view, each leader strives to develop his or her own unique approach to leadership practice (Spillane, 2006; Spillane et al., 2004). Each leader must learn when to exercise his or her influence, when to yield to a fellow leader, and how to read the situation. He or she must also learn self-awareness, self-confidence, and humility to blend his or her efforts and promote collaborative, positive action (Fletcher & Kaufer, 2003; Spillane, 2006).

This perspective generates an appealing, nonhierarchical, relationship-focused, collaborative vision of leadership activity (Fletcher & Kaufer, 2003). For this to arise, the members must develop commitment and cohesion within group (Hooker & Csikzentmihalyi, 2003). When members experience this, they can expect to feel a sense of mutuality flowing from "an understanding and appreciation of each other's capacities to lead under different conditions" (Conger & Pearce, 2003, p. 293). This means that one member can experiment with a new phase of his or her leadership secure in the knowledge that other members of the group can, and will, transition from following to leading, if the need should arise.

In practice, many real-world challenges can complicate the practice of this type of leadership. One consideration is the challenge of sustaining the collaborative dynamic. This is a concern because learning to lead is a developmental process, and members will make mistakes in the process of honing their skills (Gronn, 2002; Spillane, 2006; Spillane et al., 2004). Another challenge is that the members may not share the same goals and values. The distributed perspective posits that the critical factor is not the differences within the group but the commonalities (Harris et al., 2007; Spillane, 2006). When members are connected in a dynamic of mutual influence, conflict is a possibility.

In addition to management theory, scholars in other fields have looked at these issues from different perspectives. These include social movement studies, technology. and public policy.

Social movement scholars have investigated the move away from hierarchical social movement organizations toward untraditional social movement efforts because of technology. Earl and Kimport (2011; 2006; 2007) argue that, for at least some organizations, technology is moving to a point, which they call Social Movement 2.0. Building on a series of interesting studies of atypical social movement organizations (most notably the Nader Traders in the 2000 presidential election). Traditional theory argues for social movement operatives who have earned their right to lead in other campaigns. These organizations, because of technology, can skip both the organization building and operative socialization processes. This, in many ways, is a huge move in a different direction. Much of the practical and theoretical literature in social movements is based on these assumptions, and if they can be dismissed, even in limited situations, it begins to unravel the theoretical enterprise.

This analysis augers nicely with the work of Shirky (2008) and Benkler (2006), who discuss the idea of organizing without organizations and Internet legend Howard Rheingold's smart mobs concept (Rheingold, 2002). All of these approaches reject the idea of traditional models of management and organization. While these ideas, along with those of Brafman and Beckstrom (2006), are really more popular works (see Earl & Kimport, 2011), they do point toward an emerging scholarly dialog on the restructuring of organizations with technology and the development of network based organizations.

Yochai Benkler, a Yale law professor, champions the idea of an open source system (Benkler, 2006). Basically, open source (as opposed to closed source) means that something (originally software) is created by a community of users and developers rather than dedicated development staff. This means that the collective intelligence of the whole is tapped by the process. Because it takes advantage of a broader base of expertise, decisions are better and the end product is superior.

An excellent illustration of this idea is Raymond's (2001) notion of the cathedral and the bazaar. The cathedral is like the traditional development process where highly trained developers work in isolation. The bazaar is unprogrammed and unorganized by comparison but enjoys the advantage of a wider and more inclusive base of expertise. In the context of advocacy organizations, traditional transnational organizations are generally managed by professional managers and employ professional political operatives that make the advocacy decisions. Again, you have this narrow base of expertise that may not be cognizant of all of the resources available. This could result in serious miscalculation due to knowledge deficits or limited perspectives.

Shirky (2008, 2011) argues for organizing without organizations via technology. His work highlights the idea of pooled collective intelligence mediated by technology. He also examines the role of participation via technology. He maintains that technology-based tools make the type of organizing without organizers functions possible. This process will be an important development to international civil society (Shirky, 2011).

Rheingold (2002) postulates that technology—principally mobile digital technology—creates the conditions that make spontaneous organizing possible. He calls these "flash mobs" and argues that they have both civic and political importance. They are, of course, short-term affairs, but this type of activity opens the door for other types of organizing.

We know that information technology expands potential span of control and tends to flatten the organizational hierarchy. While the eventual impacts of social media are probably years away, it is unlikely that social media will do anything to reverse this course.

In fact, social media is antithetical to many organizational processes that characterize traditional approaches to organization and management. It also operates in opposition to many of the ideas of professional political advocacy.

The questions are, what does this mean for nonprofit theory and practice, and what can it mean for transnational advocacy organizations? Another, but no less important issue is what will this mean for nonprofit research.

NONPROFIT/VOLUNTARY ACTION THEORY

It might be useful to think of nonprofit studies as breaking down into two camps: those that only study formally incorporated nonprofits and those who look at the broader nonprofit sector that includes voluntary associations (Smith, 2000). Many of our ideas about nonprofit organizations come from the study of the first kind of organization, while studies of the second type of organization are rarer and yield fewer widely held approaches or influential theories. This not only unfortunate for the study of current nonprofit organizations but also leaves the field at a real disadvantage when dealing with emerging phenomenon. The organizations that we are interested in here are generally not incorporated and rarely, if ever, have 501(c)3 status.

These are mostly unincorporated associations that use technology to organize. What we know about formally organized traditional organizations doesn't apply or doesn't apply as well. Voluntary action theory is a much better fit. Given that some of the constraints that face traditional voluntary associations could be potentially removed by technology. In general, information technology can dramatically reduce the cost of organizing, particularly the transaction costs. It can eliminate or minimize some of the problems of distance and time. Just the few examples we have seen in the past five years point to a new form of voluntary association on the horizon.

Maybe these are harbingers of things to come. This might mean that the formally organized format that we have seen in the past might change radically or become a thing of the past. This would cast managers into a more decentralized organizer role. It would also support a move toward crowdfunding or other alternative mechanisms.

While political nonprofits are more visible (by design), a lot of things are going on under the radar scope. We might be looking at a new generation of voluntary associations that operate in health, human services, education, and the arts.

BUILDING A USEFUL SYNTHESIS

While we have had nonprofit organizations for a very long time, we are now moving into a new phase. The transition to an information society, the impact of technology on society and on organizations, and a host of smaller changes lead us to look to some new and exciting models.

Many of the ideas that we have used to build our understanding of the non-profit sector are in the process of being overtaken by events. The emerging reality will change the nature of organizations and our understanding of the sector.

REFERENCES

912 Project (2009, March 24). Mission statement. Retrieved from http://www. the912project.com/2009/03/24/mission-statement-2/

Batliwala, S. (2002). Grassroots movements as transnational actors: Implications for global civil society. *Voluntas, 13*, 393–409.

Benkler, Y. (2006). *The wealth of networks: How social production transforms markets and freedom*. New Haven, CT: Yale University Press.

Berry, J. M. (1977). *Lobbying for the people*. Princeton, NJ: Princeton University Press.

Berry, J. M. (1999). *New liberalism: The rising power of citizen groups*. Washington, DC: Brookings Institution.

Brafman, O., & Beckstrom, R. (2006). *The starfish and the spider*. New York: Penguin.

Cohen, R. (2010a, August 12). The starfish and the tea party. *Nonprofit Quarterly*. Retrieved from https://nonprofitquarterly.org/2010/08/12/the-cohen-report-the-starfish-and-the-tea-party/

Cohen, R. (2010b, September 15). The starfish and the tea party, Part II. *Nonprofit Quarterly*. Retrieved from https://nonprofitquarterly.org/2010/09/15/the-cohen-report-the-starfish-and-the-tea-party-part-ii/

Cohen, R. (2010c, October 21). The starfish and the tea party, Part III *Nonprofit Quarterly*. Retrieved from https://nonprofitquarterly.org/2010/10/21/the-cohen-report-the-starfish-and-the-tea-party-part-iii/.

Conger, J. A., & Pearce, C. L. (2003). A landscape of opportunity. In C. L. Pearce & J. A. Conger (Eds.), *Shared leadership: Reframing the hows and whys of leadership* (pp. 285–303). Thousand Oaks, CA: SAGE.

Earl, J. (2006). Pursuing social change on-line: The use of four protest tactics on the Internet. *Social Science Computer Review, 24*, 362–377.

Earl, J. (2007). Leading tasks in a leaderless movement: The case of strategic voting. *American Behavioral Scientist, 50*, 1327–1349.

Earl, J., & Kimport, K. (2011). *Digitally enabled social change: Activism in the internet age*. Mit Press.

Fletcher, J. K., & Kaufer, K. (2003). Shared leadership: Paradox and possibility. In C. L. Pearce & J. A. Conger (Eds.), *Shared leadership: Reframing the hows and whys of leadership* (pp. 21–47). Thousand Oaks, CA: SAGE.

Fisher, M. (2011, March 26). In Tunisia, act of one fruit vendor unleashes, wave of revolution through Arab world. *Washington Post*. http://www.washingtonpost.com/world/in-tunisia-act-of-one-fruit-vendor-sparks-wave-of-revolution-through-arab-world/2011/03/16/AFjfsueB_story.html

Foster, W. (1989). Toward a critical practice of leadership. In J. Smyth (Ed.), *Critical perspectives on educational leadership* (pp. 39–62). Philadelphia: Falmer.

Gaby, S., & Caren, N. (2012). Occupy online: How cute old men and Malcolm X recruited 400,000 US users to OWS on Facebook. *Social Movement Studies: Journal of Social, Cultural and Political Protest, 11*, 367–374.

Germany, J. B. (Ed.). (2006). *Person to person to person: Harnessing the political power of on-line social networks and user generated content*. Washington, DC: Institute for Politics, Democracy and the Internet, George Washington University.

Gronn, P. (2002). Distributed leadership. In K. Leithwood & P. Hallinger (Eds.), *Second international handbook of educational leadership and administration* (pp. 653–696). London: Kluwer Academic.

Hamdy, H., & Gomaa, E. (2012). Framing the Egyptian uprising in Arabic language newspapers and social media. *Journal of Communication, 62*, 195–211.

Harris, A. (2005). Reflections on distributed leadership. *Management in Education, 19*(2), 10–12.

Harris, A., Leithwood, K., Day, C., Sammons, P., & Hopkins, D. (2007). Distributed leadership and organizational change: Reviewing the evidence. *Journal of Educational Change, 8*, 337–347.

Hooker, C., & Csikzentmihalyi, M. (2003). Flow, creativity, and shared leadership. In C. L. Pearce & J. A. Conger (Eds.), *Shared leadership: Reframing the hows and whys of leadership* (pp. 217–234). Thousand Oaks, CA: SAGE.

Klimp, E. (2010). The Tea Party movement: Leftist attacks fail to stop its growing influence. Retrieved from https://capitalresearch.org/article/the-tea-party-movement-leftist-attacks-fail-to-stop-its-growing-influence/

Lang, A. S., & Levitsky, D. (Eds.). (2012). *Dreaming in public: Building the occupy Movement.* Oxford: New Internationalist.

Lepore, J. (2010). *The whites of their eyes: The Tea Party's revolution and the battle over American history.* Princeton, NJ: Princeton University Press.

Lim, M. (2012). Clicks, cabs, and coffee houses: Social media and oppositional movements in Egypt 2004–2011. *Journal of Communication, 62*, 231–248.

Londoño, E., & Wan, W. (2012, February 6). Egypt names Americans charged in NGO probe; Sam LaHood among those facing criminal charges. *Washington Post.* http://feeds.washingtonpost.com/click.phdo?i=af031ffa3d8d81d3e15458f9c510c01b https://www.washingtonpost.com/world/egypt-to-prosecute-americans-in-ngo-probe/2012/02/05/gIQAQRderQ_email.html

Madden, M., & Fox, S. (2006). *Riding the waves of "Web 2.0." backgrounder.* Washington, DC: Pew Internet and American Life Project. Retrieved from http://www.pewinternet.org/files/old-media/Files/Reports/2006/PIP_Web_2.0.pdf.pdf

McNutt, J. G., Curtis, K. O'Boyle, T., & Fox, S. (2010, November). *Coffee or tea? An examination of on-line organizing techniques of the tea party and coffee party movements.* Paper presented at ARNOVA's 2010 Conference in Alexandria, VA.

McNutt, J. G., & Flanagan, M. (2007). *Social networking choices and environmental advocacy organizations: Implications for global social justice.* Paper presented at the 2007 Meeting of the Association for Research on Nonprofit Organizations and Voluntary Action, Atlanta, GA.

Orcutt, M. (2011, November 9). How Occupy Wall Street occupied Twitter, too. *MIT Technology Review.* Retrieved from http://www.technologyreview.com/view/426079/how-occupy-wall-street-occupied-twitter-too/

Papacharissi, Z., & Oliveira, M. (2012) Affective news and networked publics: The rhythms of news storytelling on #Egypt. *Journal of Communication, 62*, 266–282.

Rasmussen, S., & Schoen, D. (2010). *Mad as hell: How the Tea Party movement is fundamentally remaking our two-party system.* New York: HarperCollins.

Rauch, J. (2010, September 11). How Tea Party organizes without leaders [Web log post]. *National Journal.* Retrieved from http://www.freerepublic.com/focus/fbloggers/2591379/posts

Raymond, E. (2001). *The cathedral and the bazaar: Musings on Linux and open source by an accidental revolutionary* (Rev. exp. ed.). Cambridge, MA: O'Reilly.

Rheingold, H. (2002). *Smart mobs: The next social revolution.* New York: Basic Books.

Rich, F. (2010, August 28). The billionaires bankrolling the Tea Party. *New York Times.* Retrieved from http://www.nytimes.com/2010/08/29/opinion/29rich.html

Sarno, D. (2009, February 27). Anti-stimulus tea parties light up Twitter, YouTube, Flickr and social media [Web log post]. *Los Angeles Times*. Retrieved from http://latimesblogs.latimes.com/technology/2009/02/anti-stimulus-t.html.

Seers, A., Keller, T., & Wilkerson, J. M. (2003). Can team members share leadership? In C. L. Pearce & J. A. Conger (Eds.), *Shared leadership: Reframing the hows and whys of leadership* (pp. 77–101). Thousand Oaks, CA: SAGE.

Shirky, C. (2008). *Here comes everybody: The power of organizing without organizations.* New York: Penguin.

Shirky, C. (2011). The political power of social media. *Foreign Affairs*, 90(1). Retrieved from https://www.foreignaffairs.com/articles/2010-12-20/political-power-social-media

Smith, D. H. (2000). *Grassroots associations.* Thousand Oaks, CA: SAGE.

Spillane, J. P. (2006). *Distributed leadership.* San Francisco, CA: Jossey-Bass.

Spillane, J., Halverson, R., & Diamond, J. (2004). Towards a theory of school leadership practice: Implications of a distributive perspective. *Journal of Curriculum Studies, 36*, 3–34.

Spillane, J. P., & Sherer, J. Z. (2004). *A distributed perspective on school leadership: Leadership practice as stretched over people and place.* Paper presented at the Annual Meeting American Education Association, San Diego, CA.

Tea Party Nation (2012).Website. http://www.teapartynation.com retreived on October 30, 2012

Tufekci, Z., & Wilson, C. (2012). Social media and the decision to participate in political protest: Observations from Tahrir Square. *Journal of Communication, 62*, 363–379.

Young, D. R., Koenig, B. L., Najam, A., & Fisher, J. (1999). Strategy and structure in managing global associations. *Voluntas: International Journal of Voluntary and Nonprofit Organizations, 10*(4), 323–343.

Warkentin, C. (2001). *Reshaping world politics: NGOs, the Internet, and global civil society.* Rowman & Littlefield.

Zernike, K. (2010). *Boiling mad: Inside Tea Party America.* New York: Times Books.

The Future

14

The Future of Technology and Social Change Practice

JOHN G. McNUTT ■

What does the future have in store for technology and efforts to create social change? In many ways, things have changed dramatically in the past three or four decades. What was once a reluctant and tentative practice is now an established part of the social change enterprise. Technology is not only a part of issue advocacy and electoral campaigns; it is a major player and may even threaten the role of traditional mass media. There are now established roles for technologists in political practice. More and more academic researchers are choosing to study this phenomenon, and many are using highly sophisticated research methodology. While it is now easy to say that technology-based advocacy has arrived, the best is yet to come.

Information and communication technology continues to develop and brings to humanity innovative capability and incredible new vistas. We can now understand the world in new ways and create things that were once just dreams. Technology allows us to cure diseases that have plagued our species for eons and extend our abilities far beyond what was possible. It also brings these capacities to those with less-than-noble aspirations. Cyberterrorism and even cyberwar are no longer vague threats and, as I write this, Americans are wondering about the 2016 election and what it means for democracy. Investigations into potential nation state involvement in hacking campaigns and election systems are raising major concerns among Americans and people worldwide.

The world is also changing. McNutt and Hoefer (2016) have argued that the rise of the information society, the environmental crisis, and globalization have united to redefine the future path of social policy and society in the United States and the world. These same forces will affect a wide range of policy arenas.

Technology use throughout the world is booming. In the United States, most of the population has access to the Internet, has a smart phone, and uses social media (Smith, 2017). Technology is a force for change throughout the world.

While there are many things that could happen, some things are more likely than others. This chapter will look at four emerging trends: new organizational forms, research to make technology-based practice more effective, the role of data science in advocacy and the development of new practitioners. Each of these topics will be discussed separately, although all four are intimately related.

NEW ORGANIZATIONAL FORMS

The traditional organization that promotes advocacy is often an interest or advocacy group, a service organization, a social movement organization, or a membership-based association. These tend to be bricks-and-mortar organizations that have both constraints and considerable sunk costs as a consequence of the way that they are organized. The fundraising necessary to keep these organizations staffed and functioning further restricts their freedom of movement. This is, to an extent, a consequence of the techniques that they use. Traditional advocacy requires a lot of resources, and these resources make the development of an organization likely.

Technology allows advocates to organize without some of these constraints. One of the approaches that has possibility (and is used in some areas) is a virtual organization. A virtual organization has a small coordinating core and outsources many of its functions. Technology makes the virtual organization operate: It makes the high degree of coordination feasible. Virtual organizations can link people and organizations with much less effort. They can mobilize much larger numbers of people without the transaction costs of traditional organizing. Microvolunteering or episodic volunteering via technology can accomplish a great deal with a smaller contribution for a larger number of participants. MoveOn is an example of a virtual organization. Started as an activist attempt to influence the impeachment of President Clinton, MoveOn grew to a huge international political force (Cornfield, 2004).

Radical organizations like Anonymous are an excellent example of a completely decentralized virtual organization (Coleman, 2014). This might be a model for a highly radical social change group. This type of organization is very difficult to counter and would have little in the way of a physical base.

There are more instances of sole practitioner advocacy (see Earl & Kimport, 2011). The Nader Traders strategic voting operators included not only one person advocacy organizations but a number of the operators had no previous social movement experience (Earl & Schussman, 2003, 2004). This creates an interesting situation for social movement professionals who must compete with new actors.

The move away from bricks-and-mortar advocacy groups might lead to the ascendency of voluntary associations, organized in cyberspace, as the expected way that advocates organize (McNutt, Brainard, Zeng, & Kovacic, 2016; see also chapter 13). It might bring members into the decision-making, reversing the trend toward managed participation.

MAKING PRACTICE MORE EFFECTIVE

The quest for evidence-based practice is a priority in many fields. Much of what practitioners in many professions do is dependent on experience. The building of empirically based practice techniques via translational research is a desired outcome. Over a decade ago, Hick and McNutt (2002) argued that technology-based advocacy needed such an approach.

The development of sophisticated research about online behavior in general and about political behavior and technology is a gratifying development. This comes at a time where researchers are beginning to apply powerful experimental and quasi-experimental designs to practical political practice (Bergan & Cole, 2015; Green & Gerber, 2016, 2008; LeRoux & Krawczyk, 2014).

Much of the current research on advocacy is limited in what it can actually explain about causal relationships between the techniques used and the outcome achieved (see Hick & McNutt, 2002; McNutt, 2011). Collecting data in an advocacy situation is difficult and often suffers from challenges to validity. Measuring the dependent variable in advocacy research is often especially difficult when that variable is a political decision.

The combination of greatly expanded knowledge about online environments and experimentally based translation research offers the possibility of a practice knowledge base that is much stronger and more robust than what we have had in the past. This is also true for traditional interventions, many of which are benefiting from the same attention.

How this will be organized is a significant issue. One of the issues that often frustrates translational research is how the intervention becomes part of practice. A mechanism for bringing together practitioners and researchers is clearly needed. This is not a new problem. Diffusion of innovation theory (Rogers, 2003) owes much of its early existence to getting farmers to use the fruits of agricultural research. What is relevant here is that creating more effective interventions will not assure that they are used. A planned process of knowledge transfer is needed.

The growth of data science has created new possibilities for research and evaluation. Coupled with sensor data that are part of the Internet of things, many variables that can only be addressed indirectly can be evaluated with these new data sources.

A related issue is the creation of a reciprocal bridge between researchers and practitioners that allows the development of new and innovative practice methodology. Many of the techniques that have been developed are things that were tried in the field and then evaluated. The creation of new practices, using research findings as a base for creating a prototype, is an alternative that promises to develop new and more capable interventions (Okpych & James, 2014; Rothman,

1980). This has been a long-standing effort in a number of fields, including social work and nursing.

Technology has the ability to bring researchers together from many far-flung locations and pool their abilities to solve common problems. The creation of research platforms that facilitates this common problem-solving would build the capacity to create and test new interventions. This would also create the capacity to involve practitioners at an early stage.

Many of the technology-based interventions use applications that were created for other purposes and then repurposed by advocates for their work. This process can be guided by research and evaluated clearly. On balance, it might be good to have applications that were written for the purpose.

To that end, the movement toward civic hacking is an excellent possible resource. Hackathons bring volunteer technologists (people with technology skills) together with people and organizations that need technology developed (see McNutt & Justice, 2016; Stepasiuk, 2014). The National Day of Civic Hacking provides an incentive for local hackathons, but different sponsors hold them throughout the year.

USING DATA IN ADVOCACY PRACTICE

The rise of data science and computational social science has changed many fields and will continue to do so. Data science fields like predictive analytics, precision medicine, and machine learning are frequently discussed in the news. Data science is an attempt to deal with the massive amount of available data that society deals with regularly.

Where do the data come from? A great deal of data about the human condition is collected regularly by many entities throughout the world. This includes administrative data, survey data, and data from economic and political organizations. New data sources such as social media, the output from technology that is part of the Internet of things, and sensor data provide a rich store of formally unavailable information. One example is license plate readers that record which cars (or actually which plates) are traveling on a road at a given time. This is much more accurate than the logs that transportation planners use to measure commuter patterns. Global position system technology in public vehicles (like snow plows and police cars) let us track these vehicles in real time. Sensors created to track water quality can help us track chemical spills. The potentially available data are almost endless.

The Open Government movement is another source of data (Justice, McNutt, & Smith, 2013). Governments throughout the world are making available data that they collect from a variety of processes. This is part of government transparency. Data repositories such as data.gov make this available to users. Many of the better developed open data efforts (such as Washington, DC; Boston; and Philadelphia) provide data that would be very valuable to local community groups. Having information on campaign contributions or contact awards are often good for opposition research or for tracking potential votes.

Improved data management and analysis techniques make this data more useful. Advanced statistical tools, machine learning, and artificial intelligence, supported by data warehousing and data curating capacity, make analysis more comprehensive and ultimately more valuable to end-stage users. Many of the older statistical systems, while still valuable, are not up to the task of dealing with millions of data points.

The data visualization capacity that is now easily available can be a huge help in educating the public and building support for a program or policy. Data visualization technology makes analysis more useful and accessible to a wider group of users including stakeholders, decision makers, the news media, and the general public. This includes sophisticated mapping programs and geospatial analysis.

Data science has obvious implications for business and public management, but its application to social change advocacy is less obvious. Nonetheless, data science is an active player in the social change universe.

One clear use of data science is the ability to understand problems more deeply and in a timelier manner (McNutt & Goldkind, 2018). More comprehensive data, analyzed with better statistical tools and presented with advanced technology, take policy analysis and policy research to a new level. Allen (2017) notes that even relatively small nonprofits can make good use of the capacity that data science can provide to support their advocacy and public education missions.

This also creates an arms race between researchers on different side of an issue (Nownes & Newmark, 2016) where less well-funded advocacy groups do not have access to proprietary data, which puts them at a disadvantage in the advocacy arena. Information is central to successful lobbying, and those with better data will have a distinct advantage.

Another use of data science is that it can enhance our ability to understand populations that advocates deal with, such as voters and stakeholders. Data science has become an important part of the management of elections (Nickerson & Rogers, 2014; Shorey & Howard, 2016), and campaigns amass huge quantities of data about the voting public. This allows campaigns to microtarget individual voters. Brown (2016) notes, "The right data collection and analytics can enable campaigns to match the specific issues and positions from the candidate's portfolio that are most appealing to specific voter groups and even individual voters." This type of information can help advocacy organizations narrowcast their appeals. Other kinds of technology make this easier to implement.

There are other political uses of data science. Large data sets of social media responses are used in sentiment analysis to gauge the mood of the public for decision makers and those they wish to influence. Knowing the mood of the constituency makes it easier for decision makers to plan for reaction to a policy. It can also alert advocates to potential bases of support.

Tools like Google Trends can be used to evaluate need for interventions and policies (Boland & McNutt, 2013). Google Trends looks at what people search for on Google. This can be used to infer interest or awareness of an intervention.

A further use of data science is studying practice, particularly online practice (Boland & McNutt, 2013). The impact of advocacy interventions can be tracked more precisely than ever before and no longer need to depend on less reliable forms of data collection. At a very simple level, analytics are available on many of the applications that advocates use. Using the network analysis tools, it is easy to see how we can evaluate these interventions in real time. Many studies of advocacy practitioners rely on observation or recall. Technology, along with sophisticated data analysis, might produce new results.

The movement toward data justice (Heeks & Renken, 2018) has created a number of new models for advocacy practice with data. Citizen science partners scientist with volunteers to conduct research on important issues (Conrad & Hilchey, 2011). Data collaboratives can provide data for community groups and nongovernmental organizations to use in their advocacy work (Verhulst & Young, 2017).

Data science can add much to advocacy technology. This is not to say that there are no issues for social justice with the movement toward massive data. Privacy and surveillance concerns are both serious and real.

The growth of data science and computational social science is a boon for technology-based advocacy. Data science will make current advocacy stronger and light the way for the advocacy of the future.

THE CREATION OF NEW PRACTITIONERS

The education accorded advocates is often on the job or in short, intensive bootcamp training situations. Practitioners are from a variety of professions; some provide advocacy training while others don't. While this has never been an optimal solution, the growth of technology means that the expected skill level has increased. This means that new training venues are needed.

The growth of online learning and the advent of massive open online courses provide mechanisms to provide training at the level that is needed. The intersection of these forces leads to a hope that programs will be available to those who need them.

This should be an expected part of the curriculum in many professional schools and programs. It is also the place for free-standing programs. There are a number of programs in applied politics that can take up the challenge.

These four trends could revolutionize the nature of technology and advocacy. In addition, the growth of technology and the massive changes to our society and our world are profound. These are also other possibilities that could push the process in different directions.

A lot of cross-fertilization is possible. A lot of work is being done by groups of people with different concerns that can benefit online advocates. Much of human energy is provided to social betterment by individuals who create things for their own purposes and to fulfill their own interests. Shirky (2010) refers to this as "cognitive surplus." The Internet and other technologies create the possibility to make use of these talents.

While there is much to celebrate about the future, it would remiss to ignore the negative possibilities. The loss of privacy is clearly a side effect of the growing sophistication of data collection. Technology can also be used as a tool of surveillance, terrorism, and repression. Cybercrime and even cyberwar are very real possibilities. Governments have used technology to repress populations and persecute dissidents.

Technology has become a cohesive part of advocacy for social change and the process of addressing social concerns. Developments in technology, practice research, new organizational forms, training for practitioners, and data science are likely to transform what we do and how we do it. These forces will interact, and the result will be more effective practice with better results.

CONCLUSIONS

We have always lived in interesting times. I am hoping that, because you decided to read this book, that you want to join me in making the world a better, safer, fairer, and more supportive place—that you share my commitment to social justice. More than ever before, we need people with the commitment and skills to make a difference.

Years ago, advocacy was different. The organizations were different, the problems were not the same, and the technology was different. Now we have new tools, strategies, organizations, and targets. We need to make that leap and take that chance.

We hope that this book has painted attractive picture of the future of social change practice. We have examined how changes in organizations, change in methodology, and changes in targets. This is an exciting, changing vibrant place to be. New developments are launched frequently.

We live in a world where there are frequent and serious threats to social justice. Advocacy is one of the means that we have to deal with these challenges. This is hard work on many levels. If technology can help advocates deal with the threats that lay ahead in a more effective manner, it will also contribute to a better life for all.

REFERENCES

Allen, J. (2017, January 13). How big data informs conservation: One example in Chesapeake Bay. *Nonprofit Quarterly.* Retrieved from https://nonprofitquarterly.org/2017/01/13/big-data-informs-conservation-one-example-chesapeake-bay/

Bergan, D. E., & Cole, R. T. (2015). Call your legislator: A field experimental study of the impact of a constituency mobilization campaign on legislative voting. *Political Behavior, 37*(1), 27–42.

Boland, K. M., & McNutt, J. G. (2013). Assessing e-government success strategies using Internet search data. In R. Gil Garcia (Ed.), *E-government success factors and measures: Theories, concepts, and methodologies* (pp. 289–307). Harrisburg, PA: IGI Books.

Brown, M. (2016, May 29). Big data analytics and the next president: How microtargeting drives today's campaigns [Web log post]. Retrieved from http://www.forbes.com/sites/metabrown/2016/05/29/big-data-analytics-and-the-next-president-how-microtargeting-drives-todays-campaigns/#1204d2c11400

Coleman, G. (2014). *Hacker, hoaxer, whistleblower, spy: The many faces of anonymous.* London: Verso.

Conrad, C. C., & Hilchey, K. G. (2011). A review of citizen science and community-based environmental monitoring: issues and opportunities. *Environmental Monitoring and Assessment, 176,* 273–291.

Cornfield, M. (2004). *Politics moves online: Campaigning and the Internet.* Century Foundation.

Earl, J., & Schussman, A. (2003). The new site of activism: On-line organizations, movement entrepreneurs, and the changing nature of social movement decision-making. *Research in Social Movements, Conflicts and Change, 24,* 155–187.

Earl, J., & Schussman, A. (2004). Cease and desist: Repression, strategic voting and the 2000 US presidential election. *Mobilization, 9,* 181–202.

Earl, J., & Kimport, K. (2011). *Digitally enabled social change.* Cambridge, MA: MIT Press.

Green, D. P., & Gerber, A. S. (2008). *Get out the vote: How to increase voter turnout.* Washington, DC: Brookings Institution Press.

Green, D. P., & Gerber, A. S. (2016). Voter mobilization, experimentation, and translational social science. *Perspectives on Politics, 14,* 738–749.

Heeks, R., & Renken, J. (2018). Data justice for development: What would it mean? *Information Development, 34,* 90–102.

Hick, S., & McNutt, J. G. (Eds.). (2002). *Advocacy and Activism on the Internet: Perspectives from community organization and social policy.* Chicago: Lyceum.

Justice, J., McNutt, J. G., & Smith, E. (2013). Understanding and measuring online fiscal transparency. In A. Manohoran (Ed.), *E-government and websites: A public solutions handbook* (pp. 22–46). Armonk, NY: M. E. Sharpe.

LeRoux, K., & Krawczyk, K. (2014). Can nonprofit organizations increase voter turnout? Findings from an agency-based voter mobilization experiment. *Nonprofit and Voluntary Sector Quarterly, 43,* 272–292.

McNutt, J. G. (2011). Is social work advocacy worth the cost? Issues and barriers for an economic analysis of social work political practice. *Research in Social Work Practice, 21,* 397–403.

McNutt, J. G., Brainard, L., Zeng, Y., & Kovacic, P. (2016). Information and technology in and for associations and volunteering. In D. H. Smith, C. Rochester, R. Stebbins, & J. Grotz (Eds.), *Palgrave handbook of volunteering and nonprofit associations* (pp. 1060-1073). Basingstoke, Hampshire, UK: Palgrave Macmillan.

McNutt, J. G., & Goldkind, L. (2018). E-Activism Development and Growth. In M. Khosrow-Pour, D.B.A. (Ed.), *Encyclopedia of Information Science and Technology, Fourth Edition* (pp. 3569–3578). Hershey, PA: IGI Global. doi:10.4018/978-1-5225-2255-3.ch310

McNutt, J. G., & Hoefer, R. (2016). *Social welfare policy: Responding to a changing world.* Chicago: Lyceum.

McNutt, J. G., & Justice, J. B. (2016). Predicting Civic Hackathons in Local Communities: Perspectives from Social Capital and Creative Class Theory. Paper read at the 12th International Society for Third Sector Research Conference, Ersta Skondal University College, Stockholm, Sweden, June 28–July 1, 2016

Nickerson, D. W., & Rogers, T. (2014). Political campaigns and big data. *Journal of Economic Perspectives, 28*(2), 51–73.

Nownes, A. J., & Newmark, A. J. (2016). The information portfolios of interest groups: An exploratory analysis. *Interest Groups and Advocacy, 5*, 57–81.

Okpych, N. J., & James, L. H. (2014). A historical analysis of evidence-based practice in social work: The unfinished journey toward an empirically grounded profession. *Social Service Review, 88*, 3–58.

Rogers, E. (2003). *Diffusion of innovations* (5th ed.). New York: Free Press.

Rothman, J. (1980). *Social R & D: Research and development in the human services.* Englewood Cliffs, NJ: Prentice Hall.

Shirky, C. (2010). *Cognitive surplus: How technology makes consumers into collaborators.* New York: Penguin.

Shorey, S., & Howard, P. N. (2016). Automation, algorithms, and politics: Automation, big data and politics: A research review. *International Journal of Communication, 10*, 5032–5055.

Smith, A. (2017). Record shares of Americans now own smartphones, have home broadband. *Pew Research Center, 12*.

Stepasiuk, T. (2014). Civic hacking: A motivational perspective. *New Visions in Public Affairs, 6*, 21–30.

Verhulst, S., & Young, A. (2017, September 28). The potential of social media intelligence to improve people's lives: How can social media data be leveraged for public good? *GovLab.* Retrieved from http://thegovlab.org/the-potential-of-social-media-intelligence-to-improve-peoples-lives-social-media-data-for-good/

Page numbers followed by *f* and *t* refer to figures and tables, respectively.